INTEGRATING KNOWLEDGE-BASED AND DATABASE MANAGEMENT SYSTEMS

M. Barrett & A. C. Beerel	EXPERT SYSTEMS IN BUSINESS: A Practical Approach
M. Becker, R. Haberfellner & G. Liebetrau	ELECTRONIC DATA PROCESSING IN PRACTICE: A Handbook for Users
A. C. Beerel	EXPERT SYSTEMS: Strategic Implications and Applications
K. Bennett	SOFTWARE ENGINEERING ENVIRONMENTS: Research and Practice
A. C. Bradley	OPTICAL STORAGE FOR COMPUTERS: Technology and Applications
P. Brereton	SOFTWARE ENGINEERING ENVIRONMENTS
R. Bright	SMART CARDS: Principles, Practice and Applications
D. Clarke & U. Magnusson-Murray	PRACTICAL MACHINE TRANSLATION
V. Claus & A. Schwill	DICTIONARY OF INFORMATION TECHNOLOGY
D. Cleal & N. O. Heaton	KNOWLEDGE-BASED SYSTEMS: Implications for Human–Computer Interfaces
I. Craig	THE CASSANDRA ARCHITECTURE: Distributed Control in a Blackboard System
T. Daler, *et al.*	SECURITY OF INFORMATION AND DATA
D. Diaper	KNOWLEDGE ELICITATION: Principles, Techniques and Applications
D. Diaper	TASK ANALYSIS FOR HUMAN–COMPUTER INTERACTION
G. I. Doukidis, F. Land & G. Miller	KNOWLEDGE-BASED MANAGEMENT SUPPORT SYSTEMS
P. Duffin	KNOWLEDGE-BASED SYSTEMS: Applications in Administrative Government
C. Ellis	EXPERT KNOWLEDGE AND EXPLANATION: The Knowledge–Language Interface
J. Einbu	A PROGRAM ARCHITECTURE FOR IMPROVED MAINTAINABILITY IN SOFTWARE ENGINEERING
A. Fourcin, G. Harland, W. Barry & V. Hazan	SPEECH INPUT AND OUTPUT ASSESSMENT: Multilingual Methods and Standards
M. Greenwell	KNOWLEDGE ENGINEERING FOR EXPERT SYSTEMS
F. R. Hickman *et al.*	ANALYSIS FOR KNOWLEDGE-BASED SYSTEMS: A Practical Guide to the KADS Methodology
P. Hills	INFORMATION MANAGEMENT SYSTEMS: Implications for the Human–Computer Interface
E. Hollnagel	THE RELIABILITY OF EXPERT SYSTEMS
R. Kerry	INTEGRATING KNOWLEDGE-BASED AND DATABASE MANAGEMENT SYSTEMS
K. Koskimies & J. Paakki	AUTOMATING LANGUAGE IMPLEMENTATION
J. Kriz	KNOWLEDGE-BASED EXPERT SYSTEMS IN INDUSTRY
M. McTear & T. Anderson	UNDERSTANDING KNOWLEDGE ENGINEERING
W. Meyer	EXPERT SYSTEMS IN FACTORY MANAGEMENT: Knowledge Based CIM
U. Pankoke-Babatz	COMPUTER-BASED GROUP COMMUNICATION: The AMIGO Activity Model
J. M. M. Pinkerton	UNDERSTANDING INFORMATION TECHNOLOGY: Basic Terminology and Practice
S. Pollitt	INFORMATION STORAGE AND RETRIEVAL SYSTEMS: Origin, Development and Applications
C.J. Price	KNOWLEDGE ENGINEERING TOOLKITS
S. Ravden & G. Johnson	EVALUATING USABILITY OF HUMAN–COMPUTER INTERFACES: A Practical Method
S. Savory	EXPERT SYSTEMS FOR PROFESSIONALS
P. E. Slatter	BUILDING EXPERT SYSTEMS: Cognitive Emulation
H. T. Smith, J. Onions & S. Benford	DISTRIBUTED GROUP COMMUNICATION: The AMIGO Information Model
H. M. Sneed	SOFTWARE ENGINEERING MANAGEMENT
M. Stein	BUILDING EXPERT SYSTEMS MODEMS FOR DATA TRANSMISSION
R. Stutely	ADVANCED DESKTOP PUBLISHING: A Practical Guide to Ventura Version 2 and the Professional Extension
J. A. Waterworth	MULTI-MEDIA INTERACTION WITH COMPUTERS
J. A. Waterworth & M. Talbot	SPEECH AND LANGUAGE-BASED COMMUNICATION WITH MACHINES: Towards the Conversational Computer
R. J. Whiddett	THE IMPLEMENTATION OF SMALL COMPUTER SYSTEMS

INTEGRATING KNOWLEDGE-BASED AND DATABASE MANAGEMENT SYSTEMS

RUTH KERRY B.Sc.
Information Systems Engineering Division
Central Computer and Telecommunications Agency

Published on behalf of
CENTRAL COMPUTER AND TELECOMMUNICATIONS AGENCY by

ELLIS HORWOOD
NEW YORK   LONDON   TORONTO   SYDNEY   TOKYO   SINGAPORE

First published in 1990 by
ELLIS HORWOOD LIMITED
Market Cross House, Cooper Street,
Chichester, West Sussex, PO19 1EB, England

A division of
Simon & Schuster International Group

Printed and bound in Great Britain
by Hartnolls, Bodmin

British Library Cataloguing in Publication Data

Kerry, Ruth
Integrating knowledge-based and database
management systems
(Ellis Horwood series in Information Technology)
CIP catalogue record for this book is available from
the British Library
ISBN 0–13–466772–7

Library of Congress Cataloging-in-Publication Data available

Contents

Preface

The UK Civil Service is the largest single user of conventional information technology (IT) equipment and services in the UK, and it is also one of the largest staff employers. There is a constant requirement to ensure that the tasks undertaken by government departments are carried out with due regard to efficiency and effectiveness. The Central Computer and Telecommunications Agency (CCTA) has a specific responsibility to research and then encourage the use of appropriate IT to assist in the administrative mechanisms of government. Knowledge–based Systems (KBS) represents one such technology which CCTA has identified as being of particular benefit. The potential rewards for effectively harnessing this technology are cost savings, which have been predicted to be of the order of billions of pounds in the UK alone, and improvements such as increased availability, consistency and quality of expertise. The primary aim in producing this book is to assist in the realisation of these benefits by drawing the capabilities of KBS to the attention of those people who are able to influence the introduction of this technology.

The ability to integrate KBS with existing IT systems will greatly affect the take–up of KBS, within and outside UK government. Current trends in IT are bringing together professionals from different domains as they are drawn into multi–disciplinary areas. This book bridges the gap between conventional IT processing, which is data oriented, and knowledge–based systems, which are information oriented.

Government departments in the UK have developed information systems (IS) strategies to underpin and achieve their business objectives. The IS strategies describe how IT will be utilised over periods of between five and ten years. The exploitation of KBS, and how they will be integrated with existing and planned systems, will be an increasingly significant feature in those strategies.

A secondary aim of the book is to stimulate vendors of information management products, especially KBS and database management systems (DBMS), to address the problems of integrating the two types of software. It is believed that standards making bodies have a key role to play in achieving an open systems architecture which includes both KBS and DBMS technology.

This book is the culmination of investigative work carried out over the last two years by the author for the Information Systems Engineering Division within CCTA. An interim report was published in the autumn of 1988 which was made freely available to government departments and the public sector. The report has been totally rewritten and an equal quantity of new material added to produce this book. I hope that readers of that report and newcomers to this material will equally find something of interest.

Readers should note that comments and views expressed in this book reflect recommendations made by the author and CCTA policy may reflect changes in the light of other policies.

Acknowledgements

I would like to thank everyone who has contributed towards the production of this book: the many software vendors, too numerous to mention here but included in annex A, for providing information about their products; CCTA for providing the facilities and time for writing the book; CCTA support staff, particularly the librarians for obtaining reference material; the reviewers, in particular Ed Dee, Michael Cumbermack and Clive Windebank of CCTA and Professor Gray of Aberdeen University, for wielding their red pens so effectively; and my colleagues for encouraging me to complete the book.

Note to readers

The reader is advised that many of the software and hardware terms used are trademarks, and are therefore the property of the companies that own them.

Ruth E Kerry
CCTA
HM Treasury
March 1990

1

Introduction

1.1 CCTA

The role of the Central Computer and Telecommunications Agency (CCTA) is to promote business effectiveness as well as efficiency in government through the use of Information Systems (IS). In support of this role its aims are to:

- encourage and assist departments in developing IS strategies to support their objectives, programmes and priorities;

- identify issues and opportunities which cross departmental boundaries in business and information systems and take the lead in addressing them;

- gather and disseminate information on government's current and future use of IS to ensure the maximum benefit to the government;

- influence, develop and promote central policy on matters affecting the use of IS in government;

- ensure that departments have the means for planning, developing and managing successful information systems;

- influence the development of an open market for products and services to meet government IS requirements;

- help ensure that the best solutions are procured with minimum timescales and cost for both government and supplier;

- assist plans and cases for investment in IS within government with the aim of ensuring maximum return on such investment.

CCTA has been carrying out work in the knowledge–based systems (KBS) field since 1983, following a visit to the United States by senior staff. Up until 1988 the work was mainly investigative, to explore potential KBS uses in administrative government computing. This included sponsorship of pilot projects in departments and provision of a demonstration workshop. By 1988 it was thought that KBS were sufficiently well established to consider how to integrate KBS work with that concerned with data management, and the Information Systems Engineering Division started to play a leading role in KBS developments. KBS should now be viewed as a component for building Information Systems, alongside fourth generation languages, data dictionaries and database management systems. The need for a method, alongside SSADM, for building knowledge–based systems is being addressed by the GEMINI project, also initiated by CCTA.

The prime focus of CCTA is on administrative computing, but there is no reason why agency guidance, such as this book, should not be applied to other areas, where appropriate. For example, integrated tool sets are also required for building real–time systems.

1.2 Background and requirement

Early in 1988 it was perceived by CCTA that there was a lack of awareness of the potential for integrating KBS (including expert systems, rule–based systems, etc) and databases, and writing a report on the subject was included in the business plan. This led to the production of Information Systems Engineering report number 29, Integration of Expert Systems and Databases, published in September 1988. It included details of twenty–six tools which could interface to databases, and described a number of ways in which the two types of software could be combined. More research has been carried out to enhance the contents of the report in the production of this book.

Government departments, like other major IT users, have systems which utilise, and are dependent upon, databases which may consist of: serial files; indexed files; network, hierarchical or relational databases; or any combination of these. It is likely that departments will want to use one or more KBS tool to develop software components which complement these existing systems. The truth of this is evidenced by several government departments already considering the use of KBS in their Information Systems strategy.

KBS tools emerged from the field of Artificial Intelligence (AI), where the emphasis was placed on *knowledge* that underlies human expertise, unlike conventional data processing tools which are primarily concerned with processing *data*. Today the term Information Systems is commonly used to embrace computerised and clerical systems, both of which will include the processing of data and the use of knowledge, to produce information.

In the early days, KBS tools were used to build stand–alone systems to solve problems which only required small amounts of data. This data was usually input by the end–user at run time, since it was frequently not available from any other source. As a result, early KBS tools tended to lack file handling capabilities and many of them did not recognise the existence of data processing tools such as: database management systems (DBMS); languages such as Cobol, Fortran and C; and Transaction Processing (TP) monitors. This was not significant while systems were self contained, possibly running on stand alone, dedicated hardware.

As KBS tools become established and are used to address problems in commercial applications, there is a need to communicate with databases and other application systems. A news article [JONE89] quoted an ICL Knowledge Engineering Business Centre spokesman as saying:

> '... (he) urges potential expert system users to identify "packets" of functionality within an application where a knowledge–based approach can be applied rather than going for an all–embracing knowledge–based approach.'

d'Agapeyeff and Hawkins [DAGA87] wrote:

> '... the scope and range of utilisation of expert systems may depend on the provision or the means of constructing the following... the ability to access existing files or databases ... '

A Butler Cox Foundation report [BUTL87] includes an appendix on the future developments of expert systems. Two of the four main areas which are mentioned are the trend towards integrating expert systems with mainstream data processing applications and the likely convergence of knowledge–bases with relational databases. It was found that:

> '... most of the suppliers that responded to our survey, and most of those we talked with, are aware of the need to integrate their products with mainstream software and applications and are working towards this goal.'[†]

An ever increasing number of KBS tools provide facilities to enable the integration of KBS applications with existing systems. The Butler Cox report mentioned above was written in 1987 and stated that 'the majority of the expert system products available today are not able to interface with conventional software'[†], naming only eight products which could interface to mainstream systems. The current situation is totally different: over 40 KBS tools are included this book and these are purely illustrative; the majority of KBS tools can now integrate with a range of conventional software tools. Three years in computing is an exceedingly long time.

[†] Reproduced by kind permission of Butler Cox plc. Originally published in Butler Cox Foundation Report 60, Expert Systems in Business.

1.3 Purpose of the book

The purposes of this book are to:

- increase the awareness of administrative computer systems implementors of the potential for integrating KBS technology with their existing and future computer systems;

- stimulate vendors to address the problems associated with integrating KBS and other technology.

These are achieved by:

- identifying and documenting the various ways in which KBS and other software can be integrated, in both development and run–time environments;

- identifying suitable KBS tools for data processing departments which have a large investment in data and information systems;

- commenting on the relative merits of methods of coupling KBS and database software;

- describing some integrated system architectures which may be used.

The products which have been included in this book are intended to illustrate various methods of integration and readers will be able to identify potential KBS products for integration with their existing systems. Inclusion or exclusion of a product in this book should not be taken as an indication of CCTA approval or disapproval of that product.

1.4 Audience

The book is primarily aimed at staff who are responsible for one or more of the following:

- Information Systems strategic planning. In the medium term, KBS will be important components in both corporate and information systems strategies. Planners should be aware of the range of products available, the ways in which they can be used and the opportunities they afford;

- maintenance of existing, computer systems. Users of KBS may require access to data and the database administrator (DBA) will need to know, in some detail, how KBS applications can interact with the database management system;

- purchasing new software for building KBS. Products need to be able to support large systems and have an open systems architecture to facilitate integration of systems built using a variety of tools, including KBS;

- purchasing KBS tools to be used for software development alongside conventional tools. Purchasers should be aware of: the ways in which KBS tools can be integrated with other development software; standards which can be applied to data management products; and how conventional systems conform to standards;

- identification and development of potential KBS applications. Staff should be aware of the capabilities of products for accessing and storing data required by an application. They may also wish to consider the contribution which existing data can make towards new applications.

Although users of systems need not, and should not, know about the software used to build computer systems, they ought to be aware of the facilities on offer and the types of application which can be built. User management could apply some of the ideas in this book to their own computer system requirements.

Some readers may be concerned about the substantial technical content of the book, but it should nevertheless be of interest to all data processing departments since the book references a number of products which run on a variety of hardware configurations and looks at the problems of implementing 'mixed' systems. Example products are given which run on micros, minis and mainframes, and which are marketed by vendors of hardware, such as IBM, ICL and Unisys, as well as software–only companies.

2

Summary of Book Structure

2.1 Introduction

This book builds upon and includes some ideas explored in a report [KERR88], which outlined four major ways in which knowledge–based systems (KBS) and databases can be integrated: firstly, data can be extracted from databases and imported into knowledge–bases for processing, and equally, data generated during the execution of a knowledge–base may be passed to a database for storage; secondly, there is a convergence of the types of facility provided by KBS tools and database management systems (DBMS); thirdly, a database can be used to hold a knowledge–base; and fourthly, rules, or knowledge, can be generated from data held in a database.

Integration of KBS and databases commonly involves other software, such as: a third or fourth generation language to link the KBS and the database; a transaction processing (TP) environment to control the use of a database; and spreadsheets on a micro or personal computer.

This book extends and reorganises the content of the early report to cover some of these wider issues of integrating KBS and databases. The book is still primarily concerned with integrating KBS and databases, but takes into account the fact that databases are often inextricably linked with development tools, such as data dictionaries, and run–time software, such as TP monitors. The main themes in the book are as follows:

- architectural issues; chapter 4;

- integration of tools used in the development of systems; chapter 5;

- integration of tools used at run–time, chapter 6;

- integration of tools within the context of open systems; chapter 7;

- conclusions based upon the previous chapters; chapter 8;

- illustration of the tools which can be integrated; annex C;

- illustration of the data access mechanisms of KBS tools; annex D.

Some introductory information about types of tool mentioned in this book is provided in chapter 3;   and some basic information about the KBS tools used as examples in the book are given in annex B, so that readers can make follow–up enquiries.

Chapters 3, 4, 5 and 6 are made up of sections (3.1, 3.2, etc), each of which describes a different aspect of the main theme.

2.2 Modelling method used within the book

Anyone who is familiar with the work of CCTA on methods will know that ERA (entity–relationship–attribute) modelling has been used as one of the main techniques to facilitate understanding and provide quality and consistency checks in the development of methods, such as the Structured Systems Analysis and Design Method (SSADM). [See reference CCTA89(2) for further information about SSADM.]

The technique can be, and has been, used to express the characteristics and underlying concepts of software tools. A simplified notation has been used here and the ER (entity–relationship) model in figure 2.1 attempts to illustrate just one characteristic for a number of tools: that is, how software components may be integrated with KBS applications during development and at run–time (chapters 5 and 6). Only entities and relationships have been shown, since this overview does not warrant inclusion of attributes. This high level overview also omits many relationships for clarity and in order to emphasise those which illustrate the main theme of the book. This book describes most of the relationships between the entity types.

Entities

Each box on the diagram represents an entity type, which in this case is a software component. The central, and most important entity types for this book, are 'KBS Application' and 'Data File'. Each entity type represents a number of instances of that type. For example, the entity type 'Knowledge–Based System Tool' represents the many tools available such as KEE, Quintus Prolog and Crystal. In the rest of this chapter an *italic style* is used for entity types.

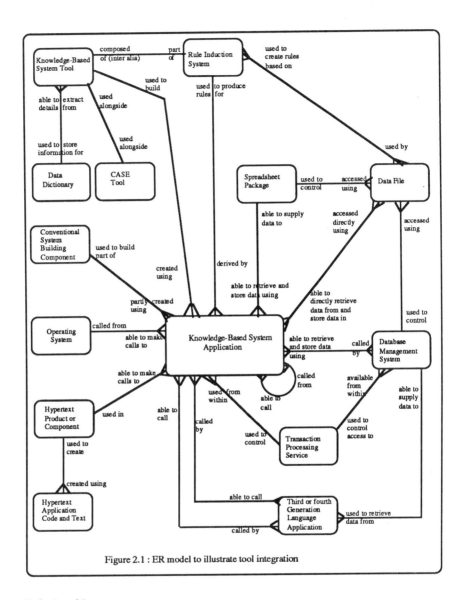

Figure 2.1 : ER model to illustrate tool integration

Relationships

Each line between entity types represents a relationship between those two entity types; the simplified diagrammatic notation does not differentiate between mandatory and optional relationships; but, in fact, all of those shown in figure 2.1 are optional. An optional relationship implies that an entity instance can exist without a relationship being established with instances of other entity types. A mandatory relationship implies that entity instances cannot exist without a relationship being established with instances of other entity types. A crow's foot (the three–prong symbol at the end of a relationship) implies that zero or more instances of the entity type which it adjoins may be involved in the relationship. In the rest of this chapter an underline style is used for relationships.

2.3 Architecture (Chapter 4)

Chapter 4 pulls together a number of issues concerned with the logical architecture of integrated KBS and DBMS. It includes a discussion about the potential for using KBS in DBMS and related software, and vice versa. Figure 2.2 illustrates these concepts, which would be transparent to the developers of KBS applications and designers of databases, and for that very reason they have not been included in figure 2.1. The following is an interpretation of the diagram and the content of this chapter.

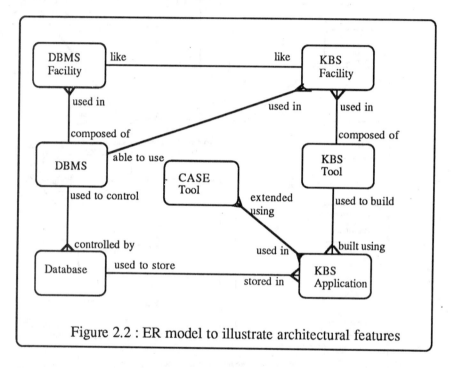

Figure 2.2 : ER model to illustrate architectural features

A *DBMS facility* may be <u>like</u> a *KBS facility,* and vice versa. Sections 4.1 and 4.2 look at the convergence of facilities exhibited by, or proposed for, both KBS and DBMS.

A *DBMS* may be <u>able to use</u> one or more *KBS facility.* Section 4.3 describes how KBS technology can be used to enhance existing DBMS facilities, such as the user interface.

A *Computer Assisted Software Engineering (CASE) tool* may be <u>extended using</u> one or more *KBS applications.* Section 4.4 describes how knowledge–base applications can increase and improve the functionality of CASE tools, illustrated by some example CASE tools.

A *database* may be <u>used to store</u> one or more *KBS applications.* Section 4.5 presents an architecture for KBS based upon database technology.

2.4 Integration of development tools (Chapter 5)

Chapter 5 is concerned with the use of conventional development tools for building components of KBS applications, particularly those which are integrated with DBMS.

Figure 2.3 highlights (by using shading in boxes) the components on the model which are discussed in chapter 5. The following is an interpretation of the diagram and the contents of this chapter.

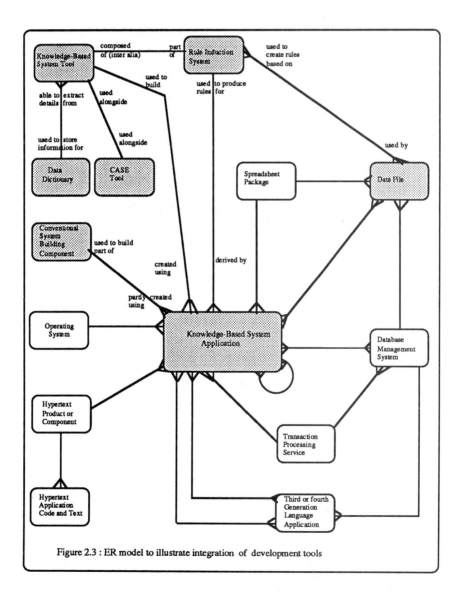

Figure 2.3 : ER model to illustrate integration of development tools

A *KBS tool* may be <u>used to build</u> one or more *KBS applications*. The inverse
relationship is a *KBS application* may be <u>created using</u> a *KBS tool*. The
optionality of these relationships is important: a KBS tool can be used to build
a KBS application, as in the majority of cases, but can also be used for other
reasons, such as prototyping conventional applications; equally, a KBS
application may, but not necessarily, be created using a KBS tool, since
conventional languages such as C are sometimes used. This is a large and
controversial topic which is not covered in this book, but it is necessary to
include the entities on the diagram in order to show how they can be integrated
with other software tools.

A *KBS tool* may be <u>able to extract details from</u> a *data dictionary*. A *CASE
tool* may be <u>used alongside</u> a *KBS tool* when building an application. Section
5.1 describes these facilities. Most KBS tools can only use a data dictionary
which is an integral part of the KBS tool rather than general purpose data
dictionaries, such as ICL's DDS. It may also be possible to use CASE tools,
particularly diagramming facilities, to design KBS applications.

A *conventional system building component* may be <u>used to build part of</u> one
or more *KBS applications*. Section 5.2 describes how this can be done,
illustrated by example tools. The section explains how application generator
components, such as a screen painter, can be used along with KBS tools to build
a single KBS application. It does not set out to explain how conventional tools
can be used to build KBS applications in total without some use of a KBS tool.

A *rule induction system* may be <u>used to create rules based on</u> one or more *data
files*. The *rule induction system* may be <u>used to produce rules for</u> one or more
KBS applications. Alternatively, these rules may be used for some other
purposes as described in section 5.3.

2.5 Integration of tools at run–time (Chapter 6)

Figure 2.4 highlights the components which are discussed in chapter 6.

A *KBS application* may be <u>able to retrieve and store data using</u> one or more
database management systems. In turn, a *database management system* may be
<u>used to control</u> one or more *data files*. The idea of extracting data from and
storing data in databases is described in section 6.1. Various methods of
coupling are discussed, illustrated by mechanisms used by KBS tools.

A *KBS application* may be <u>able to call, or be called by</u> one or more *third or
fourth generation languages*. Section 6.2 discusses issues associated with third
and fourth generation language communications.

A *KBS application* may be <u>used from within</u> a *transaction processing service*.
Many large conventional systems on mainframes utilise a transaction processing
service to control on–line systems which may use a database. Some, but not
all, KBS applications can be integrated with these large systems and section 6.3
outlines how this can be done.

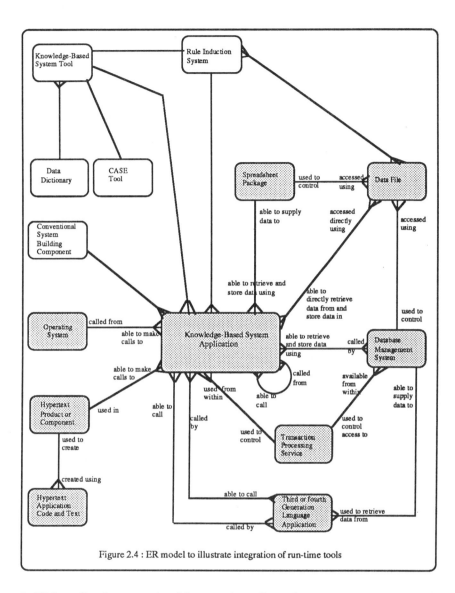

Figure 2.4 : ER model to illustrate integration of run-time tools

A *KBS application* may be <u>able to make calls to</u> the *operating system*. This is an important feature which enables applications running on different hardware to communicate. Section 6.3 also describes this type of integration.

A *KBS application* may also be <u>able to retrieve and store data using</u> a *spreadsheet package*. In turn a *spreadsheet package* may be <u>used to control</u> one or more *data files* (often termed worksheets). This facility is most likely to be provided by packages running on micros. The concepts behind this and some example software are described in section 6.4.

A *KBS application* may be <u>able to directly retrieve data from and store data in</u> one or more *data files* which may be serial or indexed files. Data files which have been created using a DBMS should never be accessed directly, but only through the DBMS. It may be possible to access worksheets created by spreadsheets if the format of them is known.

A *KBS application* may be <u>able to make calls to</u> a *hypertext product or component*, which may have been <u>used to create</u> one or more *hypertext applications*. Section 6.5 looks at the potential for using hypertext software.

Lastly, a *KBS application* may be <u>able to call, or be called from,</u> one or more other *KBS applications*. Most applications are being built as separate units, but it will be useful to be able to integrate them into a single information system (as far as the user is concerned), if required. The ability to modularise an application could also make maintenance easier. Section 6.6 discusses these issues.

3

Introduction to Categories of Software

Purpose

This chapter is intended to set the scene for the following chapters, where technical terms may be used without explanation. A short introduction to various types of software is given, so that readers can appreciate the fundamental messages of the book, without necessarily knowing about the technical details of all types of software. Those people who require more detailed and comprehensive information are directed to the references.

3.1

Introduction to knowledge–based systems

3.1.1 Definition

There is no commonly accepted definition of knowledge–based systems (KBS) or expert systems and the terms are frequently used interchangeably. The term knowledge–based systems is used in this text in a generic sense to encompass expert systems, intelligent knowledge–based systems (IKBS), rule base systems, etc. The following is given as an explanation and is not intended to be definitive.

The phrase 'knowledge–based systems' is frequently used to refer to both KBS *applications* (such as a system for diagnosing computer faults) and KBS *tools* (such as KEE and ICL–Adviser). The context of the words should give some indication of which is intended. This book is mainly, but not exclusively, concerned with KBS tools.

The British Computer Society's Committee of the Specialist Group on Expert Systems has produced the following definition for an expert system [KBS] *application*:

> 'the embodiment within a computer of a knowledge–based component from an expert skill in such a form that the machine can offer intelligent advice or take an intelligent decision about a processing function. A desirable additional characteristic, which many would regard as fundamental, is the capability of the system on demand to justify its own line of reasoning in a manner directly intelligible to the inquirer... '[†].

[†] Reprinted with the permission of the British Computer Society Specialist Group on Expert Systems (SGES).

The Butler Cox Foundation Report number 37 [BUTL83] defined an expert system [KBS] in a simpler, easy to understand way, as:

> 'a computer system containing organised knowledge, both factual and heuristic, that concerns some specific area of human expertise; and that is able to produce inferences for the user.'[†].

Paraphrasing these definitions, a knowledge–based system:

- is a piece of computer software;

- contains human knowledge which can be written down. This may be factual, such as a person under the age of 17 may not hold a driving licence, or it may be heuristic, for example, a person over 30, who owns a car, has a mortgage and is in full time employment is credit worthy. Probability weights may, on occasions, be applied to heuristics;

- consists of a task which is usually, though not necessarily, carried out by someone who has specialist knowledge, such as an insurance broker, a tax adviser or a doctor;

- is limited to a task or part of a domain and is only as good as the knowledge which was built into it. For example, a system built to diagnose faults on one manufacturer's cars may not be applicable to diagnosing faults on those made by other car makers;

- may provide an explanation facility which can justify results produced, but some people would not regard this as a fundamental requirement of a KBS. This is easy to build using most KBS tools.

A KBS *tool* is a software package which facilitates the building of a KBS application and embodies the architectural components shown in figure 3.1.2. KBS applications have been built using conventional tools such as Pascal and C compilers and conversely, it is possible to use KBS tools to build some conventional systems. This book is not concerned with this topic. It is concerned with *how* tools may be integrated and not with *the purposes* for which integrated tools may be used.

Several types of application have been successfully tackled using KBS tools, including systems for diagnosis, configuration, giving advice, product formulation and scheduling. Although the primary aim in developing these applications is to use expertise, it is sometimes necessary to include some conventional data processing, not least for data capture, retrieval and storage. In these cases neither KBS nor conventional tools provide the total functionality required. Integration of KBS and conventional system tools is the solution, so that appropriate components can be used to develop the application.

---

† Reproduced by kind permission of Butler Cox plc. Originally published in Butler Cox Foundation Report 37, Expert Systems.

3.1.2 Using KBS tools to build applications

Figure 3.1.1 gives a simplified, diagrammatic representation of how a knowledge–based system is developed and used. This diagram is referenced in some of the following chapters to illustrate the context in which a database can be used.

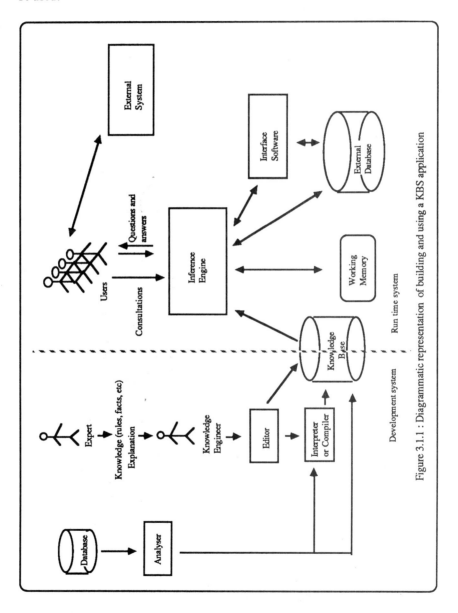

Figure 3.1.1 : Diagrammatic representation of building and using a KBS application

Experts are recognised as having some knowledge or expertise which is to be captured and used to form the basis of a KBS application. It is a knowledge engineer's job to elicit information and explanations from the expert(s) and build this into the knowledge–base. The representation of the information varies, but frequently rules are used to define aspects of process and facts define data. The knowledge–base may be compiled incrementally after each change has been made, at the end of an amendment phase or not at all, depending upon the software tool.

Optionally, an inductive KBS (see 3.1.5 and section 5.3) can be used to initially populate the knowledge–base. The software referred to as the analyser in figure 3.1.1 takes a set of examples which are representative of the domain being investigated, and generates a set of rules. The knowledge engineer can modify this knowledge–base according to expert advice. He can then build the application.

The knowledge engineer and the expert test the application to ensure that it produces the desired effects and results. Most tools provide some debugging aids to facilitate testing by displaying fact values, enumerating rules which have been fired and outputting explanatory text. Such facilities are comparable to those provided for debugging conventional systems, for example, the Interactive Testing System (ITS) used for debugging Cobol programs on ICL 2900 machines.

The end users may exhibit varying degrees of expertise. The user interface of the KBS application, which is often generated by the inference engine from information held in the knowledge–base, should reflect the level of expertise needed to drive it. The user initiates a consultation in a similar manner to starting an on–line session for a conventional system. The inference engine accesses the knowledge–base, run–time storage (working memory), and possibly databases and other systems. Run–time storage holds fact instantiations (values) and system information such as which rules have been fired. The inference engine may access an external database to provide fact instantiations as an alternative to asking the user to input details via the screen or derivation by inference; this may be done either directly using data manipulation language (DML) encoded in the knowledge–base or indirectly via an external system such as a Cobol program.

3.1.3 Theoretical model

The model shown in figure 3.1.2 is commonly used to depict the logical, conceptual components of a KBS. In practice, some of the components overlap; for example, the knowledge–base of an ICL–Adviser application will contain the text of questions and explanations (user interface specification). There is a large number of KBS tools on the market, 200 in 1988 [OVUM88], and this conceptual view will not be representative and applicable to all of them.

A fundamental component of a KBS application is the *knowledge–base*. A tool can be used to build a number of applications, that is, knowledge–bases. The knowledge–bases are usually logically and physically separate, unlike a database managed by a DBMS where the data is considered as a single, logical entity (even though the data may be stored in more than one physical file). The knowledge–base can loosely be equated to a file containing the source code of a program, such as a Cobol program, in that processes and data are defined in the knowledge–base. However, there is only a small, if any, procedural element to determine the order of execution of statements, unlike a Cobol program which would contain many 'GO TO' and 'PERFORM' statements.

The knowledge–base contains the information required to emulate expertise, which will include some facts or data, and rules or clauses which express how the facts can be manipulated and evaluated. Users of the KBS tool (knowledge engineers) must populate the knowledge–base.

The *inference engine* operates on the knowledge–base and applies laws of logical inference or reasoning to control the flow of making deductions and drawing conclusions. That is, it causes facts to be instantiated while attempting to reach goals and conclusions. All of the facts may not be instantiated; only those which are required as part of the inferencing will have values.

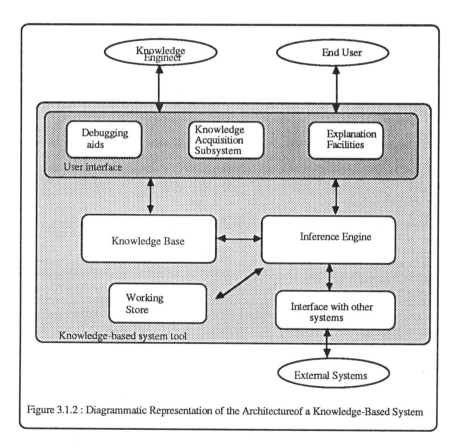

Figure 3.1.2 : Diagrammatic Representation of the Architecture of a Knowledge-Based System

The knowledge–base may contain some procedural information which guides the inference engine through the knowledge–base; this is minimal, and often not essential, but may be included for a number of reasons such as improvement of performance at run–time. A number of control strategies may be associated with the inference engine, such as forward and backward chaining, truth maintenance and conflict resolution. It is not necessary in the context of this book to know about or understand these concepts, but readers who are interested in more detail are directed to the references and general KBS texts.

Working store, or memory, is used by a KBS tool at run–time, to store transient and dynamic information, such as data values, which facts have been instantiated, which rules have been fired, etc. This is the part of the host machine memory allocated to the KBS, which will be controlled by the inference engine.

The *user interface* provides the link between the outside world, that is people, and the KBS tool. The *knowledge acquisition subsystem* is used by the KBS application builder to add facts and process details to the knowledge–base. This may exhibit varying degrees of complexity: it may be a simple line editor or a sophisticated windowed, mouse–driven interface. Some *trace and debugging aids* are usually provided to help validate and test the system. *Explanation facilities* allow the knowledge engineer to build explanations into an application about why questions are asked of the end–user, how conclusions have been reached and give general help information. The inference engine causes explanatory messages to be displayed in response to user requests or design features of the knowledge–base.

The last component on the diagram, but one of the most significant as far as this book is concerned, is the *interface with other systems*. KBS tools do not necessarily have such a facility, especially versions which were released before 1988. The interface may provide access to languages such as Cobol and C, packages such as the spreadsheet Lotus–123, the operating system, other KBS applications (allowing modularisation) and databases. One of the main themes in this book is concerned with the development and availability of such interfaces.

3.1.4 Packaging of tools

Many KBS tools provide an environment in which to build and execute knowledge–based system applications. An editor is usually provided to create and update knowledge–bases, though a general purpose editor or word processing package may be used. For example, the source of an ICL–Adviser application can be changed using the VME Screen Editor and SD–Prolog relies upon the use of a word processing package or editor for creation and amendment of the source code. A compiler or interpreter may be included in the KBS environment to produce object code from the knowledge–base content. Housekeeping facilities may be provided to allow back–up copies of knowledge–bases to be taken, security restrictions to be applied, etc.

The inference engine which controls run–time execution of knowledge–bases is included in the KBS environment. Many KBS tool vendors provide run–time only systems (at a reduced cost), in addition to the complete tool sets, which do not include the knowledge acquisition and compiler subsystem. These can be used for delivery of systems to users so that the knowledge–base is protected against permanent amendments by the end users.

Some KBS tools are loosely comparable to database management systems (DBMS), in that KBS control access to the underlying knowledge–bases at all times, just as DBMS control data files.

3.1.5 Types of KBS tool

Just as there are a number of tool types available for building data processing systems (machine code, low level languages, third generation languages and application generators) there are several categories of KBS tool. The type of tool selected should be matched to the application to be built because different tools are, in general, applicable to different application types and a mismatch may reduce the chance of successfully implementing a system.

The boundaries between the types listed below are artificial, blurred and overlapping, but enable features to be attributed to a class of tools. Some people may also argue that some of the classes can be broken down further; for example, object oriented languages could be defined as a separate class.

Figure 3.1.3 gives a diagrammatic representation of the types of KBS software available, indicating the range of applications which they can be used to build and the skill level required for using those tools. The more elongated the boxes are on the horizontal axis, the bigger the range of applications that can be built using those KBS tools. The taller the boxes are on the vertical axis, the wider the range of staff which are able to use those KBS tools, within the spectrum from user to knowledge engineer. Both the ranges of staff and application are indicators of the flexibility of the tools.

The most basic type of tool is programming *languages*. The common Artificial Intelligence (AI) languages are Lisp and Prolog, though conventional programming languages such as C, Pascal and Fortran have been used to build KBS applications. Lisp was developed in the mid–1950s with the aim of providing a language for symbol manipulation rather than calculation, the only data structure being the list. Prolog is a declarative language based on logical relationships between objects. A Prolog program can be regarded as a collection of statements of fact, called clauses, and the appropriate clause for execution is selected by pattern matching.

Programming languages offer maximum flexibility with respect to the range of appropriate applications, possibly at the cost of limiting usability to highly trained staff. The user of basic versions of Prolog or Lisp commonly had to construct the KBS framework, though many language based tools available today, such as SD–Prolog, provide high level facilities including a window mechanism, for building a user interface.

Shells were developed originally by removing the knowledge from knowledge–based system applications. A classic is EMYCIN (Empty MYCIN) which was developed from MYCIN, a KBS which diagnoses bacterial infections. Most of the shells on the market today are purpose built tools, often written in C, which generally provide a high–level interface, rule–based knowledge representation and a forward or backward, or both, chaining mechanism. There is often no physical separation between the user interface and the knowledge–base. Shells are generally considered easy to use and provide high productivity, at a cost of having limited applicability. They are commonly, though not exclusively, used to build diagnosis, configuration and advisory systems. Examples of shells include ICL–Adviser, Savoir, Crystal and CA–DB:Expert. (See annex B for details of these and other products).

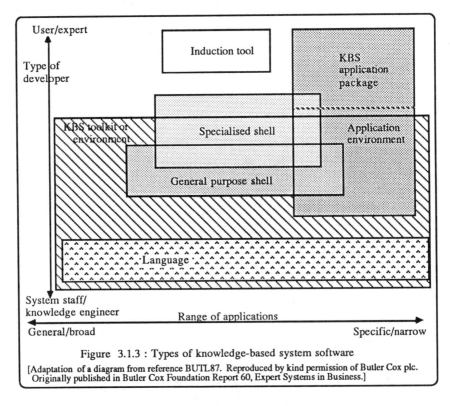

Figure 3.1.3 : Types of knowledge-based system software

[Adaptation of a diagram from reference BUTL87. Reproduced by kind permission of Butler Cox plc. Originally published in Butler Cox Foundation Report 60, Expert Systems in Business.]

Specialised shells, as mentioned in BUTL87, are designed to cater for a specific class of applications for a specific domain of expertise. These are perhaps more commonly developed by software houses by generalising applications which were built using commercially available tools.

Hybrid toolkits or *environments* contain a variety of knowledge representation techniques and inference mechanisms, which have been integrated and packaged with a high level user interface and other development aids to provide a selection of tools for the system developer. Toolkits provide the developer with the flexibility of one or more languages (usually Lisp and Prolog) without needing to explicitly write all of the code. For example, diagrammatic representations can be converted to code by some toolkits. A number of ways of approaching problems are provided: for example object oriented structures or rules. The most appropriate paradigm(s) or representation(s) can be used to populate the knowledge–base. Application builders using these toolkits need intensive training in comparison to that required for shell usage due to the complexity of the software.

Examples of toolkits are KEE, Inference ART and Knowledgecraft. They used to be expensive and only run on large machines or workstations which had a large memory capacity. However, they are becoming increasingly available on smaller machines, a version of KEE being available to run on some micros.

All of the types of tool mentioned above are examples of the generalised architecture for *deductive* KBS; the application builder who uses these tools needs to know what rules and facts are to be coded in the knowledge–base. *Inductive* KBS tools are different, in that they can generate rules to populate a knowledge–base. They can be presented with a series of decision examples, which would be made under a variety of representative conditions, then rules underlying the decision making process are induced. In other words, inductive tools develop rules from examples or generalise from the particular. These rules can then be fed directly into a knowledge–base associated with a deductive KBS or be re–coded using a language, shell or toolkit. Examples of induction tools are ExTran and XpertRule. For more details see section 5.3.

The final type of KBS product shown in figure 3.1.3 is *application packages and application environments*. KBS application packages include a basic knowledge–base for a subject domain and a set of inference rules. An application environment enables users to change a KBS application package to suit their needs. For example Parys from Unibit is an application environment designed for human resource managers and it provides a set of tools for customising an application to organisational needs. Parys can be used to store data such as personnel records, and elicit and store information such as job requirements. The system can then be used for recruitment, job evaluation, training assessment, etc, according to the criteria laid down by that organisation.

A number of products from each of these categories will be used in the following chapters to illustrate ways of integrating KBS with other software.

3.1.6 Comparison of KBS and conventional system software

Figure 3.1.4 compares conventional applications software with KBS software. The architecture of KBS tools available today is rapidly moving away from that shown for 1987 towards that suggested for the 1990s, although the use of a knowledge encyclopaedia has not yet emerged. Figure 3.1.4 shows that KBS decoupled the application logic from the application control (1987 column), but at the same time incorporated data definition and storage into the application logic. The four software elements, application logic, application control, data definition and stored facts, are unlikely to become totally distinct in 1990 and beyond. A knowledge–base will inevitably continue to include some facts which are unique to the application and some data definitions. In the database world there is a trend towards inclusion of some application logic in the data dictionary (data definitions) and databases (facts). Data definitions will perhaps include some logic such as integrity constraints and data such as range values; and databases will be extended to store more than just items of data.

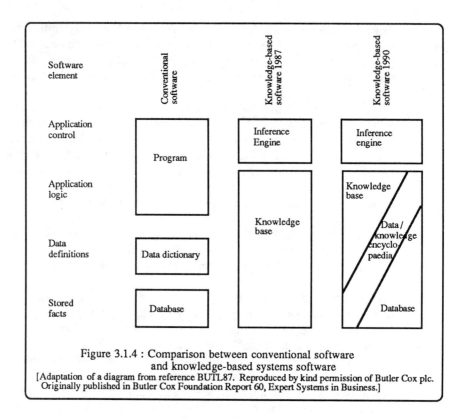

Figure 3.1.4 : Comparison between conventional software
and knowledge-based systems software
[Adaptation of a diagram from reference BUTL87. Reproduced by kind permission of Butler Cox plc.
Originally published in Butler Cox Foundation Report 60, Expert Systems in Business.]

3.1.7 'Expert database systems'

This phrase seems to have been coined to describe various combinations of KBS and databases, which are described in this book. 'Expert database systems' represent architectures of the future, on which some research projects are working. Kerschberg [KERS87] described them as follows:

> 'Expert database systems represent the confluence of concepts, tools and techniques from diverse areas: artificial intelligence, database management, logic programming, information retrieval and fuzzy systems theory... Basically, an expert database system supports applications that require "knowledge–directed processing of shared information".'

It is unfortunate that information system engineers coin new terms without adequately defining them. I believe that 'expert database systems' could be used to describe a number of the architectures discussed in this book. So reader beware: if you see the phrase 'expert database system', be prepared for anything!

3.2

Introduction to database management systems

3.2.1 Definitions and functions

There are numerous definitions of a *database*, including the following given by James Martin:

> 'A database is a collection of inter–related data stored together with controlled redundancy to serve one or more applications in an optimal fashion; the data are stored so that they are independent of programs which use that data. A common and controlled approach is used when adding new data or when modifying or retrieving existing data.'[†]

The data is controlled by a database management system (DBMS) which is proprietary software for handling the storage and retrieval of data. A DBMS provides the following:

- data independence. The DBMS separates specification of processing from the data. Processing works on a logical view of the data and the DBMS maps the logical view on to the physical representation of the data. There are a number of advantages associated with this approach, not least that data can be re–organised, and possibly re–structured, with minimal impact on the programs;

- data integrity. Checks on the consistency of the data can be encoded within the data description; the DBMS will ensure that the data satisfies these checks. The DBMS also automatically maintains indexes and chains (which represent sets in a network database). Without these facilities the processing would need to be included in all the applications that update the data;

[†] Reproduced by permission of James Martin Associates.

- data concurrency and consistency. Since the database is a shared resource the DBMS allows a number of users to access the database concurrently. The DBMS can inhibit concurrent access to the same data instances by setting locks on data. A second user is then prevented from reading logical sets of records which have been partially updated by another transaction, thus maintaining consistency from the database point of view;

- recovery. The DBMS logs changes made to the database by all users; if a user aborts the current transaction then all changes made within it are automatically undone by the DBMS. A DBMS also provides facilities to back–up the database (by copying all or parts of the data). If at any time the database is corrupted, a back–up copy can be used and changes which have been logged since that copy was taken be applied to the replacement database. This mechanism provides resilience against loss of the database;

- access control. The DBMS controls who can access which parts of the database and in which mode (read or modify). Access control is important when all the data is held as one logical unit;

- controlled data redundancy. By maintaining complex data structures and access paths automatically, the DBMS allows the database designer to reduce and control data redundancy. Reduced data redundancy minimises the possibility of inconsistencies between copies of data;

- centralised control. The DBMS facilitates treatment of data as a corporate resource. Standards, such as locking of records at table or set level when updating, and error checking with appropriate output of messages, can be enforced through the DBMS. Data which is physically distributed across several machines can be centrally controlled using a DBMS;

- data maintenance. Facilities to unload and reload, re–organise and re–structure data are generally supplied with a DBMS.

When the number of data types, which may be simple or complex objects, within a system is small, the facilities provided by a DBMS are not needed to control storage of them. However, the above features of a DBMS become more useful and essential, not just desirable, as the complexity of a data structure increases and when several people require concurrent access.

3.2.2   Architecture

An overview of the architecture of a DBMS is given in figure 3.2.1. There are three logical views of the data in a database, the descriptions of which are usually held in a central repository, such as a directory or dictionary, in association with the database. The ANSI–SPARC 3 level architecture uses the terms External schema, Global schema and Internal schema, though they are commonly referred to as subschema, schema and storage schema respectively.

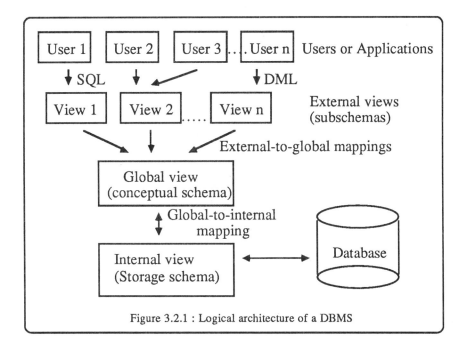

Figure 3.2.1 : Logical architecture of a DBMS

The *internal view* (storage schema) defines the physical structure of the data, specifying where records should be placed, clustered, scattered, etc, across physical files and how they should be physically accessed, such as by using an index or a serial search.

The *global view* (conceptual schema) provides a logical view of the database, specifying such things as record layouts, data item definitions and set membership and ownership. There is a mapping between the internal view and the global view, which is often implicit in the use of common names.

A number of *external views* (subschemas) define different views of parts of the global view; logical record definitions can be defined, made up of data items from one or more global record types, in addition to records and sets in the global view. New data items can also be generated through calculations based on one or more data items. Mappings between the global view and external views must be defined. Often synonyms are included in the mappings so that the external view can define data items using terms which the end user can understand.

The external views provide an access control mechanism for processing, since only those data items which are essential for an application to function are included in the definition to be used. All the other data items and record types, which are not included in the view, are hidden and unavailable to the application.

The internal, global and external views are described using a Data Definition Language (DDL). The syntax of this language may be product specific, as is the case of IDMS(X) on ICL machines. Alternatively, it may be based on an international standard such as SQL.

Users and applications access data through an external view using a DBMS specific language, generally termed a data manipulation language (DML). Some databases have a language which has unique syntax, but most relational databases have standardised on the database language SQL.

3.2.3   Client/server architecture

A client/server architecture, in database terms, logically (and sometimes physically) separates application functions from the database management functions. Figure 3.2.2 shows the client/server architecture as implemented by Sybase. The user can work with the client (front–end) on a terminal and only use resources of the server (back–end) when data is required. A client/server architecture allows more users to access a database than would be possible with other architectures.

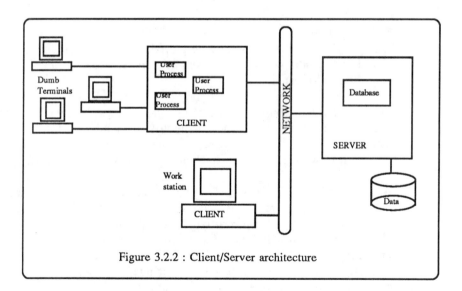

Figure 3.2.2 : Client/Server architecture

A client/server architecture easily maps on to a network of machines, each machine carrying out the tasks to which it is best suited. For example, the client machines could support sophisticated user interface software and the server machine could have high processing power.

3.2.4   Types of databases

There are basically three main types of DBMS, hierarchic, network and relational, which differ in the way data is viewed. They serve equivalent applications, in that a relational or a network database could be used to store the same data, unlike KBS tools which are generally better suited to particular types of applications. A fourth category, free text databases, has been included in the report as there is at least one KBS product which can interface with such a database. Free text databases are not usually associated with the other types of database since they specifically support information retrieval applications and are not usually applicable to transaction type applications. A fifth category, object oriented databases, is beginning to emerge from research; see section 4.2 for further details.

A *hierarchic* DBMS has a number of data units (record types) organised in tree structures; each data unit has one and only one owner, but it may have one or more member units. IBM's Information Management System/Virtual Storage (IMS/VS) is an example of such a database management system.

Network DBMS implement a network view of data. Records can be inter–connected in general networks as well as in hierarchies, thereby providing a more flexible structure. However, once a particular network structure has been implemented as a database, it is very difficult to modify that structure. Integrated Database Management System (IDMS) which runs on ICL machines under the VME operating system is a network DBMS commonly used within government.

A *relational* DBMS is perceived to hold data in a series of two dimensional tables, where each table maps on to a record type and consists of a number of rows (record occurrences) and columns (attributes). Relationships between rows in different tables are represented by the storage of foreign keys (attributes from other tables) within a table. New tables can be formed by selecting rows or columns from existing tables or by joining tables. Relational DBMS are considered to have the most flexible structure in terms of data access and the data can also be relatively easily restructured. The penalty for flexibility is usually poor performance, though most new releases of products attempt to address this problem. There are numerous examples of relational databases. Oracle and Ingres are perhaps the best known products, but there are others such as Sybase and Rdb.

Free text databases, as implied by the name, allow the storage and efficient searching of data in English language or free format. The databases usually have a logically flat file structure, in that all records have a similar structure. Records consist of fields which can hold text. Most free text databases have a more detailed hierarchic structure where text consists of documents, containing sections, made up of paragraphs, consisting of sentences constructed of words.

The physical structure of a free text database varies with the product, but as a minimum, there must be a text file and an index file containing significant words and pointers to occurrences of those words in the text file. The indexes allow data to be accessed by matching of key words or phrases within a field.

Free text databases are usually associated with retrieval rather than updating applications, such as library help systems. STATUS, CAIRS and BASIS are examples of text retrieval databases.

3.2.5   Microcomputer DBMS

The above information about DBMS generally refers to those which run on workstations, minis and mainframes, with possibly a version for microcomputers. Such DBMS are intended to be used for relatively large applications which have large volumes of data and many users. A number of DBMS have been developed specifically for microcomputers which, in general, are intended for single user systems which store smaller volumes of data. However, the separation of these types of DBMS is blurred, not least because of the increasing power and storage capacity of microcomputers and the ability to link machines as networks.

DBMS aimed at the microcomputer user would not be expected to exhibit all the features described in earlier parts of this section, because they are not required. For example, a single user DBMS does not need concurrent access features and access control need not be so elaborate. Conversely, they may have facilities (or add–on packages which provide facilities) which do not exist in the larger DBMS products, such as word processing, spreadsheets and desktop publishing.

In this book dBASE III has been used as an example of a microcomputer DBMS, not least because many knowledge–based systems which run on microcomputers can access dBASE III data files. dBASE III:

- can store 128 fields and 4000 bytes per record, over a billion records per file (limited by hardware capacity) and have up to 10 files open simultaneously;

- has a data catalogue and fast sorting and indexing;

- can import and export files in a number of formats including ASCII, DIF and Lotus–123.

dBASE IV has been released which has greater functionality than dBASE III, including: multi–user features, such as record locking and rollback; connectivity with minicomputers and mainframes; dBASE/SQL for data query and manipulation; and up to 99 files can be open simultaneously.

3.3

Introduction to data dictionaries

3.3.1 Origins

Data dictionaries originated as simple directory systems supporting the definition of data structures for file management or database management systems. Facilities were then rapidly added to make the data dictionary the repository for all information about data, as illustrated in figure 3.3.1. Some systems allow the documentation of many kinds of file and database and even of manual document structures. Generation facilities to produce data definitions for use by database management systems were provided and used to justify the cost of entering definitions into the data dictionary.

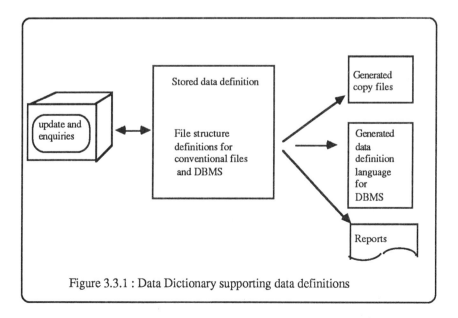

Figure 3.3.1 : Data Dictionary supporting data definitions

Data dictionaries were extended to document details of processing. The typical report to aid the planning of maintenance is 'Tell me all the programs that use Customer–Number'. However, in a Cobol environment, this type of cross–reference information, invaluable for impact analysis, often has to be entered manually rather than being deduced automatically as a program is compiled. The effect is that the cross–reference is rarely maintained.

The release of application generators such as ICL's Application Master, Computer Associates' ADS/Online and ADR/Ideal extended the scope and usefulness of the data dictionary considerably. All application data definitions, screen layouts and application logic can now be held in the data dictionary. Working application code can be generated by the back end of the application generator as shown in figure 3.3.2. Impact analysis is automated to a higher degree because the application logic is held in the data dictionary.

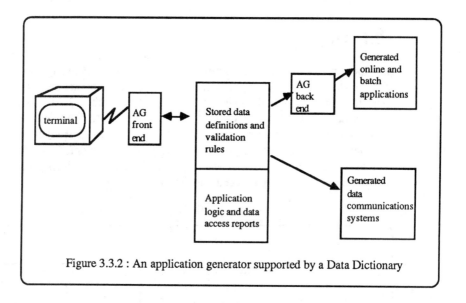

Figure 3.3.2 : An application generator supported by a Data Dictionary

3.3.2 Architecture

Database management systems, application generators, query languages, and more recently analyst workbench or computer assisted software engineering (CASE) tools all have at their heart a data dictionary. This records the information captured during the various system development phases that they support. A data dictionary is simply a container of information about data and processing.

Some of the current mainframe data dictionary products support both analysis and design, notably ICL's DDS. Analyst workbench products support analysis and some are beginning to support design. These products also contain data dictionary facilities, although most of them are micro based. The contents of a

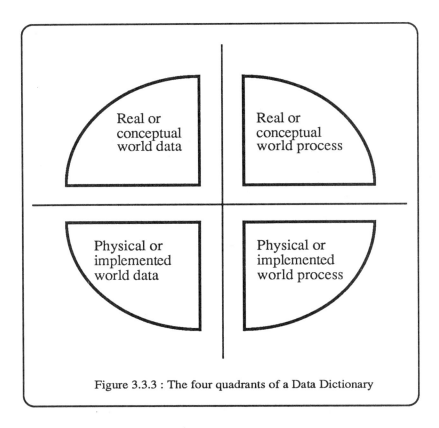

Figure 3.3.3 : The four quadrants of a Data Dictionary

data dictionary to support analysis and design can be viewed as in figure 3.3.3. The two upper quadrants support the analysis work providing separate structures and syntax for describing the data and the processing. The two lower quadrants support design, again separating data and process descriptions. There are logical relationships which cross the boundaries of the four quadrants, for example to show how the entities and attributes of analysis map on to tables and columns of a relational database design.

3.3.3 Information Resource Dictionary System (IRDS)

There is a need for a standard to facilitate interworking of application development tools because the lack of such a standard holds back effective use of existing tools. The appropriate vehicle for such a standard is the data dictionary. Development has been underway in the USA since 1980 and at the British Standards Institute (BSI) since 1985, the latter in support of an International Standards Organisation (ISO) IRDS standard.

Current work on the IRDS standard includes drafting of a framework and a services interface. It is anticipated that standards will be in place by 1990 and 1991 respectively. Import and export facilities to and from IRDS are being specified in consultation with developers of CDIF (CASE Data Interchange Format) and they are likely to be delivered in the next three years.

3.3.4   Benefits

A data dictionary provides a number of benefits to analysts, designers and programmers during the development and maintenance of systems. A data dictionary cross–relates a business view of a system with the detailed data and procedural specifications used by computer specialists. Three major benefits are realised through the provision of facilities to control definitions, enforce standards and carry out impact analysis.

A centralised repository for data and process definitions ensures that everyone uses the same definitions. It is possible to carry out integrity and consistency checks across the collection of documentation held in the dictionary. Furthermore, a dictionary can help the configuration manager to control versions and releases of the definitions.

Since all the system analysis and design documentation is held in electronic form it is possible to use the controlling data dictionary software to enforce standards. These may be in house standards, such as naming conventions, SSADM standards, such as diagramming conventions, or international standards such as SQL and Cobol syntax.

Impact analysis, during development or maintenance of a system, through use of a data dictionary is more efficient, and possibly more effective, than manually checking paper–based documentation, providing that appropriate information has been added to the dictionary contents. 'What–if' queries can provide an assessment of the impact of a change.

3.4

Introduction to third and fourth generation languages

3.4.1 Third generation languages

The term 'third generation languages', or 3GL, became popular when the term 'fourth generation language', or 4GL, came into use. The term encompasses those languages which are of a higher level than assembler or machine instructions and are mostly procedural, which emerged in the 1960s and 1970s. Cobol is perhaps the best known 3GL in administrative computing, but Fortran, Pascal, Algol and C are other well known third generation languages.

It is likely that most readers of this book will be familiar with one or more of these languages, therefore a detailed description has not been included. Those people who require information about third generation languages will find numerous books on specific languages in the computer section of libraries.

3.4.2 Move towards fourth generation languages

Third generation languages emerged when data processing was based upon serial and indexed files and they continued to be used (and are still used today) for accessing data held in databases, particularly those based upon hierarchic and network architectures.

A number of packages became available in the 1970s, often termed report writers or parameter driven applications, which allowed the developer to create limited types of application quickly, since less coding was required. These packages were invariably marketed separately from data management software.

When relational database management systems (RDBMS) emerged in the 1980s it became common to market application development software with them. Indeed some proprietary names, such as Oracle and Ingres, refer to both the database management system (DBMS) and the application development software, which can cause confusion. This was the first major step towards integrated development and run–time environments.

ionally, the processing associated with RDBMS is different to that
iated with hierarchic and network databases. The processing is set–based,
r than record or tuple based: that is to say, a process specifies *what* should
be done to a *group* of records rather than what should be done and also *how* the
records should be read and *individually* processed. As a result, there is less
processing code to write, which increases developer productivity. (A set in
relational terms means a group of related records which are processed together,
and this should not be confused with a set in a network database, which
represents a relationship between two entity types.)

In the 1980s it was realised that integrated development environments were
required for the future, not least so that development costs could be minimised
and large system development could be controlled. Computer assisted software
engineering (CASE) tools are beginning to be incorporated with DBMS and
application generator software, as illustrated by Oracle software. In the 1990s it
is likely that this trend will continue and with the advent of automatic system
generation from a design specification, development tools will become even less
distinct.

3.4.3 Fourth generation languages within application generators

It is impossible to give a universally acceptable definition of the terms 'fourth
generation language' and 'application generator' because of the multiplicity and
contradictory nature of the terminology used by product vendors.

Consider integrated tool sets such as Ingres or Oracle, which commonly
incorporate fourth generation tools. A distinction can be made between the client
application oriented elements and the server data management (database) elements
(see section 3.2), with some form of data control or query language providing
cohesion and integration. Typically, the client component will include a number
of different elements, used initially for developing applications and subsequently
by the application when it is running. These elements may be grouped together
and sold as a package, often collectively being called the *Application Generator
(AG)*, or they may be sold individually or in small groups. The set of client
elements may be marketed as a Fourth Generation Environment (4GE), or as a
Fourth Generation System (4GS).

Typical client tool elements are:

- forms: screen images of forms can be designed and constructed which
  can be used for data entry into the database, and subsequent update,
  query, or deletion, and help information;

- menus: hierarchies of logically associated forms can be built. (The user
  interface to the AG might be menu driven, possibly being an
  application built using the AG);

- query facility: to enable end users to formulate their own database queries and input them directly. The query facilities may be forms based, Query–by–Example, a natural language or some other interface to aid the user in building a query language statement;

- fourth generation language (4GL): a high level or declarative language is commonly provided. Examples of these can range from systems enabling complex form and report definition, menu control etc from within the 4GL, to products containing little more than commands to control the flow through the processing code, the ability to embed query language commands and to provide access to forms, menus, etc;

- 3GL pre–compiler: this enables query language commands, and in some cases forms and menus, to be embedded in a third generation language such as Cobol, C or Fortran;

- report writer: a mechanism for extracting data from the database and formatting it into structured reports may be provided;

- database global view editor: changes to the database global view or schema can often be made. Commonly this facility is a forms application;

- data dictionary: this can take many forms, from being the repository of the business analysis and hence of the original system specification which can potentially be used for automatic system generation, through to simply being the directory or catalogue recording the database structure. The data dictionary usually utilises a database management system for the physical storage of its contents. Further tools such as analyst workbenches provide input to the data dictionary;

- decision support tools: these include facilities to draw graphs or use spreadsheet–like calculators.

Whilst all these tools may be bundled together and sold as a single package, some of them may be sold as separate, add–on packages.

3.5

Introduction to transaction processing monitors

3.5.1 Requirements

Transaction processing systems are required to:

- enable multiple users to concurrently access common resources in an efficient manner;

- control a number of processes as a single service.

A Transaction Processing (TP) Monitor allows multiple users to access all the facilities of which it is in control, including a database management system (DBMS), allocated store and application code. See figure 3.5.1.

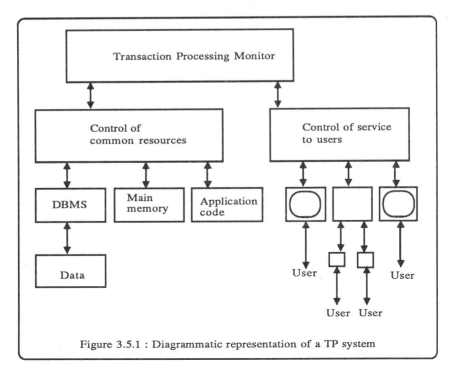

Figure 3.5.1 : Diagrammatic representation of a TP system

It is possible to provide multiple users with access to common resources without a TP monitor. A DBMS can allow multiple users to access a database concurrently, providing that a shared service can be declared. An operating system allows many users to access main memory and backing store, seemingly in a concurrent fashion; and applications can be 'publicly loaded' so that the same code is used by everybody, rather than each user having a separate copy of the code. However, it would be difficult to ensure that the service to all users of these common resources was efficient, since the operating system which is controlling all processing would be using scheduling algorithms which maximise efficiency of the whole machine.

The second requirement of a TP monitor, to control a number of processes as a single service, allows users to view the applications to which they have access as a single system. Commonly, a menu driven interface will be provided from which the user can select services; the access control mechanism will hold details about which applications each user may access and menus will be adapted accordingly.

3.5.2 Transaction processing services and systems

A transaction processing service allows many people to hold simultaneous dialogues with application programs about some business they have in common. A transaction processing system, or monitor, is a software package which controls this concurrent processing, ensuring that responses to enquiries are directed to the correct terminals and that there is no interaction between users of the entire system.

A transaction processing service will be set up such that:

- system routines route input and output messages between the terminal operator (end user), the application programs and other elements of the TP system;

- messages can be scheduled, so that a priority system can be applied to messages. For example, some users or applications might have priority access to the database;

- resources are scheduled in such a way that an efficient service is provided to users;

- application programs will service one or more different types of input message;

- a spooler will route output from the TP service for printing;

- intermediate information (partial results in ICL parlance) in multi–phase transactions will be stored. That is to say, data input by the user, retrieved from the database or calculated by a program will be stored while a response from the user at the terminal is awaited and before further processing can take place, freeing resources for use by other people;

- databases and files can be shared, the DBMS providing the locking mechanisms for update transactions;

- the required screen definitions are available for display in accordance with terminal descriptions;

- an audit trail of all transactions is maintained so that in the event of a machine fault or an error the system can be recovered with minimum user intervention.

3.5.3 Transactions

A *single–phase* transaction consists of a single output message and a reply. A *multi–phase* transaction consists of a series of logically connected message–reply pairs. Consider the following example: a user logs on to a TP service in a library and is offered a choice of browsing through the catalogue, selecting a book synopsis by author, title or ISBN, or leaving the system. The display of this choice information (output) and the user's decision to leave the system (reply) is a single phase transaction. If, however, the user chose to select a book by author, he might be starting a multi–phase transaction, which is like a conversation. He may be asked to input the author's name; if this is not unique the user might be then asked to select the author's initials from a retrieved list which has been displayed; the author might have written a number of books so a list of titles might be displayed; only when the user selects a title will the book synopsis be displayed and the multi–phase transaction be completed.

If a multi–phased transaction performs tasks which cannot be undone, such as updating a database, then *success units* must be identified. A success unit consists of the execution of a sequence of operations which transform a database from one logically consistent state to another. Actions between the start and end of a success unit can always be aborted or undone. There is a trade–off between long success units, such that the user can abandon the transaction, and short success units, which minimise loss of intermediate results, should the TP service go down (the service, when resumed, will restart after the last success unit which was logged). Necessarily, success units and database commits must be synchronised.

Some operations, such as writing lines to a report or sending messages to other terminals, must be linked with success units since these operations cannot be undone. Commonly, such processing would be executed at the end of a success unit, along with database updates.

3.6

Introduction to spreadsheets

3.6.1 Origins and architecture

Spreadsheets were developed from the requirements of financial planners, who used pencil and paper to develop matrixes or worksheets. Much of the terminology has been carried over into spreadsheet software.

The software package is generally referred to as a spreadsheet. Common examples are Lotus–123, Symphony and SuperCalc. A worksheet is equivalent to a large grid or matrix, which can be developed using a spreadsheet package. Columns divide the worksheet vertically and rows divide the worksheet horizontally. Cells are formed by the intersection of rows and columns, and each cell has a unique reference. Figure 3.6.1 gives a very simple example of a worksheet.

	JAN	FEB	MAR	APR	....	1990			
Salary JB	50		7						
Salary AA		8							
Salary BD	6		6						
Total Salary	11	8	13						
Terminals									
Comms									
.									

Figure 3.6.1 : Sample worksheet

Some multi–sheet packages are available so that three–dimensional worksheets can be developed. This is like having a pad of paper with a worksheet on each page. The software allows access to cells across, in addition to within, the worksheets.

The data which is entered and displayed in worksheet cells can be stored in a number of files. Separate physical files may be used to store subsets of data in tabular form, from logically associated cells. It may be possible to specify the format of data, such as a comma separated value (CSV) and DIF format file. Some spreadsheets can read data created by other software: for example Logistix can load data from Lotus–123 and SuperCalc files, in addition to dBASE III files.

3.6.2 Functionality

A cell may contain an expression, number, date or text in most spreadsheet packages. An expression is a formula which combines various elements (numbers, column or row references and mathematical functions) to calculate the value of that cell. Many functions are provided to be used in expressions, such as average, total and date calculations. Some packages allow graph commands which relate to characteristics of a graph to be associated with cells.

Many spreadsheet packages can manipulate large worksheets; for example, release 2.2 of Lotus–123 allows up to 256 rows and 8 192 columns per worksheet. The software provides a window on to the worksheet, which can be moved around to view different areas.

A variety of functions are generally provided to manipulate the worksheets and underlying files: rows and columns can be inserted or deleted; worksheets can be linked; data can be extracted or stored in files; rows can be sorted; worksheets can be printed; the window on the worksheet can be moved; and so on.

A very useful feature of spreadsheet packages is the automatic re–evaluation of cell values, when cell values on which they depend are changed, so that 'what–if' type queries can be made. For example, a spreadsheet might contain pay calculations, such that the rows represent staff and a total on columns, and columns hold values for annual salary, monthly pay, NI contribution, tax deduction, net pay each month, etc. The effect of a 10% increase in annual salary on pay per month and total of salaries paid could be tested, by just changing the annual salary cell values. A graphic display of the data, if one was associated with some of the cells, would also change as the cell values were re–calculated.

All advanced spreadsheet packages have macro facilities which enable programs to be written to manipulate spreadsheet data, extending the capabilities provided as standard functions.

3.7

Introduction to hypertext

3.7.1 Concept

The hypertext principle was developed in the 1960s. It describes how someone would use a document such as a software manual; that is, they would be unlikely to read it sequentially but would skip around, cross–referencing sections, jumping to the index or glossary, looking at diagrams, leaving markers in various pages to get back to them easily, and probably scribbling comments in the margin.

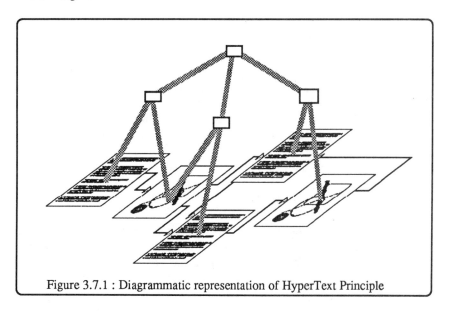

Figure 3.7.1 : Diagrammatic representation of HyperText Principle

Hypertext is intended to have similarities to the way we think. Consequently it is claimed that implementations of the principle are easy to use and conceptually suitable for beginners. The basic premise is that starting from one particular piece of information it is simple for the user to follow trails of information that interest him, and ignore detail or other areas of lesser interest.

Traditional software, such as a word processor, treats subject data, in this case a document, as a sequential object. Movement through the document is sequential – up, down, next line, next page, beginning of document, etc. A word processor based on hypertext principles would allow the author to impose his own structure in any way he wished.

The hypertext principle is that information is not sequential and can be stored as a network of interconnected information elements or objects – that is, as a number of separate, small pieces of text or pictures, with links between them. It is likely, however, that such elements can also be grouped, and consequently a hierarchical structure can be imposed on top of the network, as shown in figure 3.7.1.

3.7.2 Object orientation

There is a similarity between implementations of the hypertext principle and object oriented design. Object oriented design and programming enables software developers to create reusable code, by allowing the construction of software systems as structured collections of abstract, data type implementations. In object oriented programming, data and operations are bound tightly together and computation is performed by one object sending a message to another object. Objects that have similar behaviour can be grouped together to form classes; classes can be linked hierarchically and lower classes inherit properties from the higher classes. [See section 4.2 for more on object orientation.]

In hypertext systems, text and pictures can be viewed as objects which have associations with each other. Moving from a display of one object (A) on the screen to another (B), is effected by the current object sending a message to another (B), which a method interprets and causes the object (B) to appear on the screen.

3.7.3 Hypertext implementations

There are a number of products which claim to implement the hypertext principle, including Apple's HyperCard and Xerox's NoteCards. HyperCard is briefly described below to show the features of a hypertext system.

HyperCard

Apple describes HyperCard as an Information Environment application where the user can store information – words, numbers, charts, pictures, digitised photographs, sound, etc, and can look through the data in a structured, but not predetermined way. Any recorded information can be linked to any other data,

with the association saved for future reference. This is analogous to having
multiple card indexes with related items of information joined by wires. The
user can look at any card and then follow the wires to study the associated data.

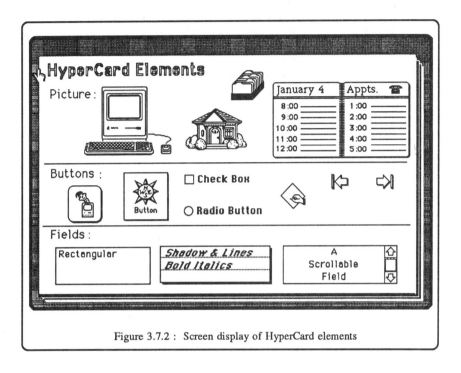

Figure 3.7.2 : Screen display of HyperCard elements

The basic object of HyperCard is the card which can contain three different types
of element:

- graphic pictures, painted onto the card;

- button objects, primarily used so that when the mouse is clicked on
  them a link to another card is followed;

- field objects, used to store text data.

The cards are contained within stacks. The cards may have a background, which
contains the three elements listed above and there may be one or more
backgrounds in a stack. The associations behind the buttons can link to any
card in any stack.

Buttons, Fields, Cards, Backgrounds and Stacks are all HyperCard objects. They
all possess 'scripts' which are written using a fourth generation language called
HyperTalk. The objects form a hierarchy and HyperTalk works by the creation,
sending and handling of messages.

Messages are created either by the user, for example by clicking the mouse, by HyperCard or explicitly by coding in HyperTalk. The messages are sent up the hierarchy of objects until a script is found for an object which contains a handler for that particular message. This handler may have been coded in HyperTalk, may be one of the HyperCard in–built commands or functions, or could have been coded in Pascal or C and linked to HyperCard as an external resource.

3.7.4 Uses of hypertext

There are likely to be many uses for hypertext other than the purely automated card index type applications. Some examples are :

- representation of rules and regulations: the Civil Service has many handbooks containing cross–referenced text and hypertext could be used to provide a better user interface to this structured information;

- company information: staff hierarchies and responsibilities, office layouts, etc could be entered on stacks with links between employees, departments and offices. New staff could use the system to familiarise themselves with the company;

- exhibition directories: an exhibition layout could be displayed and information about each stand be obtained by clicking the mouse on the appropriate stand;

- instruction manuals: for example, a detailed breakdown of how to repair a car could be supplied in hypertext form. The user could enter key words for a particular problem, see cards with relevant information, and navigate the stack in useful ways;

- computer aided learning: the user could proceed at his own pace, moving through the topics as he wished, following up interests or repeating sections at will;

- presentations: a machine can be connected to an overhead projector, thus enabling the screen display to be projected. Using hypertext with such a projection system can provide many benefits in terms of being able to adapt the presentation to the audience, particularly in response to particular lines of questioning;

- catalogues: for example, lists of items for sale or a spare parts catalogue.

4

Architecture

Purpose

This chapter covers a number of issues concerned with the logical architecture of integrated knowledge–based systems (KBS) and database management systems (DBMS) as depicted in figure 4.1. Building upon the assumption that there is merit in attempting to integrate the architecture of the two types of system, a number of approaches are investigated.

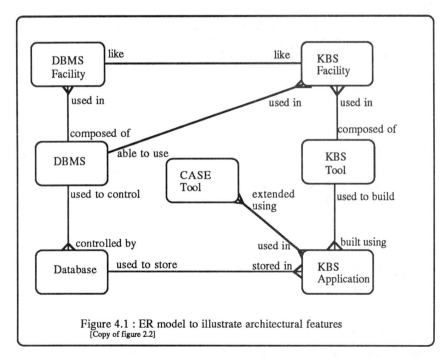

Figure 4.1 : ER model to illustrate architectural features
[Copy of figure 2.2]

Section 4.1

Section 4.1 considers the convergence of facilities exhibited by, or proposed for, both KBS and DBMS, as shown in figure 4.2. Similar facilities have been developed along different evolutionary paths, by different people. The old adage 'great minds think alike' seems to be true here.

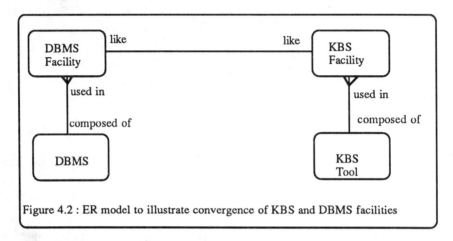

Figure 4.2 : ER model to illustrate convergence of KBS and DBMS facilities

Section 4.2

Section 4.2 considers the paradigm of object orientation which transcends not only KBS and DBMS, but programming languages and other software. Object orientation could potentially be such an important integrating mechanism for KBS and DBMS that a section has been devoted to the topic.

Section 4.3

Section 4.3 describes the use of KBS technology to enhance DBMS by improving and building upon existing facilities; see figure 4.3. The users of DBMS, both developers and end–users, should not be aware that KBS are being used in the underlying software.

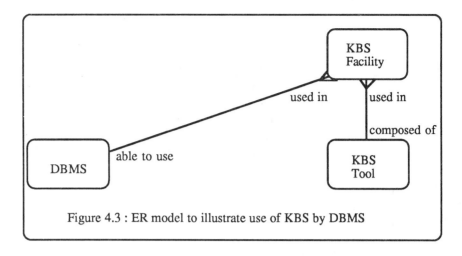

Figure 4.3 : ER model to illustrate use of KBS by DBMS

Section 4.4

A number of CASE tools are known to use KBS technology internally and it is very likely that most of them will in the future. The functionality can be extended by adding new applications to carry out first–cut database design for example, or be improved by rewriting some modules using KBS tools. See figure 4.4.

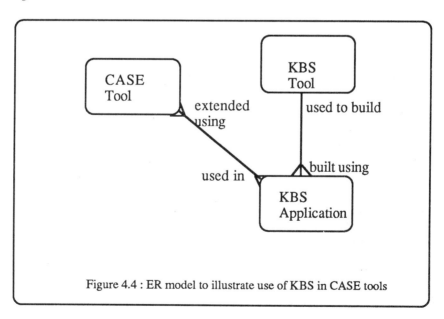

Figure 4.4 : ER model to illustrate use of KBS in CASE tools

Section 4.5

Section 4.5 presents a fundamental change in the architecture of KBS by exploiting database technology. It is suggested that a DBMS can be enhanced to produce a knowledge–base management system (KBMS), so that all knowledge is stored in a database and can be managed and controlled by the KBMS software; see figure 4.5. The components of a KBS (user interface, inference engine, etc) can then be made more distinct and facilitate a move towards open systems.

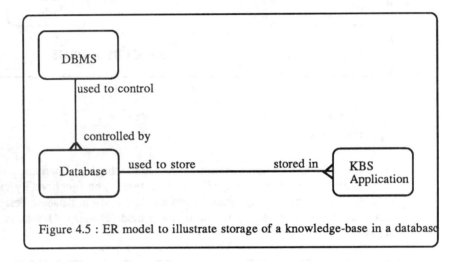

Figure 4.5 : ER model to illustrate storage of a knowledge-base in a database

4.1

Convergence of KBS and DBMS facilities

4.1.1 Introduction

This section is concerned with the convergence of facilities exhibited by knowledge–based system (KBS) tools and those exhibited by, or proposed for, database management systems (DBMS), as shown in figure 4.1.1. The term 'expert database systems' has been used [KERS87] to represent the confluence of concepts, tools and techniques from a number of areas including artificial intelligence, database management, logic programming and information retrieval, but the term is believed to be misleading.

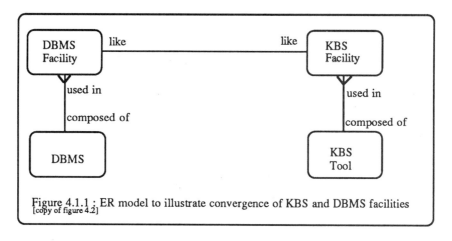

Figure 4.1.1 : ER model to illustrate convergence of KBS and DBMS facilities
[copy of figure 4.2]

A Butler Cox Foundation report [BUTL87] states that:

> '... the similarities are not surprising because both relational database theory and logic programming (the basis of expert systems) have their roots in predicate calculus, a branch of mathematics and logic.'[†]

[†] Reproduced by kind permission of Butler Cox plc. Originally published in Butler Cox Foundation Report 60, Expert Systems in Business.

It is interesting to observe what appear to be similar facilities, in that DBMS exhibit features which could be expressed using KBS technology, and to speculate upon how developers of the two technologies could learn from each other. Some DBMS product developers are using KBS technology to implement some of the facilities described in this chapter, as illustrated by the products Ingres and Generis. Extensions and enhancements are being developed for some DBMS, and these are discussed in section 4.3. New products are likely to emerge which exhibit some of the best features of both KBS and DBMS, and which may become difficult to classify as one or the other.

4.1.2 KBS facilities

This sub–section has been included to introduce and recap on some of the relevant features of KBS technology, in the context of convergence of KBS and DBMS facilities.

Rules

Rules provide the most common format for specification of knowledge and knowledge processing in a knowledge–base of a KBS application. A number of shells use rules exclusively; and some sophisticated toolkits provide rules as one of several specification formats. Rules are declarative, stating *what* is to be done and not *how*, using variations on the format:

> IF condition
> THEN action,

where the condition evaluates to true or false, and if it is true the action is carried out. This is a much simplified notation, in that: the condition may be complex (including simple conditions linked by AND, OR and NOT); many actions may be specified; different actions may be specified if only some of the conditions are true; an action may be specified for the case when the condition evaluates to false; and so on. However, the above is intended to convey the means of specifying a rule–based system, not to provide an all–embracing syntax.

Examples of simple rules are: 'IF raining THEN take_umbrella_to_work' or, 'IF cheeks–are–rosy THEN health–of–patient = "good"'.

Inference mechanisms

The inference engine provided with each KBS tool is complex and employs a number of strategies for managing the use of knowledge–base components at run–time. The strategies determine the *order* in which the processing will be carried out. That is *how* rules will be invoked and if there is a conflict, *which* rule will be fired and *when* it will be fired. The following describes forward and backward chaining, demons, hypothetical reasoning and truth maintenance, and backtracking.

Forward chaining, or data driven inferencing, occurs when an attempt is made to reach a goal or conclusion using facts which have already been evaluated. All facts which can be derived, directly or indirectly, from some known facts are evaluated in an attempt to derive a goal value. A number of facts may be evaluated for no purpose, that is they cannot be used to solve the problem. Forward chaining can be thought of as a bottom–up approach to problem solving.

This mechanism is commonly used when there is a very large number of possible solutions, given a large combination of possible fact values. For example, consider a system which generates a machine configuration: a very large number of configurations are possible in terms of the number of disk drives, tape decks, printers, cables to connect them, etc. However, when some significant constraints are specified, the number of possible configurations can be drastically reduced. By evaluating some of the important requirements (facts) at the start of the consultation, a manageable number (possibly zero) of options may be generated.

Backward chaining, or goal driven inferencing, occurs when an attempt is made to evaluate a conclusion or goal by resolving or evaluating a limited number of facts relevant to a line of reasoning. This is a more structured, top–down approach to problem solving. Backward chaining is commonly used when values of some key facts eliminate the need to evaluate a number of other facts, and when there are fewer possible goal values. Backward chaining is often the default inferencing mechanism of shells; for example, it is used by ICL–Adviser, Savoir and XiPlus.

Example applications which are suited to a backward chaining approach are diagnosis (of medical problems, machine faults, etc), selection systems (for choosing a DBMS, a document type, etc) and advisors (such as law and regulation interpreters).

Demons, or event driven actions, are available to be executed at any time and can interrupt processing. A condition (which might be complex, involving ANDs, ORs and NOTs) associated with each demon determines when it should be executed by the inference engine. Demons can be thought of as free standing, globally applicable actions; some operating systems allow such actions to be specified, for example 'WHENEVER condition... action' can be used in ICL VME job control language to trap error conditions in job control procedures. Demons are commonly used to identify unusual situations and specify remedial action.

There are no KBS tools which solely use demons for reasoning. They are usually provided in addition to backward or forward chaining, and are employed to interrupt the chaining mechanism.

Hypothetical reasoning and truth maintenance: Some KBS tools allow a number of options to be explored simultaneously in order to arrive quickly at a solution. Multiple hypothetical situations can be explored and the software maintains a number of states, sometimes referred to as viewpoints, worlds or contexts. Truth maintenance systems keep track of truth and contradictions, and eliminate viewpoints which violate constraints.

Consider the problem of trying to identifying the two quickest routes on the London underground from station A to station B, with minimal line changes. A KBS application might attempt to solve the problem by exploring a number of options simultaneously if the two stations are not on the same line. It could consider all options with a single line change (assuming there is more than one option), two line changes and so on. The truth maintenance system could eliminate all but the quickest two routes throughout the processing, to minimise the follow up on options which do not fit the criteria.

This mechanism is commonly used for simulation, scheduling, planning and some real–time applications. Versatile toolkits such as ART, KEE and Knowledgecraft use this mechanism for solving complex problems.

Backtracking is a feature of the language Prolog, Prolog–based tools and production rule systems. Such systems instantiate facts once and use this value whenever the fact is referenced, unless instructed to find an alternative value for a fact, in which case backtracking may be used. Backtracking consists of reviewing what has been done (in terms of satisfying goals) and attempting to re–satisfy the goals. Values for goals, which have already been found, are undone up to a point where an alternative path can be taken.

Backtracking may occur because the current line of reasoning does not evaluate the goal when some facts cannot be evaluated, or it may be initiated by the end user requesting that another answer be found. Backtracking might be used to read records from a database, a single record being returned each time. The backtracking mechanism is analogous to someone trying to get out of a maze: if he comes to a dead–end, he retraces his steps to the last place at which there was a choice of direction, and he then takes a different path.

4.1.3 Database integrity constraints

Integrity constraints

Integrity constraints, when applied to data, define the set of valid states for a database. They are considered to be meta–data since they describe data, and they should be defined in a schema (global view) with the data descriptions. To clarify this point consider the following examples:

- Smith; WK; Mr; 0362 608241; Norfolk; 241042; are instances of data;

- a person record type, made up of the attribute types name, initials, title, telephone number, county of residence, and date of birth, is an example of meta–data. (This data description could be applied to the data given above.) A number of occurrences of person details (instances of data) will map on to this format;

- dates of birth are in the range 010118 to 010190 and must be valid dates in the format DDMMYY, are examples of integrity constraints. These constraints might apply to all dates included in data definitions or be associated with given dates in some record types.

Integrity constraints may be of varying complexity and may:

- pertain only to particular attribute occurrences, such as the managing director's salary, not affecting the salary of all other people;

- constrain a subset of attribute instances, such as the salary of executive officers;

- restrict all instances of an attribute to a permissible subset of possible values for the given data type. For example, 'all salaries must be rounded to the nearest £10', even though the type of the attribute is integer. Similarly, values such as NULL may not be allowed for a primary key attribute in a relational database, to uphold one of the referential integrity rules for relational databases;

- refer to attributes in a number of entity types; for example, 'a teacher can only teach two different classes of pupils at the same time if they are taught the same subject, in the same classroom', where teacher, pupil, location of class and subject are attributes of different entity types;

- uphold the second referential integrity rule for relational databases, to ensure that foreign keys held in one relation exist as a primary key in another relation;

- include arithmetic, such as 'a customer's credit limit must be greater than or equal to the value (sum of the price multiplied by the quantity) of all items ordered';

- restrict relationships; for example, 'the cardinality of a relationship between salesman and customer must not exceed 20', that is, a salesman can only have up to and including 20 customers;

- be time based, for example historical data (which may in turn be defined as a comparison of two date fields in a relation) cannot be amended but current data can be changed;

- involve recursive processing, for example, 'a person cannot work for more than one person of the same grade' assuming that matrix management is not allowed, or 'a person cannot at the same time work for and supervise any other person'.

Many of the relational, network and hierarchical DBMS in use today could not support some of the more complex integrity constraints given above. This may be because it is difficult to specify complex constraints descriptively. The original Codasyl proposals included database procedures so that complex constraints, for example, could be defined, but few vendors implemented them in a useful way.

In existing systems many of the integrity constraints are embedded in the processing rather than the data description schema. For example, a Cobol program which assembles customer order records for insertion in a database would check that the customer number existed (foreign key referential integrity), that the order number did not exist (unique value) and so on. It is likely that similar checks will be (or should be) included in a number of Cobol programs which deal with customer and order details, unless it has been coded as a separate module to be called by all programs.

Specifications of integrity constraints could be included in the schema and integrity checking could be done by the DBMS, using KBS facilities. There would be a single specification which would be executed every time the relevant data items were changed. The constraints in the schema would be applied consistently and with the same rigour; this may not happen when constraints are coded in Cobol programs by different people. The constraints on the data would reside in a logical place; that is, with the data descriptions in the schema.

Integrity constraints and action rules

Action rules are mechanisms which make permanent changes to data. One use of such rules is to link them with integrity constraints so that when a constraint violation is identified, remedial action can be taken. These action rules could be linked directly with an integrity constraint or be globally available. For example, a referential constraint on a customer orders system would be that all 'order lines' must belong to an 'order header'; an action rule would cause all order lines to be deleted when the order header is deleted. An over–riding global action rule could specify that if all other remedial actions fail to satisfy all of the integrity constraints the database should be rolled back to the state before update began. Some types of action rule are included in the SQL2 and SQL3 standards.

ISO and ANSI SQL2 and SQL3 standards

The ISO and ANSI SQL3 standard is not likely to be available until after 1993 (and implementations are not likely to be available until some time after that), but the SQL2 standard will be available earlier. The drafts of the two standards include some specification mechanisms which could be used to implement most of the above constraints, including those which involve recursion. Two new schema constructs, ASSERTION (a simple form in SQL2) and TRIGGER (SQL3). Extended syntax on table and column specifications has been included in SQL2.

Constraints define valid database states. Unless the constraint is defined as deferred, whenever a value in the database is changed, the constraint is checked. Deferred constraints are checked when a transaction attempts to execute a COMMIT (end of transaction). This is needed when multi–phase transformations are required and intermediate database states will be invalid.

Constraints can be defined as an integral part of a table or column definition or they can be free-standing, in which case they are referred to as ASSERTIONs in SQL.

ASSERTIONs in SQL are *passive* mechanisms for maintaining database integrity. That is, they check whether the data violate the constraints; if so, the database changes will not be executed and the user will be given some explanation. TRIGGERs, however, are *active* mechanisms concerned with changing the data content in order to maintain integrity; that is, they may cause data to be deleted, updated or inserted. Triggers can also be actioned before or after the triggering event.

Updates to data, caused by triggers or integrity constraints on columns and tables, can cause further updates to be actioned or checks to be run. The use of the term 'CASCADE' in SQL2 syntax describes the situation well, in that an update on a column can be propagated through the entire database. This is particularly useful for maintaining referential integrity on foreign keys and ensuring that columns used in joins remain consistent. Deletion of related details can also be caused by a single SQL delete statement. For example, all details concerned with a particular customer (orders, order details, etc) could be deleted by actions on integrity constraints which implement 'all orders must belong to a customer' and 'all order lines must relate to an order', etc.

4.1.4   Convergence

There are at least four types of rule which are being, or have been, incorporated into DBMS:

- integrity constraints, which are rules about data (meta-data);

- action rules, which can make permanent data changes, including creation and deletion of data;

- transformation rules, which can only transform the values of *existing* data;

- inference rules, which can generate temporary or virtual data.

Implementations of these types of rule and associated inferencing are discussed in the following sub-sections.

4.1.5 Integrity constraints and action rules

SQL is a declarative language and the integrity constraints described in 4.1.3 above could be mapped on to a rule format. Assertions and triggers, for example, specify when an integrity constraint should be run (IF condition) and what is to be done (THEN action). SQL is notoriously difficult to learn and write, therefore users may prefer to specify constraints in a simple rule format.

One SQL statement would probably map on to a number of simpler, related rules. It is conceivable that an interface could be developed to carry out the transformation (see section 4.3).

The SQL2 and SQL3 constraints do not just specify *what* is to be done, but sometimes indicate *when* actions should be taken, relative to the changes which trigger the checks. For example, it is possible to specify that a check should be run at the next COMMIT, immediately before or immediately after an update, insertion or deletion, or on request if the constraints are switched off. However, the majority of the details about implementing these facilities is left to the discretion of the developers of relational database management systems. The following speculates on how inferencing mechanisms used in KBS could be employed.

The most obvious of the inferencing mechanisms which could be used is *demons*. To recap, demons are executed immediately a condition becomes true. Demons are called triggers in SQL3; referential actions in SQL2 are also equivalent to demons. Update, insertion or deletion of a column or table, as specified in the integrity constraint, would cause the demon to fire, running the integrity check and possibly initiating actions. A more sophisticated system (which could be implemented using more complex conditions) is needed to deal with delayed actions, such as running checks before the next COMMIT rather than immediately, and the choice of running the check before or after the update which triggered the check. An event/trigger mechanism (ETM) has been described [KOTZ88] and the syntactical constructs are similar to those of demons found in many KBS tools.

CASCADE in SQL2 propagates changes through a database and effectively all the cascaded operations resulting from an action take place simultaneously. Unless parallel processing is employed, which is unlikely at present, the operations must be reduced to a sequence of operations. Although, in theory, the order in which the actions take place is immaterial, this can be difficult to implement in practice. A *forward chaining* inference mechanism could be employed to cause execution of updates, rather than using demons which can affect run–time performance.

Theoretically, it is possible that triggers which cause propagated updates (which is similar to a forward chaining mechanism) could cause the system to loop and never reach an integral state. (The definition of triggers and referential actions in the SQL2 and SQL3 draft forbids the possibility of a loop.) That is, trigger–1 might be initiated by an update on table–A and cause table–B to be updated; trigger–2, triggered by table–B changes, updates table–C; trigger–3, triggered by table–C changes, updates table–A and so on. Some KBS compilers, such as that in ICL–Adviser, can detect circular reasoning. DBMS must similarly be able to recognise data descriptions which would cause looping.

Update, deletion or insertion of data might trigger more than one integrity check, yet the SQL proposals do not include syntax for specifying *precedence*. Precedence rules used by a KBS inference engine are usually documented. For example ICL–Adviser will attempt to evaluate a fact by using relevant questions and rules in the order in which they are written in the source code (knowledge–base). It also maintains a stack of outstanding actions, which might be built up while the system is backward chaining, and actions will be cleared on a last–in, first–out basis. The rules can also have associated priorities which enables queue jumping, and so on. Some systems, especially those which include several inferencing mechanisms, may have very sophisticated techniques for determining the order in which to execute actions when there is a choice. DBMS developers may be able to use these techniques for determining precedence on integrity constraints.

Performance

Demons are known to incur performance overheads in KBS applications and it is usually recommended that knowledge engineers should use them sparingly. The inference engine has to check whether any demons should be fired after every fact evaluation. It is likely that the inference engine will hold information about which facts trigger which demons, but there can still be a significant overhead in carrying out these checks. A DBMS which incorporates the integrity constraints outlined in the SQL proposals is likely to have a similar problem, in that update of columns or tables can necessitate running checks. The syntax of assertions may incur tremendous processing overheads. Given that assertions can be specified to be run at COMMIT time, the system will need to determine whether it is necessary to run these assertions on every commit. The DBMS will need to internally modify such integrity constraints to add conditions which identify the need to run a check, such as only when referenced columns and tables have been updated.

When integrity constraints are embedded in code such as Cobol, the programmer can determine when checks should sensibly be executed (although he may get it wrong!). Consider an application which stores customer orders and order lines using a cursor for record processing. Typically, the application will check that the customer number exists and that the order number does not exist; and if this is the case, store the order and the order lines without further checks. It is likely that a DBMS in control of integrity constraints, such as customer number matching on customer and order records and unique order numbers, would check that the order number existed every time a new order line was inserted. A DBMS could execute integrity constraints more efficiently if it can be guided on when to run checks, although embedding such knowledge may not be an easy task.

The database administrator (DBA) may choose to have a facility to enable him to run all or some integrity checks at will, so that at intervals he can reassure himself that the database is consistent. For example, he may wish to check that the database has been recovered correctly following an error, or after system programmers have amended the database. An integrity checking facility is provided by some DBMS, such as IDMS (the network DBMS running under VME on ICL machines), to enable the DBA to check such things as: the pointers on sets have not been corrupted and all members of a set occurrence form a closed loop; and all mandatory relationships actually exist, that is no order records exist without being attached to a customer record. A forward or backward chaining mechanism could be used to propagate the execution of selected integrity constraints.

Advantages of extending the DBMS

Enforcement of integrity constraints through the database management system has the following advantages:

- reduced system development costs since integrity checks are written once and shared by applications;

- reduced maintenance costs, since only one set of central constraints need be modified;

- improved reliability and consistency, due to centralisation of control;

- increased DBA control, since rules are centrally enforced and cannot be circumvented.

Transference of integrity constraints from code into DBMS incurs significant performance overheads, since DBMS are general purpose integrity handlers. However, there is considerable scope for using inferencing mechanisms and knowledge specification methods for improving DBMS handling of constraints.

4.1.6   Other possible uses of integrity constraints and action rules

Kotz refers to integrity constraints and action rules as semantic rules [KOTZ88]. It is suggested that they can additionally be used to:

- trigger output of snapshots of the database;

- collect statistical information;

- initiate data reorganisation;

- handle alarms;

- set savepoints for recovery;

- initiate actions on other nodes within a distributed DBMS.

The DBA or a user could be given up–to–the–minute information about the state of the data in the database. These states need not be invalid but may be of particular importance. For example, a database and KBS combination could be used to support tactical situation assessment for the army or navy. Static information about maps, vehicles, weapons, etc and dynamic information about positions and actions of vehicles would be stored and updated. Integrity constraints (or thresholds) could be used to identify threat situations which arise as a result of changes to the dynamic data, and cause messages to be displayed to the users, alarms to ring and real–time applications to be run to determine a response to the threat database state.

Action rules need not just be associated with maintaining database integrity. For example, a change to the database, such as insertion of a new customer record, could cause mailshots to be prepared for sending to that customer. The most likely way of dealing with this is by the DBMS calling an external sub–routine to carry out the detailed actions.

External events, in addition to changes to the database, could trigger action rules, such as a call from a Cobol program, a parameter from the operating system or a query input by an end user. The external event could be a date or time; actions such as purging of data at the end of the month could be initiated in this way.

4.1.7 Transformation rules

Transformation rules, as specified in 4.1.4 above, transform existing data values without amending the database and can be used in conjunction with a DBMS as a translation mechanism. These rules would be associated with subschema processing, such that the internally stored data is transformed into external views.

In non–database systems, it is common to code and decode data. For example, a stock control system might use a six digit code instead of a 30 character item description, and a look–up table would store a list of matching codes and descriptions. This mechanism is generally used to save storage space when replicating large fields in serial files. In a database, the fields such as item descriptions are only likely to be stored once, but translation mechanisms may still serve a purpose. A translation might be needed if, for example, several NULL states are implemented as suggested in SQL3. Null values, which represent such things as not yet evaluated and not relevant, will need to be decoded on retrieval.

Some CASE expressions have been, or are being, introduced in SQL2 for representing complex conditions, using the syntax COALESCE and NULLIF. COALESCE(v1, v2, v3,... vn), where v1, v2 to vn are values (column specifications or constants), translates into the rule:

```
IF v1 NOT NULL
THEN v1
ELSE  IF v2 NOT NULL
         THEN v2
      ELSE IF v3 NOT NULL
              THEN v3
              ELSE...
```

A transformation could be used to find a value for next–of–kin. COALESCE (husband, wife, father, mother) would use the values of data types husband, wife, father and mother, in that order, to find a non–NULL value for next–of–kin.

NULLIF(v1, v2) means:	NULLIF(boolean–1, 'FALSE') means:
IF v1 = v2	IF boolean–1 = 'FALSE'
THEN NULL	THEN NULL
ELSE v1	ELSE boolean–1

The NULLIF function is used for storing the correct database values when external representations do not support NULL values. In the above example a false value for a boolean could be stored as a NULL value.

Transformation rules could be activated or triggered by retrieval of column values and therefore could be implemented using backward chaining on data retrieval. Alternatively, they could be implemented using demons which trap access to the appropriate columns.

4.1.8 Inference rules

Inference rules, as defined in 4.1.4 above, can be used to generate virtual or temporary data, from real, existing data. Therefore, data produced as a result of executing these rules would only be available within the current session, for the user who initiated generation. The data would not be part of the database, but end users need not be aware of this, other than that they could not update it. DBMS external views (subschemas) can include generated data such as totalled values.

Specificity of rules

Inference rules could be specified in the subschema to operate at different levels. They may work on instances of data; for example, it could be specified that only the monthly salary of employee 'Mr Smith' should be calculated according to a specified algorithm. The algorithm would be associated with Mr Smith and no–one else, since it does not generally apply to all occurrences of the entity type 'employee'. 'Monthly salary' is a derived value and will not be a permanently stored data item.

Alternatively, inference rules could apply to selected or all entity types (record types or object classes). For example, the salary of accountant employees may be calculated by a given algorithm (which is different to that for other staff), or the amount of leave given to all employees may be associated with the person record type and be based on grade and years of service. In an object oriented database these generic inference rules could be attached to an object or class at any level in the object hierarchy, in which case a precedence mechanism is required. For example, if there are algorithms for calculating any employee's salary, accountants' salaries and Mr Smith's salary, and Mr Smith is an accountant, then which rule should be used? The general rule–of–thumb applied in object oriented systems is that the most specific rule is applied, that is the rule at the lowest level or that inherited through the least number of levels in the hierarchy. If two rules have the same specificity, then the end user may be asked to decide which rule should be used. The problem of deciding which rule to apply in a non–object oriented database is not likely to arise since the rules would be associated with entity or attribute types and the conditions would determine whether or not a rule applies.

Applications

Inference rules can be used in a number of ways to enhance DBMS. They could be used to populate (virtual) columns or attributes. For example, a timetabling application might populate a schedule of tutors for course occurrences using attributes in tables of tutors and courses. Attributes such as availability, qualifications, etc could be used by the inference rules. If the schedule was not satisfactory, the inference rules could be changed (by authorised people) and the tutor schedule be re–populated.

Another possible use for inference rules is in extending the dynamic nature of RDBMS, to provide support for changes to the data description. For example, new, permanent columns can be added to table descriptions, where the tables already contain tuples. Inference rules may be complementary, in that new rules for derived data items can be added dynamically with the added benefit that no changes need be made to the underlying physical data (since the rules are executed at run–time to create temporary data).

Execution

Execution of inference rules could be triggered in a number of ways. Derived data items, which are the goals of inference rules, may be declared in external views of the database, so that the end user is unaware that the data items are not actually stored (in the same way that an end user does not realise that a view may represent a join on a number of tables, rather than represent a single physical table). However, the user must realise that they have read only access to this virtual data. When a user requests data (that is, they input a query) via a view then the inference rules would be triggered through forward or backward chaining. Equally, an end user may directly ask for inference rules to be run, to perform chosen calculations. For example, a display of course tutors may be requested.

It would be possible to incorporate hypothetical reasoning into the mechanisms used to derive data. For example an end user might request that all possible combinations of timetables (tutors and courses) should be produced. Associated with the inference rules would be a number of integrity constraints which affect truth maintenance, such as a lecturer cannot be in two different places at the same time, eliminating impossible timetables as early as possible.

The permanence of virtual or generated data during a user session would need to be clarified. The simplest implementation would generate values once, which would remain for the entire session. However, it would be possible to use demons to cause recalculation of values when the underlying variables within the database changed (updated by other people in a shared service) within a session. This mechanism could be switch–driven to enable users to control recalculation.

Squirrel

Waugh [WAUG89] has designed an extended SQL, Squirrel, for deductive database systems, which permits *clauses* to define values in a relation, unlike relational databases where the database population consists of tuples (data) defined by table types. This incorporates some of the above ideas on adding rules to the data definition of a database.

He distinguishes between the definition of values in a relation and the actual values found in a relation, referred to as syntactic (rules and facts) and semantic (data) objects respectively. Syntactic objects define semantic objects under some resolution strategy. For example, syntactic objects might be (using Prolog–like syntax in a male–only database):

son(bill,john)	[bill is the son of john]
son(X,Y) if father(Y,X)	[X is the son of Y if Y is the father of X]
father(simon,mark)	[simon is the father of mark]
father(martin, tom)	[martin is the father of tom]

The following semantic objects (data) can be generated from this:

son(mark,simon)	[because simon is the father of mark, mark is the son of simon]
son(tom, martin)	

This ability to specify syntactic objects and generate implicit data is equivalent to using inference rules.

Waugh also permits the definition of integrity constraints which apply to the semantic values. They can show dependencies of values from more than one relational table. For example, a message can be displayed if the declared integrity constraint is violated:

> INSERT INTEGRITY CONSTRAINT ic2
> MESSAGE IS 'No teaching load for all teaching staff.'
> FOR teaching_staff
> IMPLIES THERE EXISTS teaching_load
>   SUCH THAT teaching_staff.name = teaching_load.name

This syntax is equivalent to that described for integrity constraints and action rules above.

4.1.9 Products

Four example products, three of which are purchasable, are described briefly below, to show that the ideas set out in this section are not purely theoretical. It is likely that new products will emerge and existing products be enhanced during the shelf–life of this book.

Generis

Generis has evolved from The FACT System which is claimed to be the world's first Intelligent Knowledgebase Management System, which uses the Generic Associative Technique to 'combine the power of relational database technology with user–defined inference and action rules which are held in the same database'. Data can be viewed in tables or in frames based on a subject class (object oriented view, see section 4.2). The System links all tables in an application into a semantic network (based on common columns) enabling referential integrity to be maintained within the schema and complex joins to be performed automatically. Generis has been developed as an integrated system encompassing database, KBS, AI representation and 4GL technology. It provides an environment for both the development and operation of applications using knowledge–based technology.

Generis incorporates a number of features described in this section:

- facts can be held at all levels in an object view. Details may relate to individual entity occurrences or to an entire class. Generic facts are automatically inherited by members of the class and the system will attempt to resolve conflicting values;

- restrictions can be defined which determine the validity of data;

- rules can be specified and processed. A query specifies a goal and the system backward–chains to evaluate the goal using the rules and existing data;

- new data items can be computed from existing values on request;

- action rules can cause permanent changes to the database or activate external processes or programs. These are triggered by external events, a time value, a change in the database or the execution of a command.

Generis is marketed by Deductive Systems Limited (see annex B).

Ingres – Knowledge Management Extension

Ingres Ltd has released two extensions to the Ingres DBMS for object management (see section 4.2) and knowledge management. The Knowledge Management Extension allows referential integrity constraints, business rules and resource and access control rules to be stored.

Rules are created using a new SQL command 'CREATE RULE' and the associated procedures are standard database procedures coded in the Ingres 4GL and SQL. An unlimited number of independent rules per table is allowed. The Rule System enforces referential integrity constraints ensuring that primary and foreign keys match, and business rules, such as 'orders must be associated with customers'. Rules are fired when data is changed, to meet the activation criteria associated with rules. Marketing material suggests that Ingres rules forward chain, such that: changes made by rules can fire other rules, and recurse; and changes made by a rule can refire the same rule to DBA–defined depths.

The database administrator can specify rules which control resource usage by queries. For example, limits on the number of rows returned and disk input/output can be specified. Queries which exceed these limits are aborted. See section 4.3 for more about query optimisation. Access control rules can also be stored and used by Ingres, to grant permissions to groups of users and applications.

Ingres is marketed by Ingres Ltd, formerly Relational Technology Inc (see annex B).

Postgres

Postgres is a relational database management system which has been built as the successor to Ingres. Six main design goals have been named [STON86], one of which is 'to provide facilities for active databases (that is, alerters and triggers) and inferencing including forward and backward chaining'. An alerter may, for example, draw attention to a problem or a trigger may propagate (cascade) updates. In the data definition, columns (attributes) in one relation (entity) can be inherited from other relations, which in some ways creates a structure like an object hierarchy. [This research is thought likely to have provided input to the development of the Knowledge Management Extension of Ingres.]

POSTQUEL query language has been developed to allow specification of iterative queries, alerters, triggers and rules. Iterative queries, such as retrieve all people managed, directly or indirectly, by Mr Smith, use an asterisk to denote that repeated processing is required. 'Always' is added to alerter and trigger queries which are fired and propagated using forward chaining. Backward chaining supports evaluation of virtual columns (derived fields) for which no values are stored but which are derived using inference rules.

Sybase

Sybase is a relational database management system designed for on–line applications. There are two major components, the DataServer which handles data management functions and the DataToolset which provides visual tools for building and running applications. The DataServer provides enforced integrity, among other things, in three ways:

- rules may be applied to individual fields. The rules can contain any expression that is valid in an SQL 'WHERE clause'. Rules can be changed or dropped at any time, but they are not retroactive, that is data entered before the rule is defined is not checked;

- stored procedures, which are collections of SQL statements and control–flow language, can execute conditional logic. They can call or be called from other applications. Queries in the stored procedures are optimised for using indexes before compilation, based on statistics about the distribution of key values in each index generated by the DataServer. A description of the processing plan for the query can be generated and at run–time performance statistics can be requested for display;

- triggers, which are a special type of stored procedure held in the central dictionary, are executed whenever attempts to insert, delete or update data are made. These triggers implement data–driven integrity and enforcing referential integrity. They can rollback transactions and issue messages to the on–line user.

Examples of the usage of triggers, as given by Sybase, are:

- update an author's identification number in all tables in which it occurs, causing cascade updating and enforcing referential integrity;

- allow a user access to a database only between 9am and 5pm;

- back–up the database at midnight or when there are fewer than three users on the DataServer, (this is considered to be an action rule);

- generate a royalty check if 'sales * royalty * price > $500'.

Sybase is marketed by the company Sybase, based in Bracknell.

4.2

Object orientation

4.2.1 Introduction

This section is a continuation of section 4.1, in that it is concerned with the convergence of knowledge–based system (KBS) and database management system (DBMS) facilities, but object orientation is considered sufficiently important to warrant a section on its own. There is, however, a subtle difference between sections 4.1 and 4.2: section 4.1 observes similar features of existing KBS and DBMS technology; this section observes features of existing KBS technology and early DBMS developments with a view towards convergence in the future.

The paradigm of object orientation seems to have infiltrated many areas of software development: there are object oriented languages such as C++, object oriented database management systems, such as V–Base and G–Base, object oriented knowledge–based systems such as KEE and Nexpert Object, object oriented methods and techniques, and so on. This section makes no attempt to cover the subject matter in detail, but addresses those issues concerned with convergence of KBS and DBMS. A concepts sub–section is included to provide a context for the rest of the section.

4.2.2 Concepts

There are five concepts which are important in understanding object orientation: objects, classes, messages, methods and inheritance. Some specialists would add a sixth concept, encapsulation, which is the combination of data and procedures in a single element, though this is achieved through the use of classes, methods and messages.

Objects and classes

Objects are entities that contain both data and procedures (methods) which act upon the data. An object is a discrete unit of data and processing. The term 'object' is commonly used to refer to both *classes* of objects and *instances* of objects, in the same way that the word entity is used to mean both entity type and entity instance. The context in which the word is used should indicate whether instances or types are appropriate. A class defines the structure of an object, that is the data description and procedures. A frame is an implementation structure for a class, used in many tools. A class is made up of slots (which are the equivalent of attribute types) and methods (no equivalent since these define the procedures which can act on instances and the class). Slots can store information which might be defined in a data dictionary for DBMS attribute types, including the name, data type, constraints and a default value.

Classes are often arranged in hierarchies, to represent generalisation at the top through to the specific at the bottom of the hierarchy. An example hierarchy is shown in figure 4.2.1 with a data model interpretation in figure 4.2.2 using entity sub–typing. One of the major differences between object hierarchies and data models is that occurrences of data can be mixed with data types (meta–data) in the former, but only meta data is ever included in a data model.

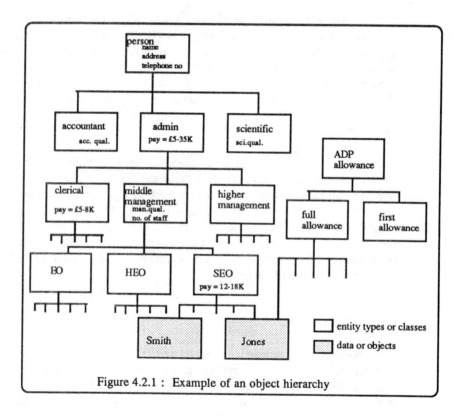

Figure 4.2.1 : Example of an object hierarchy

Messages and methods

Messages invoke attached procedures (methods) to act upon object data. Objects respond to messages they receive by determining the appropriate procedure to execute. A procedure or method is a specification of action on data contained in the object. For example, a message called 'Print–object' could invoke a function to cause the data in an object to be printed.

Messages are identified by selectors, which are names recognised by receiving objects. When a message is sent to an object, the object responds by locating an attached procedure associated with this message and executes it. Different objects might respond to the same message in different ways, because different procedures are defined as methods for the objects. For example, a 'Print–object' message might cause the person object in figure 4.2.1 to execute a 'print' method to display the default values for the class on a screen; the same message might cause the Jones object (an instance) to execute a 'print' method (same name but a different underlying procedure) to print all Jones' personal details.

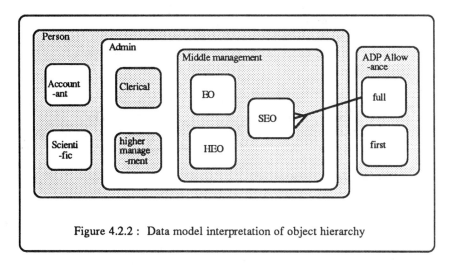

Figure 4.2.2 : Data model interpretation of object hierarchy

Inheritance

A facility which is fundamental to object oriented systems is inheritance of characteristics. Slots and methods can be inherited from parent classes; if a class is a son of two or more classes then it can inherit characteristics from both parents (multiple inheritance). If the same characteristic is defined for both parents, but the definitions are different, then a default mechanism may determine what is inherited, which can usually be modified by the developer.

4.2.3 Advantages

Object orientation offers a number of advantages to implementors of some types of system during development and maintenance, because of the following features:

- data structures are flexible due to the hierarchy from generalisation to specificity, in that data and its attributes can be stored at the appropriate level of abstraction, with no clear distinction between typing (classes) and occurrences (objects);

- there are rich facilities for describing data, for example it is common to store with a slot such information as constraints, sources, prompts, a default value, etc, in addition to the usual description;

- data values can be inherited rather than duplicated across related objects;

- complex models can be built, which take into account all the exceptions rather than just the generalised rule;

- processing which is related to objects is associated with those specific objects;

- code, that is procedures, can be associated with many different object types enabling reusability and controlling replication.

Encapsulation, that is the combination of data and procedures within a single element, is often claimed to be advantageous, in that a user need not know what an object contains, only what message to send to it in order to achieve the required effect. Others might argue that this is a retrograde step, since over the last ten years separation of data and processing has been advocated. Perhaps the novel way of expressing procedures, using messages and methods, enables processing to be viewed in a similar way to data, so that separation of the two is no longer necessary.

4.2.4 Object oriented knowledge–based systems

There are many object oriented KBS tools, such as Natural Expert, KEE, Inference ART and Goldworks to name but a few, which have been available for a number of years. The use of object orientation is often optional, in that systems can be built using other mechanisms such as rules, particularly in the mainframe KBS tools. The following brief descriptions of objects in ADS and BIM Prolog show how objects may be implemented.

ADS

There are five ADS objects, class, slot, method, instance and rule, and each type of object has its own editor. A class acts as a template for other objects, and within a class instances, slots, methods and procedures can be created. Other ADS objects, such as functions, messages, reports and graphs, can also be defined in a class. Class variables, that is data associated with a class rather than an instance, are called parameters. A subclass can be created from a class, and it automatically inherits slots and methods. The inherited slots and methods can be modified, and new ones can be added. A slot description includes a sourcing property: it is possible to specify that a slot is a value retrieved from a database.

A number of ADS objects can be attached to a method, including functions, messages, reports and graphs. Methods which are inherited by subclasses can be specialised; the common part of a method is stored in the parent object rather than replicated, which will reduce maintenance effort.

Rules used in inference based applications can also be used in object oriented ADS applications. A traditional if... then rule specifies actions on a single object instance, such as:

IF amount > 100 THEN send (excessive_amount to display) END

A pattern matching rule specifies actions on a set of instances, from one or more classes as follows:

IFMATCH
amount > 100
credit_limit = 100
THEN
credit_status = 'maximum'
END

A pattern matching rule could be used to process a set of relations retrieved from a database.

BIM Probe

BIM Probe is the object oriented extension to BIM Prolog and it is made up of three modules: a core object oriented system, a Prolog constraint language and a human computer interface. Probe implements the basic features of an object oriented language, in terms of classes, instances and slots. A slot may be a property which defines the static state of the object, a constraint which specifies the integrity requirements or a method which describes the behaviour. Slots are defined by a set of facets.

Objects are organised in hierarchies or networks, since multiple inheritance is allowed. Conflicts caused by inconsistent definitions in parent classes are detected and the user requested for a solution.

Procedural attachments can be defined for objects: active values are procedures triggered under certain conditions; methods are procedures which must be explicitly called by sending a message to the object. Procedural attachments can be specified using Prolog Constraint Language (PCL), Prolog or C. PCL is based on a modified form of predicate calculus and is therefore well suited for specifying integrity constraints.

4.2.5 Object oriented database management systems

Some object oriented DBMS (OODB) have emerged from research comparatively recently, such as V–base and G–Base, but they are by no means in common usage. The better known relational database management systems, such as Oracle, Ingres and Sybase are unable to directly implement object hierarchies at current releases. However, data held in relational tables can be translated into object hierarchies as shown by the link between KEE and Oracle, described in annex D.

Beech (BEEC88) describes a correspondence between relational and object database models: a relational table corresponds to a type (class) or a function; and a column name and type correspond to the name and result type of a property function. He points out that in an object oriented database it would not be necessary to generate unique keys for objects and therefore referential integrity problems cannot arise. Also, the user does not need to specify joins by matching keys to navigate between objects.

It is conceivable that a DBMS external view mechanism could be built, to present the user with an object oriented view of relational tables. SQL3 includes a proposal for subtables, which could be used to represent object hierarchies. The Object Management Extension of Ingres, as described below, could be enhanced in this way. Spiers suggests that the quickest way to deliver object oriented databases will be to build on existing technology, providing it is a suitable foundation [SPIE89]. Relational DBMS seem the most likely candidates for that foundation.

The rest of this sub–section describes some developments concerning OODB.

G–Base

G–Base uses a 'property–value' representation; the DBMS can be viewed as an interpreter of a set of properties, each being described as a property–value list. While processing data, the presence of any property in a data stream can activate associated functions.

An entity can either be a Model (definition) or an occurrence of a Model. The characteristics of an entity are properties or fields which store information. Properties are declared at the occurrence level and can therefore be manipulated independently of Models. This is claimed to have the advantage that entity Models can evolve without the database contents having to be restructured, although this could impact on maintenance.

Terminal properties allow values to be assigned to an entity occurrence. Structural properties are used to represent relationships between entities. A relationship can involve a one–to–one (father) or one–to–many (brother(s)) within an entity type, or one–to–many and many–to–many between two entity types.

Lisp applications can access G–Base databases using functions to open and close a database, retrieve entities, and update and delete entities.

Ingres – Object Management Extension

Relational database management systems have in the past been limited to storing data types such as characters and numbers. Complex data elements and unconventional data, such as coordinates, arrays, vectors and bitmaps, have generally been stored outside the database. The Object Management Extension of Ingres now allows user defined data types, functions and operators to be used by the DBMS server, in a client/server architecture.

The Database Administrator (DBA) can write procedures in any third generation language to specify how to store and manipulate new data types. Such procedures will handle sorting, input and output formats, default values and valid ranges of values. At run–time, these procedures are invoked when a user–defined data type is used.

User–defined functions and operators can be written to manipulate user–defined data types (and others). The functions are add–ons to SQL for manipulating data; the operators provide new meaning for conventional operators such as addition and subtraction using + and – respectively.

This Object Management Extension effectively only allows new data types to be defined and manipulated. It does not provide a superstructure for manipulating data as objects, in the way that objects are described in 4.2.2 above. That is, there are no class hierarchies, inheritance, methods or messages.

Sembase

Sembase [KING86] is a DBMS based on an object oriented model. The model represents an application environment as a collection of objects: types and subtypes are arranged in hierarchies according to type–subtype relationships. Descriptor objects are atomic values of strings, integers, booleans and real numbers; abstract objects are defined in terms of their relationships with other objects.

Database manipulations are performed by data operations: databases can be retrieved and saved; objects can be created, amended, deleted and read; and some functions allow the user to navigate through the database.

4.2.6 OODB requirements

It has yet to be seen whether OODB, such as G–Base and V–Base, will be as successful as relational DBMS are proving to be, and network and hierarchic DBMS have been in the past. It is thought that object orientation could provide the unifying mechanism for KBS and DBMS, and thence facilitate the integration of KBS and conventional, DBMS–based systems.

OODB will need to provide the following:

- a rich collection of complex data structures, such as images, lists, etc;

- new data types, such as booleans and coordinates;

- the facility to build named, user–defined data structures, including hierarchies, networks and arrays, which are then re–usable;

- storage mechanisms for poorly structured data, such as text, sound and graphics, which may be used as part of a user interface;

- a facility for amending the structure of data (the data definition) without having to restructure and reorganise existing data. One of the advantages of a relational database over a network is that the data description can be extended without needing to unload and reload existing data (data independence);

- a facility for extending existing objects by adding new slots (properties) and methods (procedures) without necessarily affecting classes or applications which access existing parts of objects (a new aspect of data independence which is not possible in relational DBMS);

- storage mechanisms for rules and procedural attachments to data, so that methods can be encapsulated in objects within the database;

- a simple, but powerful, user interface for manipulating the data. This could be a natural language interface, possibly built on top of SQL or a formal language;

- performance which is comparable to that of relational, if not network, databases.

What this is basically saying is that all the advantages of object orientation should be built into a DBMS without losing existing, good features, such as data independence. All the usual features of DBMS, such as access control and security against loss of data would also be required.

4.2.7   Unification

It seems that the paradigm of object orientation could provide the unifying mechanism for KBS and DBMS technology. The basic concepts have been defined (though the terms are frequently misused), such that mismatches at the logical level should not occur. There are likely to be differences in physical implementations, but interfaces could be sufficiently well documented to prevent loss of data or accuracy of values. The concept of encapsulation would enable 'black boxes' to be built with well–defined interfaces, implemented using messages.

The level of functionality provided in object oriented systems (both KBS and DBMS) will vary across products. For example, the types of integrity constraint which may be associated with a slot will vary. A minimum level of functionality could be specified, which could potentially become a standard.

The SQL standard is trailing behind products, in that the features implemented in DBMS, such as Ingres and Oracle, are beyond the minimum laid down in the standard. When such facilities are documented in the standard, vendors will be reluctant to change their products if this is necessary to conform with the standard. There is a timely opportunity here, to develop an object orientation standard which will lead mainstream products, particularly OODB, to pull products up to a baseline.

4.3

Enhancement of DBMS using KBS

4.3.1 Introduction

There is the potential for using knowledge–based systems (KBS) applications to enhance database management systems (DBMS), see figure 4.3.1. That is, a number of the functions of a DBMS could be augmented by the application of KBS technology.

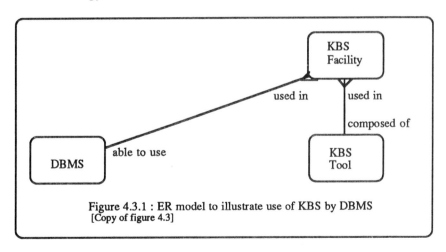

Figure 4.3.1 : ER model to illustrate use of KBS by DBMS
[Copy of figure 4.3]

EUSIDIC suggests that artificial intelligence (AI) will develop through three identifiable phases [EUSI88]:

- for four or five years AI will contribute improved convenience to the user by taking over such functions as on–line dialogue management and defining the search;

- in the next phase there will be full provision databases. Text as well as data will be available on–line, and they will be usable by the machine as well as by the user;

- in perhaps ten years time the development of a corporate knowledge resource in which information, both public and private, analysis, knowledge and skills will be combined.

To date, most applications have concentrated on four aspects in the first area listed above:

- specification and checking of integrity constraints in the DBMS;

- subschema or external view generation;

- improving the end user query interface through the use of a natural language, so that the casual user does not need to learn the syntax of a query language such as SQL;

- optimisation of queries to improve the response time.

Inclusion of integrity constraints in the DBMS is described in section 4.1. It has been reported [JONE89(3)] that Oracle believe one of the keys to the success of products like Oracle is portability, and this could be compromised by embedding AI techniques. This may be true, unless one of the portable KBS tools, such as KES which is written in C, is used. Their approach, perhaps like a number of other companies, is to build AI capabilities on top of the relational environment in the form of extensions to SQL. This section describes some developments which could be, or have been, implemented in this area.

4.3.2 Easier syntax and appropriate query formulation

The target user population for database query languages is changing to include managers and application specialists, who have a high degree of application knowledge but little patience to acquire familiarity with programming concepts. Such users require high level query languages which perform powerful operations without requiring technical skills. Many 'natural language' packages exist which allow end users to input queries or questions in an English–like format.

Some users master query languages such as SQL and can write relatively simple queries; however, problems arise with complex queries which involve several tables (hence joins) and selection criteria which are connected using 'and', 'or' and 'not'. The user might write a syntactically correct query, but he remains unsure about whether it will retrieve the information which he needs. A user may only realise that the query was wrong when data has been retrieved and displayed. This is a classic case where a KBS application might provide a number of variants on the query (with full English explanations and examples) so that the user gets what he wants, rather than what his initial query specified.

It is not unusual for a wrongly worded query to cause a large proportion of the database contents to be retrieved unintentionally. This, in turn, can cause scarce resources to be tied up in fruitless searches of the database. A KBS could present the user with an interpretation of each query and an indication of the number of records which will be retrieved, before it is actioned.

KBS have been used to improve the user interface of a number of existing software packages, for example a regional gas board has developed a front–end to Querymaster using ICL–Adviser. In general, the KBS application obtains information from the user in a less machine–oriented fashion than the package requires, then translates the requirement into a call to the Querymaster software package. The latter is used to interrogate IDMS databases.

4.3.3 Query tools which use KBS

Db–edge

Db–edge is a personal computer front–end for DB2 mainframe databases, which uses rules to hide the complexity of the database from the user. The system stores a customised view of the database on the personal computer, simplifies the user's enquiries and generates optimised SQL statements to fetch the required information from the database. The view is customised by adding high–level rules in Prolog, describing relationships between columns in terms which the user can understand.

Easytalk

Intelligent Business Systems Inc has developed a product, Easytalk, which is an expert system that translates a 'user's plain English request into SQL' [KULL89] and navigates a database to find the most efficient statement. The system can interrogate Oracle databases, and there are plans to support Rdb and DB2.

The Easytalk system includes a knowledge–base that describes the application databases and a component which can use this database to determine the best path through the data. The software automatically extracts information about tables, columns and indexes from the DBMS catalogue. Database developers and administrators then add their own understanding of the database.

The user organisation also builds its own thesaurus for natural language translation on to the thesaurus of common business terms provided with Easytalk. The developer can use this facility to build business rules into the query system, such as a 'good customer' might be one who pays for goods within ten days of delivery. Developers can continue to refine the knowledge–base using information logged by the system in response to user requests or through feedback from users.

Figure 4.3.2 shows the architecture of the system. The database user phrases a query in English; the 'meaning representation' expresses the entities included and the database search criteria. A 'retrieval specification' is produced using the knowledge–base which holds information about database access and where data is held; this is then translated into SQL via a meta–query language.

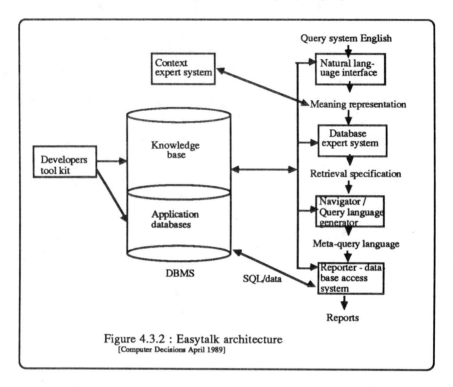

Figure 4.3.2 : Easytalk architecture
[Computer Decisions April 1989]

Intellect

The natural language package Intellect, marketed by AI Corp, provides a front–end to most commercial DBMS which run on IBM machines; this includes Adabas, DB2, Focus, and SQL/DS. PC–Link allows Intellect to down–load the results of queries to micros. Intellect is also available on VAX machines and can therefore interrogate Rdb databases. Intellect is used to access data for KBMS (the KBS tool marketed by AI Corp) applications.

Intellect is an expert system which embodies programmers' knowledge and knowledge about the English language. It uses a lexicon made up of a built–in dictionary of basic English words and grammatical rules, and names of data fields extracted from the DBMS schema. Users can add synonyms and concepts to the lexicon. Intellect paraphrases queries and echoes them back to the user to make sure that the query has been interpreted as the user intended, before accessing the database. Intellect/DB2 generates optimised SQL using a minimum number of lines of SQL code; other interfaces generate the appropriate command language for data retrieval. The results may be presented as histograms, pie charts, etc, using an interface to IBM's Graphical Data Display Manager.

Intelliscope

Intelliscope was developed by Intellicorp, who also market KEE. It is described as a database assistant which helps users to get information out of relational databases without writing SQL or understanding how the data is structured. Intellicorp is built upon KEE so it can be used to analyse and reason about data which is extracted. It can be used with any SQL database which can be accessed by KEE.

Intelliscope has an interactive graphic interface which uses mouse–and–menu operations. At each step in the query formulation process, it displays an example and uses its knowledge of the structure of the database to suggest options for refining the query. As the user changes the query Intelliscope highlights new and relevant information.

Data can be displayed as histograms, scatter plots and tables. Overlaying windows enable the user to view the query, listed data and graphic displays on a single screen.

KIRA

The ESPRIT project KIWI worked on a methodology for information retrieval to assist consumers in accessing databases [KIWI88]. A prototype system, Knowledge–based Information Retrieval Assistant (KIRA), implements the methodology. The KIWI team perceived that information consumers need help in solving fuzzy problems. The user's initial statement of his information need usually consists of several subject concepts that are more generic than his actual need. Therefore the assistant must carry out an iterative process of interview, interpretation, presentation of possible answers and getting feedback as to the relevance of the answers he actually needs.

Q&A and Intelligent Assistant

Symatec's Q&A database has an English language front–end, Intelligent Assistant. It has a 450 word vocabulary to start with, but words can be added during use. Synonyms can be included for 'jargon translation'.

Full text retrieval

Gauch describes an expert system for searching in full–text [GAUC89]. An intelligent search intermediary is being developed to help end users to locate relevant passages in large, full–text databases. The expert system reformulates queries to improve search results and presents retrieved passages in decreasing order of estimated relevance. The system uses search strategies which are domain independent.

The user interacts with the system using a high–level query language. The system deals with the technical details of the database and works with the user to refine the query if an initial search is unsatisfactory. If the search would retrieve too many texts, the expert system tightens the constraints on the query; conversely, if too few are produced, the constraints are loosened or expanded. When an appropriate number of texts have been identified, they are ranked in terms of probable interest based on several criteria including the number of different concepts in the text and word types for each concept. Microarras is the text retrieval package used.

4.3.4 Single interface to many DBMS

Although a standard for SQL has been produced, this is the tip of the iceberg for standardisation of query languages. If a user wants to consult a number of databases, managed by different DBMS, it is likely that he will have to use different query languages or at least variations of SQL. Maraschini suggests that 'what is really needed is a system that contains the knowledge that is usually found in database directories, operator guides and the like, and that utilises this knowledge in order to connect with the proper host, send to it correct command code and interface to the user in an intuitive and consistent way... ' [MARA88]. He continues, '... it must have knowledge of the databases that are available and their contents; ... it must have a detailed knowledge of the retrieval system query language... '.

A project, *Easyfind*, was started in an attempt to simplify the use of Find, an information retrieval system used by the Italian Supreme Court for the distribution of its databases [MARA88]. One of the criteria of design for Easyfind was to generalise the interface in order to possibly interface different database distribution systems. The system is structured to allow the definition of the structure, commands and characteristics of other database access systems.

Howells describes a source to source translation system between pairs of database query languages, which is table driven and implemented in Prolog [HOWE88]. This makes access to any remote database much easier. A common intermediate query representation based on relational algebra is used.

4.3.5 Development of user profiles

A KBS application which recognises common expressions and words used by an individual or a group of individuals, over a period of time, could be used to build up user profiles regarding their use of a database. This knowledge can then be used to build specific, tailored interfaces for those users.

Some researchers at Tome Associates set out to build an expert system which would model some of the skills and knowledge of librarians and other expert intermediaries [DURH89]. Many large companies have a number of such people, who use their knowledge of databases to search out information on behalf of users. Some of the requisite knowledge consists of strategies for writing boolean queries required by most on–line text databases, and for broadening, narrowing or modifying a query when necessary. Most of the other requisite knowledge is domain dependent, particularly vocabulary.

Building the knowledge–base is very labour intensive. Typically, an experienced information scientist is able to add about 1000 terms per week. Tome has a built–in editing tool which can be used when the source books are already in electronic form.

The research project revealed that a thesaurus is potential raw material for the knowledge–base of an expert system. For this purpose, the information is stored as a semantic network. Each word or phrase is linked to others by pointers which can be traversed in either direction. Behind the scenes Tome Searcher (the product) rephrases the query to exploit special features of a particular query language and the user may be asked to choose the best of numerous suggestions of words made by the system. [Tome Searcher is not on sale but custom systems can be built by Tome Associates.]

4.3.6 Explanation of data

A database and the associated catalogue contain a highly impoverished description of a part of the real world. Sometimes, but not always, names in the database are English words, but often they do not impart much information. Also one man's invoice number might be another man's receipt number. A thesaurus built to facilitate query formulation could include synonyms and explanations about data types. A KBS application could potentially explain the relationship between terms used within the database and real world, business terminology, as relationships may not be straight forward synonyms.

Explanation of the *meaning* of data is difficult, since this requires an interpretation to be placed on the data. However, the meaning of the original query and the amount of data retrieved could be used. For example, relational database queries sometimes find no tuples and hence no data is displayed. It is important that the user knows what the implications are of this lack of output. For example, a request to list customers who purchased a particular item might produce no results; but this could be because the item is not sold by the company, rather than because nobody bought the item. Motro recognised that it is unsatisfactory for users to get null answers and proposed a solution of generating more general queries until some answer is obtained [MOTR84]. He went on to develop the FLEX system which is a user interface that is tolerant of incorrect input and cooperative in the case of null answers.

Data retrieved from databases can be misleading, in that it might be out of date, incomplete or ambiguous. An SQL query will only cause the items which satisfy the selection criteria to be displayed. Information about data which was read in order to satisfy a query (for example values used in joins) might provide a missing link.

Error messages output to the user are rarely meaningful to someone who is not familiar with the database content and the DBMS. The query language analyser may not be able to interpret a query and therefore displays an error message; the user may not understand the error message and may not know what changes should be made to the query. A KBS application could provide simple explanations for errors and suggest possible actions to be taken as a result of an error. A user support team may well be able to provide a number of classic cases, based on experience, to be incorporated into such a system.

4.3.7 Query optimisation

A query optimiser standardises, simplifies and transforms a query to enable the application of fast, special purpose algorithms and achieve efficient execution of a query. Rules may guide the choice of query transformation rules, for example they may identify detachable sub–queries. Alternative query evaluation strategies may be generated from rules, so that evaluation costs based on knowledge about storage structures and database statistics can be compared.

A basic data selection instruction might be:

SELECT customer–name	[data to be displayed]
FROM customer–table, order–table	[tables to be used in the query]
WHERE customer–table.customer–number = order–table.customer–number	
AND order–date > 010288	[selection criteria]

The query optimiser must determine how this query can best be satisfied. It could join all permissible combinations of records in the two tables (on the common column, customer–number) and then select those tuples with the required date; alternatively, order records which satisfy the date criterion could be selected and joined with the appropriate customer records to obtain customer name; or there may be other variations on these themes.

One way of handling this is to treat optimisation as a problem of search. The query is converted into a lower level representation than SQL and a number of plans are generated with the cost of satisfying each plan. Statistical information about the database, such as number of records in each table, index distribution and location of data in a distributed database may be used to calculate the costs. For any given query there is likely to be a number of possible plans and KBS technology could be used to help prioritise these plans.

Shan describes an optimal plan search strategy for the Iris DBMS, which generates an initial plan based upon a set of heuristics rather than searching for the optimal plan directly [SHAN88]. One of the objectives was to provide extensibility, so that the system could be dynamically tuned to support different system configurations and functional requirements. The mechanism works as follows:

- the original query is translated into a query tree of extended relational algebra operators;

- the optimiser uses a set of catalogued rules to produce an equivalent tree by examining the node configuration of the query tree. Relational transformation rules and access plan computation rules are used to generate an initial plan;

- the relational transformation rules are based on relational algebra laws or semantic calculus;

- access plan computation rules describe the correspondence between logical operators and physical access methods and associated cost formulae;

- the last phase attempts to minimise a cost objective; a reasonable execution plan for the query is used as a basis for cost comparison with searches for the optimal plan. Heuristics are also used to prune the search space.

Gray [GRAY89] suggests that Prolog is a good language for query optimisation. He discusses various forms of optimisation, from simple re–ordering of goals to the total transformation of a query from a tuple–at–a–time form to a set–based form expressed in an SQL–like language.

4.3.8 Query optimisation in tools

Details about the internal workings of proprietary DBMS are always likely to be confidential, since a company will not want a rival to gain knowledge of their ideas, particularly if those ideas provide competitive edge. Optimisation procedures for SQL fall into this category. They are frequently alluded to in marketing literature by some vague information. Documentation of query optimising mechanisms which might be used are likely to be documented in research papers.

Ingres Ltd give some information about their Ingres query optimiser in an 'Overview of Ingres'. It is said to be an AI–based query optimiser that automatically determines the fastest way to satisfy a database request. The cost–based optimiser uses information such as:

- a maximum cost set by the user or database administrator (DBA);

- data distribution, storage structures, keys and indexes;

- strategies, data location, cost of network and cost of processing. The statistics–based optimiser determines the number of rows returned and the amount of disk input and output necessary to process a query;

- resource control rules stored via the Knowledge Management Extension.

The optimiser produces an annotated query plan or the query might be rejected as being too costly.

4.3.9 Other facilities

As stated at the beginning of this section, most work has been channelled into providing a better user interface. However, there are other potential applications for KBS technology, associated with the DBMS:

- provision of facilities for database developers, see section 4.4 where the use of KBS technology in CASE tools is discussed;

- facilitating integration of independently developed databases, which are controlled by the same proprietary DBMS, by reasoning over separate data descriptions where standards may have not been applied;

- building of intelligent gateways between two or more DBMS so that a user need not be aware of the different types of DBMS being used. This might be useful to existing users of ICL's IDMS network DBMS who would like to extend their data storage using the relational products now available, such as Ingres and Oracle;

- development of efficient search strategies for locating data in a distributed database;

- implementation of a more sophisticated access control system, such that the DBA can store rules about access (as implemented in Ingres Knowledge Management Extension);

- providing information to database administrators, in addition to statistics, to enable them to tune the database and improve performance. For example, common values could be identified or columns which ought to be indexed.

4.4

Using KBS in CASE tools

4.4.1 Introduction

The analysis, design, implementation and maintenance of computer systems are essentially tasks carried out by experts who have knowledge about how to use methods, techniques, and implementation tools, and during these processes they learn about the system under development. Computer Assisted Software Engineering (CASE) tools are emerging to support these experts by: overseeing the procedural aspects of methods and enforcing the use of standards; providing drawing tools which are tailored for given techniques; checking consistency across documentation generated by different techniques; automatically generating code from a detailed physical design; and so on. It is not surprising that CASE tool developers are starting to use knowledge–based systems (KBS) technology to facilitate these knowledge–oriented tasks; see figure 4.4.1.

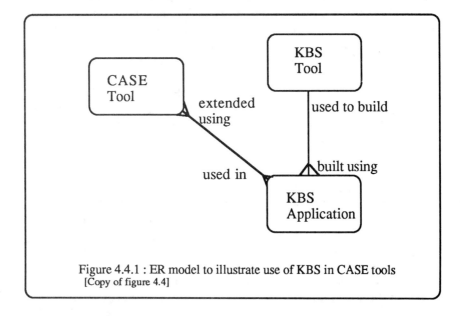

Figure 4.4.1 : ER model to illustrate use of KBS in CASE tools
[Copy of figure 4.4]

This section is concerned with incorporating KBS applications into CASE tools, rather than the use of CASE tools to build KBS applications, which is discussed in section 5.1.

4.4.2 Application of knowledge in CASE

It would be difficult to provide an exhaustive list of all the potential applications which could be built into CASE tools; any task within system development which requires expertise may be considered, but criteria for selecting a suitable KBS application should be applied. This sub–section gives an indication of areas of application. There are four major topics to be considered:

- analysis and design;

- code generation and the programming environment;

- maintenance of systems;

- project support and management.

The last point might be deemed to be outside the province of many CASE tools, but support for project management would be provided in an integrated project support environment (IPSE).

Analysis and design

A lot of the KBS work on CASE tools has concentrated on this area. In order to build KBS support into a CASE tool to facilitate the use of an entire method by inexperienced people, such as the Structured Systems Analysis and Design Method (SSADM), it is necessary to document the rules, data and tasks of that method. Although there are many books and training courses which describe and teach methods respectively, it is unlikely that there will be a comprehensive, consistent, unambiguous, detailed description of any method, because methods are large, complex and not *totally* understood by many people. People are very good at using incomplete information, filling in the gaps from past experience or by asking questions, and can therefore use methods without having a detailed description. Unfortunately computer systems, including KBS, cannot do this.

CCTA started to produce a formal description of SSADM as part of a CASE prototyping project. The work was extremely successful and a set of rules for SSADM now exists. However, it was found to be easier to document some parts than others; for example, the rules, tasks and data (notation) of Logical Data Structuring (LDS) or Entity Modelling can be written down using a formal notation, although it is difficult to specify all the integrity constraints associated with the technique. In any method, explicit definitions for dialogue design and how to modularise a procedure in the system for example, are likely to be more difficult to produce.

At present, therefore, CASE tools must compromise and use KBS to support the techniques or stages of a method which can be formally specified. Some of the following could be provided:

- support for user, business and technical requirements analysis and specification, with question lists, what–if queries, rule induction, etc;

- integrity, consistency and completeness checking within and across data flow diagrams (DFDs), logical data structures (LDSs) and entity life histories (ELHs);

- advice and guidance on drawing DFDs, LDSs, and ELHs;

- streamlining of dialogues and transactions within processes;

- prototyping, based upon system documentation (dialogues and screen outlines, calculations, etc) which has already been captured;

- guidance on documentation of the system, such as what type of information is expected to be supplied when defining an entity type;

- generation of a database schema design for a proprietary database management system (DBMS) from a logical data design, and tuning of the design to meet performance criteria;

- explanation of faults in a data description (as described in KELL86, through the use of a prototype, KM–1);

- performance predictions for processes, based upon the database schema design.

Loucopoulos gives an introduction to some papers which document research in a number of these areas [LOUC88].

Code generation and the programming environment

Transforming a process specification into code, or automatic system generation (ASG) as it is sometimes called, increases productivity in system development. Vendors of CASE and application generator tools have already provided some facilities in this area, not necessarily using KBS. For example, some Application Master (ICL's application generator) code can be generated from specifications held in a data dictionary (DDS). The process specification will need to be comprehensive and unambiguous for ASG, which is often not the case when programmers produce the code from written specifications. If the simpler programs, such as those which produce reports, can be automatically generated, then programmer skills can be applied more productively to the complex processing.

Testing and debugging code is perhaps another area where KBS technology could be applied: to detect circular reasoning and redundant code; to suggest approaches to testing after an analysis of the code; producing regression test data from test shots, for use during maintenance; and maintaining a log of code changes and retesting as part of a quality control process.

Maintenance of systems

There is a lot of interest in reverse engineering; that is, producing a specification from code or a data design from a physical data description, such that it can be changed and re–engineered using the same or different implementation tools. Providing that code is well structured or a physical data design was produced from a logical data model, the task is not too difficult.

A well known KBS tool vendor has produced a system for use in the conversion of code; that is translating Cobol programs into a different 'dialect', so that the code can be ported to another machine. Until portable systems come of age, conversion can be a problem if non–standard, machine specific syntax is used.

Maintenance is tedious and uses a large percentage of a company's IT resources. This seems to be a ripe area for the use of KBS technology, since one of the claims for KBS is that the mundane jobs can be automated, freeing the expert's time for more complex and interesting tasks.

Project support and management

In the context of CASE tools, facilities for version control of 'documents', once they have been reviewed and accepted, could be provided using KBS technology. Configuration management on large projects could be an automated process rather than a manual one, linked with the access control mechanisms.

Production of design metrics has been investigated for the MASCOT development method [LOUC88]. Estimates of cost and resource requirements frequently have large, built–in 'fudge' factors to allow for the inevitable. KBS applications could provide a consistent method of estimation, although they would only be as good as the expertise used to build them.

4.4.3 CASE tools and research

Some CASE tools already use KBS technology or AI techniques in limited areas. It is thought that one proprietary CASE tool may offer support for transforming logical design into physical implementations [JONE89(3)]. The Oracle CASE tool also provides this facility, generating program structures from data structures, but without using AI–approaches. Netron/CAP from Netron Inc includes an expert system for generating program structures.

ASPIS

The Application Software Prototype Implementation System (ASPIS) was developed as part of an ESPRIT project [PUNC88]. The ASPIS environment includes tools to support tasks in the early phases of the software development life cycle: requirements definition, analysis and design. Four 'assistants' were developed: the Analysis Assistant and the Design Assistant embody knowledge about the method and the application domain; the Prototype Assistant verifies and executes the specification; and the Reuse Assistant helps developers to reuse specifications and designs. See figure 4.4.2.

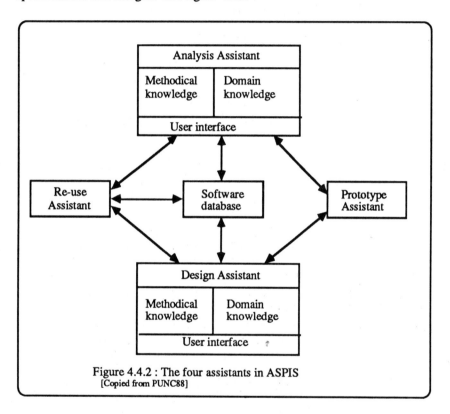

Figure 4.4.2 : The four assistants in ASPIS
[Copied from PUNC88]

The methodical knowledge in the Analysis Assistant contains the rules of the analysis method and some 'rule–of–thumb' expertise. The methodical knowledge consists of syntax, criteria of the method and heuristics gained from use of the method.

Bachman Re–Engineering Product Set

The Bachman Re–Engineering Product Set includes tools for advanced data modelling and database design, to help the developer to create new data structures focussing on business information and then produce optimised database designs. Knowledge–based processing is included to support the data modelling and database schema generation functions.

The Product Set can reverse engineer from existing IMS, Computer Associates' IDMS or DB2 data structures to produce a data model or models which can then be forward engineered into DB2 or IDMS database designs.

GESDD

Dogac describes a two part generalised expert system for database design (GESDD) [DOGA89]: one part generates methodologies for database design (ESGM); the other part designs a database (ESDD) using a selected methodology. ESDD is responsible for obtaining information about the business for the requirements specification phase (in accordance with the rules generated by ESGM), invoking test rules after a conceptual schema has been generated and producing a logical schema for a hierarchic, network or relational database.

Knowledgeware

The Knowledgeware tools support the Information Engineering methodology. The Information Engineering Workbench (IEW) toolset supports business planning, analysis and design, including database design. The IEW/Analysis Workstation captures user requirements and system specifications. The IEW/Design Workstation uses the specifications to create physical data and process specifications; this includes an option for DB2 design. The IEW/Cross System Product Enablement Facility allows generation of code (Cobol). A rule–based 'Knowledge Coordinator' underpins the IEW toolset, to check consistency during development and to integrate the development phases.

4.4.4 Future

The use of KBS applications in CASE tools is a fast growing area, but vendors are unlikely to reveal much information if the applications provide competitive edge. Current CASE tools are generally built to support one method or a collection of techniques. In the future, it is likely that customisable tools will be built, so that an organisation can input its own methodology rules. A base set might be provided for techniques such as data flow diagramming and entity modelling, but new rules about these techniques, or totally new techniques, could be added. This would be the advent of CASE shells.

It is possible that CASE tools may be customised for particular types of application, perhaps including some of the domain knowledge. This would be a novel way of presenting software packages, such as payroll systems. The CASE tool could contain the generalised specification, the organisation would add its own rules, and with automatic system generation produce a customised package.

4.5

Storing a knowledge–base in a database

4.5.1 Introduction

This section looks at the possibility of using a database to store the details of a knowledge–based system (KBS) application, which are included in the knowledge–base; see figure 4.5.1. The general idea is to exploit database management system (DBMS) capabilities for storing knowledge (rules, facts and so on) and to suggest a new architecture based on DBMS. Some KBS tools already exhibit *some* of the features included in DBMS which are discussed below, but they are a minority. KBS could be enhanced through the exploitation of DBMS technology, which has absorbed many man years of development effort.

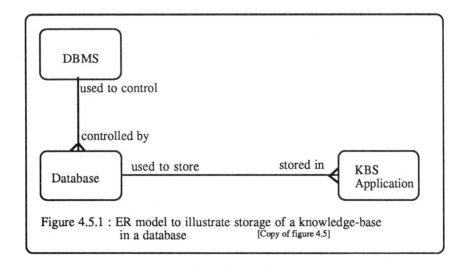

Figure 4.5.1 : ER model to illustrate storage of a knowledge-base
in a database   [Copy of figure 4.5]

A diagrammatic representation of using a KBS, as given in figure 3.1.1 in section 3.1, would need to be revised to include a DBMS as given in figure 4.5.2 below. The knowledge–base database would be controlled by a DBMS during creation and update by the knowledge engineer. It would be possible to compile the knowledge–base contents to produce run–time code, to be used by the inference engine; alternatively, the inference engine could access the knowledge–base–database via the DBMS. The former is likely to give better performance.

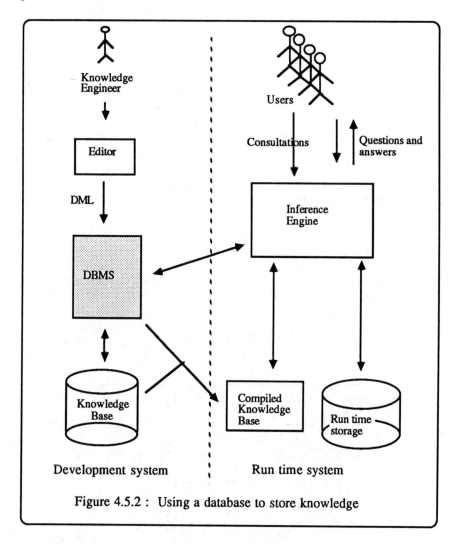

Figure 4.5.2 : Using a database to store knowledge

Natural Expert is thought to be the only KBS tool which currently acknowledges the use of a database (Adabas) for storing knowledge. Held suggests that 'eventually, expert system knowledge–bases will require database management system support' if multi–user, multi–functional, general purpose KBS applications are to be developed [HELD89].

4.5.2 Gains

The concept of storing a knowledge–base in a database is not intended as a mental exercise, but it is a serious suggestion for an improved open systems architecture. The following outlines what could be gained by adoption of this architecture.

Database management systems (DBMS) are used to *manage* data; that is, they provide *centralised control* of operational data, where operational data is one of the most valuable assets of an organisation. Another important asset of any business is the staff employed, upon whose expertise and experience the organisation depends. If some of the expertise and experience (knowledge) is to be captured and used within knowledge–based applications, then it is important that this should be managed just as effectively as any other corporate resource such as data.

Extending this line of reasoning, it is suggested that a DBMS could be enhanced to become a knowledge–based management system (KBMS) and thereby provide the following strategic features for an organisation:

- establishment of a corporate view of a number of physically separate, knowledge–bases;

- shareability of knowledge, in that tasks, rules and facts which are common to several applications can be re–used, rather than replicated, thereby increasing consistency and reducing redundancy of knowledge;

- integration of knowledge–bases from independently developed applications;

- enforcement of standards, which facilitates the interchange of knowledge through open systems. Standardisation might be at company, national (BSI) and international (ISO and ANSI) levels;

- management of *large*, corporate knowledge–bases. As the size of knowledge–bases increases so does the need for consistent, integrated facilities to manage the knowledge contained therein [SALV89(2)];

- the potential for integration of conventional applications with KBS.

In addition, a number of control features may be of interest to developers of KBS applications:

- automated consistency maintenance, such that integrity constraints could be specified and automatically enforced when a knowledge–base is created and updated;

- security restrictions can be implemented through the DBMS access control mechanisms. This may be of particular importance if sensitive or confidential rules and facts are held in a KBS application;

- recovery and back–up (logging, rollforward, etc) procedures are provided;

- the same knowledge–base could be accessed concurrently by a number of users, but locking facilities would ensure that only one person could update a part of the knowledge–base at any one time;

- the physical storage can be tuned to improve performance;

- distributed knowledge–bases could be created.

A knowledge–base management system would generally increase and improve the flexibility and versatility of the knowledge–bases within an organisation. A company developing a number of independent knowledge–based applications would be able to view them as a corporate resource.

The above gains are available at a cost: an existing DBMS could not be used effectively to store knowledge without some additional processing features, and the following would need to be developed:

- a generic schema to represent the end user's view of the knowledge–base, including rules, objects, classes, etc and to include the associated integrity constraints;

- an internal mechanism for translating this schema into data to be stored in a database;

- processing capabilities which can manipulate the high level components in the knowledge–base.

Before these three topics are discussed in more depth, the next section outlines how knowledge could be stored in an existing database, though this is not thought to be a satisfactory solution.

4.5.3 Storing knowledge as data

It is *not* suggested that knowledge (rules, facts, methods, etc) should be transformed into data, such that the processing mechanism is lost. The following example explains what is meant by this. A machine fault diagnosis system may contain a number of rules which process symptoms to deduce the possible cause of a problem. Some of these rules and combinations of symptoms could be reduced to a table of data, (see figure 4.5.3), assuming that this part of the system is sufficiently simple. The application would look up symptom values for given problems in the table, instead of using rules. This method of implementation might then be more effectively written using a 4GL or a decision table preprocessor, rather than a KBS tool, since the problem has been reduced to *data* processing.

There are a number of problems associated with this approach:

- a complex data model for each application would be required to support this method of storing knowledge;

- the interaction and cross–referencing of rules may be lost when rules are reduced to separate rows in tables;

- the explanation associated with rules, which the inference mechanism uses, will be lost.

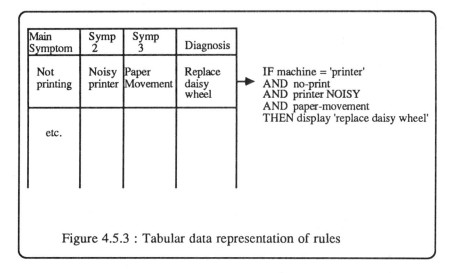

Main Symptom	Symp 2	Symp 3	Diagnosis
Not printing	Noisy printer	Paper Movement	Replace daisy wheel
etc.			

IF machine = 'printer'
AND no-print
AND printer NOISY
AND paper-movement
THEN display 'replace daisy wheel'

Figure 4.5.3 : Tabular data representation of rules

It would be a backward step to take this approach, and it is unlikely that it could be done for complex problems. The next section explains how knowledge could, and should, be stored in a database.

4.5.4 Storing knowledge as logical data structures

If knowledge is to be stored in a database, then at some point it must be reduced to data. However, users of the knowledge should be able to view it using logical structures (rules, frames, etc), in the same way that external views (subschemas) can be used to present data in a format which is different to its physical storage (internal view). The mapping between an internal storage representation (integers, strings, etc) and a user's logical view of knowledge is likely to be more complicated than it is for data, as shown in figure 3.2.1 in section 3.2. There are two fundamental, inter–related problems: what should be included in the external view and how can this be mapped on to data structures?

Jansen and Compton in Australia [JANS89], Held and Carlis in the United States of America [HELD89] and Salvini in the UK [SALV87 and SALV89(2)] are working on topics that will facilitate the storage of knowledge in a database. Jansen and Compton are working on The Knowledge Dictionary which 'utilises the relational data model to store the heuristics in a data form rather than in an executable code form'. Held and Carlis postulate that 'Eventually, expert system knowledge–bases will require database management system (DBMS) support' and they are working on data models to support knowledge systems.

The Knowledge Dictionary

A conceptual, entity–relationship model is presented in reference JANS89, which includes object types such as rule, fact, kb_task and kb_data_structure, and relationships between objects such as [kb_task] is a collection_of [rule]. Each object type is intended to be treated as a set of data or a table. It is suggested that 'a relationship could be pointer– or set–based, as in a Codasyl database, relational– or value–based, as in the relational model, or even function–based, where the membership of a relationship is dependent on the evaluation of some function returning a true or false condition, as appropriate'.

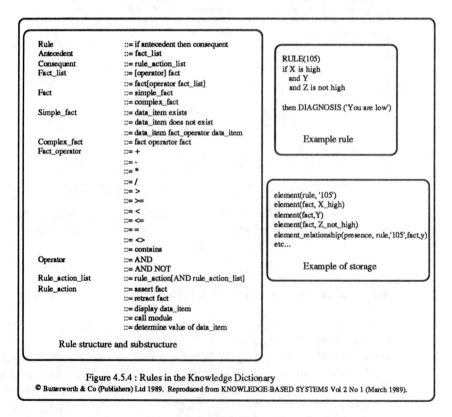

Figure 4.5.4 : Rules in the Knowledge Dictionary
© Butterworth & Co (Publishers) Ltd 1989. Reproduced from KNOWLEDGE-BASED SYSTEMS Vol 2 No 1 (March 1989).

Each task (object) is a collection of rules (object). A rule structure and an example of how an instance of a rule could be decomposed into this structure, for storage of a database, is given in figure 4.5.4 above. A rule tests for the presence or absence of a set of facts, and if the fact profile is matched then some rule actions are performed. This rule structure does not allow ORs to be specified between facts (only ANDs), which means that some rule instances would need to be decomposed. However, internal processing between the logical view and the data representation could break down and rebuild rules.

The model which has been developed as part of this work does not encapsulate all the formalisms and types of syntax used by the many KBS tools which are available. However, the model could be extended to produce such a model.

Conceptual modelling

Held and Carlis have produced a logical data structure for an existing KBS application based on Lisp. Some of the objects identified are:

- scratch–pad, which is a data structure containing all the objects relevant to the current problem solution;

- hypothesis, which is a guess about a classification;

- primitive element, which is a single word or number that forms part of the information of a contextual object.

The attributes and relationships for each of these (and other) objects are defined.

Salvini's ESKIR[†]

Salvini has devised a representation format called Expert System Knowledge Internal Representation (ESKIR). A number of formalisms including rules and frames can be translated into ESKIR. The following shows a rule and the internal ESKIR format:

```
rule6:
        if
                        diagnosis/group/abscess
        and
                        pocketing/depth/'>5mm'
        and
                                pain/character/'sudden onset'
                        or
                                tooth/'pulp test'/positive
        then
                        patient/diagnosis/'Acute Lateral Abscess'
        with
                        certainty(0.9).
```

[†] Reproduced by permission of S Salvini, Heriot–Watt University, Edinburgh, reference SALV89(2).

```
patient(dentest, esrule, [0.9], diagnosis('Acute Lateral Abscess')):–
       patient(group, abscess),
       pocketing(depth, '>5mm'),
              (pain(character, 'sudden onset');
               tooth('pulp test', positive)).
```

CCTA modelling work

The above three pieces of work are based on specific KBS applications. These are valuable contributions, but a great deal more work must be done in order to produce a generalised knowledge description or global view, which can be used for all application types, to be implemented using all KBS tools. Some work in this area is being carried out by CCTA, attacking the problem from a different angle to the above researchers.

CCTA has produced a number of conceptual entity–relationship–attribute models for some KBS tools, to represent the functionality and characteristics of the tools. A generic model is being produced, based upon these individual models, to represent the superset of functionality provided by KBS tools. This model will be validated against some other KBS tools which have not been modelled, to ensure that it includes as many features as possible.

Using this model, it should be possible to specify the totality of objects and relationships required to represent knowledge which can be stored using any of the existing KBS tools. And this model could provide the universal schema, for storing knowledge in a database.

Integrity constraints

Some integrity constraints will be defined as part of the entity–relationship–attribute model of the global schema. For example, relationships such as [task] is a collection_of [rule], would suggest that every rule must be associated with a task; boolean facts may only hold the values true and false; etc. However, more subtle integrity constraints may be specified, such as: there may be a limit to the number of ANDs and ORs specified in the conditional part of a rule; classes and objects cannot have recursive structures; names of all facts, rules, etc must be unique; and so on.

It is likely that there will be some integrity rules which hold true for the global schema, and others which are imposed by individual KBS tools. It is the former which are of most concern here, but the latter cannot be ignored.

4.5.5 External knowledge to internal data mapping

Assuming that it is possible to produce a universal global view of knowledge, and the above work suggests that it can be done, then the problem of mapping this into data remains.

Knowledge can be considered to consist of facts and the processing of those facts. It is unlikely that there will be a problem in mapping the fact descriptions on to data storage. The differences between facts and data are discussed in section 6.1 and the problems associated with storing facts in a database also apply here. Some fact types which are not generally stored in databases, such as booleans, will need to be transformed into DBMS data types. For example, a single digit integer could be defined as having two possible values, one and two, where a value of one represents true and two represents false.

The internal representation of the fact processing is likely to be more difficult. Abstract data types will be needed to support rules, demons, explanation, etc, which constitute the processing of facts. Abstract data types involve user–oriented constructs or representations. A graphic design package for example, will use abstract data types for storing shapes such as lines, circles and cubes. The system is likely to store an indicator for the object type, such as circle, and attributes such as diameter, colour, fill pattern, etc, for each circle occurrence. Basic data types such as numbers and strings can be used to hold this attribute information. When such an object is retrieved the graphic designer is not concerned with how the data was stored, but the system will present a circle of the correct dimensions, colour and so on.

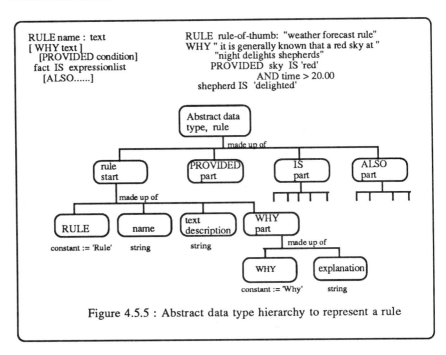

Figure 4.5.5 : Abstract data type hierarchy to represent a rule

The abstract data types in a KBMS would be those defined in the global view or schema. Each of these must have a definitive structure, such as that given in figure 4.5.4 for a rule, so that the most detailed constituent parts can be defined as data items. Figure 4.5.5 gives an illustration of how part of an abstract 'rule' data type may be defined based on the rule syntax of ICL–Adviser. The complex data type which represents the rule can be built up from a number of simple data types and constants.

From the above, it is possible to see how a rule can map on to a collection of ordered data items which make up a complex data type to be stored in a relational database. Complex data types are the equivalent of record types and their descriptions would be true for all knowledge–bases for a given KBS tool, or ideally for all tools. A complex data type in the internal view (storage schema) would define the physical storage of an abstract data type which has been defined in the global view. A processing mechanism will be required to translate internal view data to knowledge on retrieval of information; and to translate external view knowledge into data on storage. The integrity constraints must be observed by these processes to ensure that inconsistent data is never stored.

An external view or subschema is a view of part of the global schema. The presentation of components in the external view need not be the same as those in the global schema; for example, in conventional systems it is common to create views of record types, which omit data items not required by an application. External views could therefore be used to define the constructs used by individual tools, since any one tool will include a subset of the global view. The processing mechanism to map external views to the internal view, and vice versa, will be similar to that which translates the global view into data.

Salvini [SALV87] has defined an expert systems interface (ESIF) which stores and retrieves knowledge stored in ESKIR format (see section 4.5.4 above). It maps any given external knowledge representation formalism into ESKIR. It also generates query language statements to carry out demands such as 'retrieve all rules about tax'.

4.5.6 Processing considerations

The last paragraph of 4.5.2 mentioned that it would be necessary to develop processes for the developer which can handle the abstract types defined in the global schema. Developers will want to manipulate rules, objects, facts, etc just as they can with existing tools, rather than the complex internal representations. This means that:

- KBMS specific editors must be used so that internal processing mechanisms maintain an integral database (knowledge–base);

- the editor must manipulate the global view (when using CASE tools) or external view (when using KBS specific tools) constructs and not the internal representations;

- diagrammatic facilities which KBS tools currently include must interface with the appropriate external view of the knowledge–base.

If the knowledge–base is always maintained in a consistent state, then it is possible to have incremental compilation of an application, which can be an advantage when testing and debugging applications. Also, it is almost certain that a developed application will run first time due to the high degree of integrity maintained in the database–held source, even if it does not produce the expected results.

Knowledge sharing

If knowledge is stored in a KBMS then it can be shared, during development and at run–time. For example, a set of rules which validates some user input might be used by more than one KBS application. Without a DBMS to control sharing of information, it may be necessary to code the rules using a KBS shell, then re–code using Prolog, for example if more than one KBS tool is being used. In theory, using external views for the shell and Prolog, the two systems can utilise the same underlying knowledge held in a database.

Salvini [SALV89] has identified some problems with this concept, in that it is not possible to guarantee to be able to translate from one format to another, particularly when handling uncertainty. He classifies knowledge, for knowledge sharing, as:

- private knowledge, to be used by the originating application only;

- shared knowledge, which can be used by two or more named KBS;

- common knowledge, which can be used by any KBS.

It would therefore only be necessary to be able to convert common knowledge to all formalisms and shared knowledge into one or two formalisms.

The classification system is similar to the concept of scoping of facts and blackboard systems (see section 5.8), but access to the source code is being restricted rather than run–time information.   The classification system would need to be included in the knowledge–base and administered by the authorisation and external view facilities of the DBMS/KBMS.

4.5.7 Current situation

KBS tools

Each and every KBS tool provides some of the features outlined in 4.5.2. The toolkits and mainframe tools tend to provide most of these features, though they have been implemented in a variety of ways. For example, KEE and Inference ART use object orientation, providing reusable, shared methods. ADS is well integrated with conventional systems, using the security features and concurrent access controls of TP monitors which run in the same environment.

Current thinking suggests that choice of a tool for building a KBS application is dependent upon the features of that application, therefore it is likely that an organisation will use more than one KBS tool. It would be difficult to integrate KBS applications which have been developed using more than one tool, particularly if some applications are integrated with conventional systems. Maintenance of these systems will be even more difficult and the idea of managing them as a corporate resource will be a problem.

Move towards KBMS

As already indicated above, some tools are showing signs of moving towards a KBMS architecture. The specification for Natural Expert suggests that knowledge will be stored in a database. 'After compilation, rules are stored in the knowledge–base, which is contained in an entity relationship object base (Adabas Entire) designed to manage large, structured data objects with multiple attributes. Rule interconnections are automatically maintained and can be queried dynamically during the creation and maintenance of the expert system model as well as during execution.' [SOFT89]

Documentation for the product Prospect (which consists of Flex and Aspect) suggests that knowledge might be held in a database: 'The Aspect database–engine can be accessed directly by the Flex expert system which gives you the ability to maintain frames, programs etc, within the overall database. Conventional database management techniques, for example reports, can then be run against expert system data and programs'.

DBMS–KBMS

Database management systems have the potential to provide all of the requirements specified in 4.5.2. There are many tried and tested products available, which represent a large development investment. There is no doubt that it would be possible to develop new KBMS architectures, which at the end of the day might be better than any of the DBMS products on the market. It would, however, seem to be more efficient to take the best features from existing DBMS products, particularly relational DBMS, and build upon them.

Separation of the knowledge–base (*what* can be done) and the inference engine (which determines *how* to achieve results) is depicted in the theoretical model of a KBS tool, see figure 3.1.2 in section 3.1. However, the architecture of some KBS tools is not so clearly defined as some of the components are tightly integrated. The approach suggested here, that the knowledge–base is stored as a database, would build upon this separation of concerns. A parallel to this is illustrated by current trends in DBMS, to separate the data storage and data processing as a client/server architecture, as a move towards open systems.

Additionally, other data management software provided with a DBMS could potentially be used in the development of KBS applications. For example, a data dictionary could be used to design and document the system (see section 5.1); and query languages, such as SQL, could be used to make enquiries on the knowledge–base.

4.5.8 Summary

A DBMS could be enhanced to produce a KBMS and satisfy a number of corporate business requirements. In addition, a move towards an open systems architecture would be facilitated as shown in figure 4.5.6.

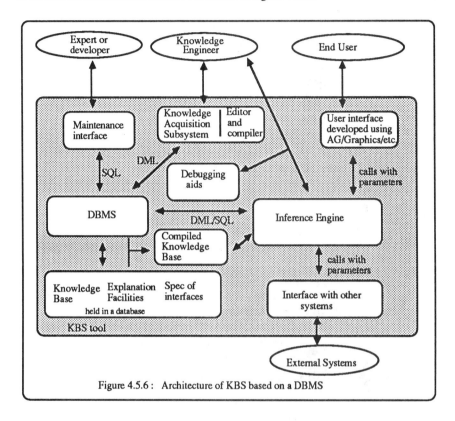

Figure 4.5.6 : Architecture of KBS based on a DBMS

In summary, the components would be as follows:

- the knowledge acquisition subsystem would be a combined editor and incremental compiler. A number of tool specific editors could be used, each having a different external view of the same database–knowledge–base; alternatively, a general KBS editor might be used in conjunction with the universal global view;

- the maintenance interface could be a new component, providing a higher level interface to the knowledge–base than the above component, which is likely to be tool–specific. This could be a KBS application in itself which can generate SQL queries from information provided through a natural language interface;

- there would be a separate user interface component for each application in the knowledge–base, possibly developed using an application generator or implemented using a graphics package;

- the DBMS would be a proprietary product;

- debugging aids would be similar to existing ones, though an incremental compiler might facilitate changes to the knowledge–base during testing;

- compilation of the knowledge–base is optional, but could provide a high performance run–time system, since access to the knowledge–base could prove to be a bottleneck and an unnecessary overhead. An incremental compiler would be closely linked with the DBMS and editor, so that components of the knowledge–base can be compiled immediately after amendment;

- the inference engine would be almost the same, except that it would lose control of formatting of user interface screens and would possibly communicate with the interface software through a standard parameter driven interface;

- there would be a single database (KBMS) to hold all the knowledge–bases, explanation for any number of applications and user interface definitions;

- the interface to existing systems might call or be called from the inference engine. The interface would have the same format as that for the user interface, as a move towards open systems standardisation.

All of these components would be identifiable as physically separate parts of what would become a KBS environment. The KBS tool and the applications would be tightly integrated with the exception of the interfaces.

5

Integration of development tools

Purpose

This chapter looks at the use of conventional tools alongside knowledge–based
system (KBS) tools in the development of KBS applications which are linked to
conventional data processing applications; see figure 5.1.

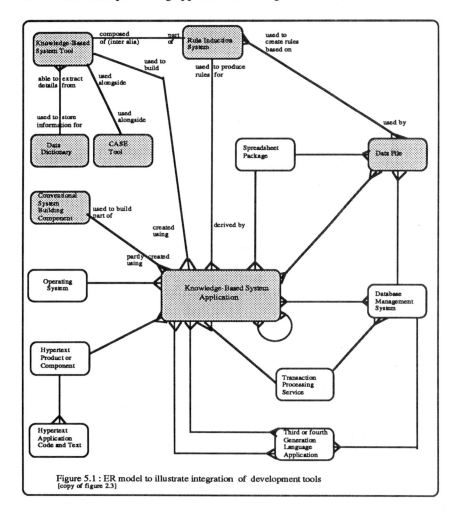

Figure 5.1 : ER model to illustrate integration of development tools
[copy of figure 2.3]

Ideally, system implementors should have at their disposal a set of integrated tools in a single environment, so that appropriate components can be used to develop applications (assuming that the implementor knows how and under what circumstances to use them). One of the prime advantages of application generators (or fourth generation environments) compared with third generation languages is that an integrated set of tools is provided for system development. Inclusion of KBS development tools within the environment is desirable. Existing Computer Assisted Software Engineering (CASE) tools generally cater for conventional system development only, though there are already moves to include KBS as illustrated by IBM's AD/Cycle (see section 5.1).

The implementor of a conventional system will usually have the following tools available, in addition to a database management system (DBMS):

- an application generator (AG), which might be a set of tools in a single environment or a fourth generation language (4GL), which may be used to develop large parts of the system;

- a third generation language (3GL), such as Cobol, to be used when the application generator is not suitable;

- a data dictionary to hold system documentation, which can be selectively extracted for inclusion in 3GL, 4GL or AG applications;

- editors and compilers for creating source code and building third and fourth generation language applications;

- debugging and testing tools;

- housekeeping facilities for tidying filestore.

It is envisaged that KBS tools will be accepted as components in this development environment, as another type of implementation vehicle alongside third and fourth generation languages, and be integrated with these existing tools. This chapter investigates three aspects of an integrated development environment, as shown in figure 5.1.

Section 5.1

Section 5.1 considers the use of data dictionaries for storing information during KBS application development and the use of CASE tools; see figure 5.2. It may be possible to use existing CASE tools in the short term, though new CASE tools which include KBS facilities are likely to provide better support for development in the future.

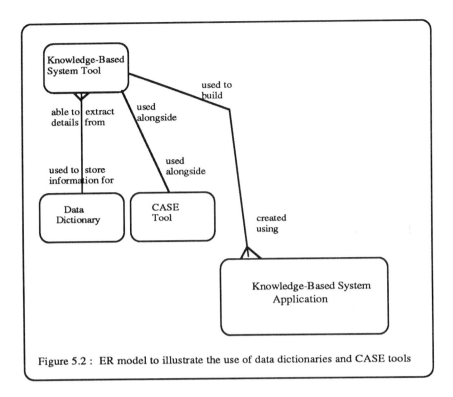

Figure 5.2 : ER model to illustrate the use of data dictionaries and CASE tools

Section 5.2

Section 5.2 describes how some conventional system building components, such as screen painters in fourth generation environments or general text editors, can be used to build part of a KBS application. The ability to export a knowledge–base as third generation language code is also included. See figure 5.3.

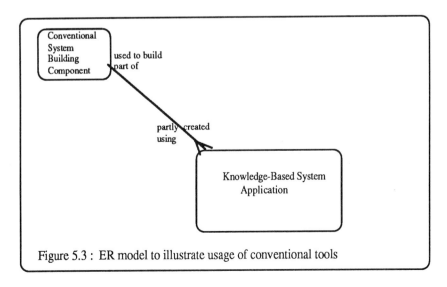

Figure 5.3 : ER model to illustrate usage of conventional tools

Section 5.3

The use of inductive components of KBS tools is covered in section 5.3, see figure 5.4. The possibility of using inductive systems in an unconventional fashion to produce management information, as well as using them as intended for deriving a 'first–cut' of a KBS application, is described.

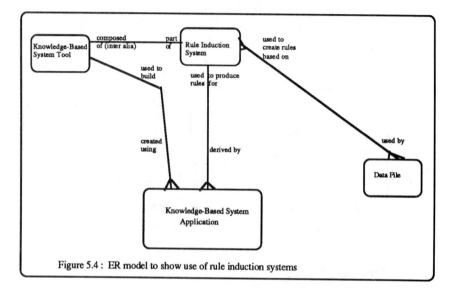

Figure 5.4 : ER model to show use of rule induction systems

5.1

Using data dictionaries and CASE

5.1.1 Introduction

This section discusses the use of data dictionaries and Computer Assisted Software Engineering (CASE) tools in an integrated environment for both conventional system and knowledge–based system (KBS) development; see figure 5.1.1. If integrated systems are required, then the integration philosophy should be visible in the design and development of those systems.

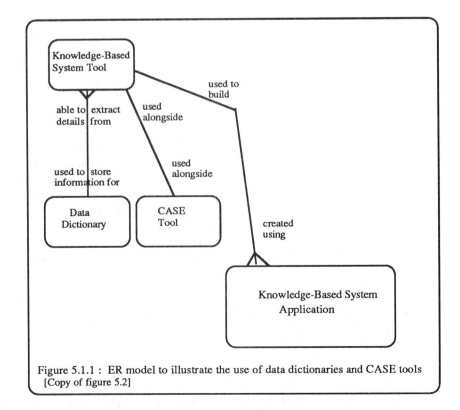

Figure 5.1.1 : ER model to illustrate the use of data dictionaries and CASE tools [Copy of figure 5.2]

The rest of this section covers three main areas: using a data dictionary as a repository; using existing CASE tools; and new CASE tools which incorporate KBS development.

5.1.2 Data dictionary usage

A data dictionary is a repository for information about data and processing. 'Data' dictionary is a misnomer and is perhaps a hangover from when dictionaries were used to simply store data definitions; most dictionaries actually store information too, such as how data is manipulated, and how real world concepts relate to technical concepts. A proposal for a new standard in this area has, quite correctly, called them 'Information Resource Dictionary Systems'.

Data dictionaries store analysis and design information; such things as data specifications, screen layouts, dialogue outlines and transaction processing (TP) service descriptions may be held. This information can be used, to a limited extent at present, for automatic system generation; that is, generation of compilable code from a design specification. More commonly, a dictionary is used as a central source of information, items of which can be copied into applications under development. For example, a database external view or subschema may be held in a data dictionary and copied into a number of applications which use this common data set.

The concept of a data dictionary is only starting to permeate into KBS development. This may be due to the parentage of KBS in Artificial Intelligence, which is separate and distinct from conventional data processing. The Butler Cox Foundation Report 60 [BUTL87][†] suggests that 'in the future knowledge encyclopaedia products are likely to contain a knowledge–base schema where the process model describes the problem solving process'. Some research has been done in this area and is described in 5.1.5 below.

Examples of the few KBS products which have been identified as mentioning data dictionaries are Natural Expert using Predict; Prospect using a dictionary associated with an Aspect database; and Today using the dictionary associated with the 4GL Today. These KBS tools are relatively new and have been released by vendors which have a data management background. Some emerging KBS tools store application details in databases (a data dictionary is a database at heart) which offer some of the facilities of data dictionaries; this was covered in section 4.5. However, such architectures do not facilitate integration with existing systems, which are documented, at least in part, in a conventional data dictionary system.

It is perceived that some benefits gained from using a data dictionary in conventional system development could be translated into similar advantages for KBS development.

[†] Reproduced by kind permission of Butler Cox plc. Originally published in Butler Cox Foundation Report 60, Expert Systems in Business.

5.1.3 Benefits of using an information repository

Integration with conventional development

The theme of integration is re–iterated throughout this book: a central, shared repository of information will facilitate integration of systems which have data and/or processing in common. The description of a corporate database will usually be held in a data dictionary. It is desirable that all processes which use the database, including KBS applications, should derive the description of appropriate data from this central source.

When using the Structured Systems Analysis and Design Method (SSADM) for conventional system analysis and design (or any other method for that matter), the documentation for the system can be stored in some data dictionaries. For example ICL's data dictionary, DDS, includes element types which directly support SSADM; also Oracle's dictionary, SDD, supports a number of techniques used in a variety of methods. Most fourth generation languages have interfaces to SSADM. All this allows the easy transition from requirements analysis to code production.

An equivalent method to SSADM for KBS does not exist, but the General Expert Systems Methodology Initiative (GEMINI) project is working to produce one. GEMINI is a joint government and industry venture which will deliver a standard method for analysing and designing KBS over the next two years. Furthermore, this method will interface with conventional analysis and design methods, in particular SSADM. Therefore, it will be desirable to store the documentation produced by both KBS and conventional methods in the same repository, particularly for 'mixed' systems designed using a combination of types of method.

When GEMINI becomes available, potential users will expect tool support which is at least as good as that provided for conventional system development. Vendors of KBS tools who can provide an integral data dictionary may well have an edge on the market at this time and the basis for a CASE tool.

Version control and a single, definitive repository

Anyone who has worked on old, conventional systems will be aware of the problems of version control; it was not unusual to find that several copies of program sources were available (held on the machine and listed on paper) and no–one would know which was the most recent version or the source of the live running object code. When a data dictionary is used to store the results of analysis, design and code, everyone should be assured that it contains the definitive version of information. Paper copies and working documents which do not agree with the data dictionary copy should be assumed to be wrong or not yet implemented.

More than one version of information can be held by some data dictionaries. A new version can be created, such that only the new version can be amended, old version being read only. In this way, configuration management control can be exerted over documentation. It may also be possible to time stamp changes to individual elements in the dictionary and journalise changes (in the same way that database updates can be logged).

A single, shared copy of information also avoids duplication. This not only reduces the risk of using the wrong version but saves resources: fewer hard copies for documentation purposes should be required. And the only person who should take copies of the contents of the dictionary should be the data administrator, for security purposes.

Standards

Organisation–wide standards can be enforced through the use of a data dictionary. The format of documentation can be enforced by the rejection of non–standard information; for example the use of some properties may be disallowed and naming conventions be endorsed. The sequential procedures for analysis and design can be controlled to some extent, by ensuring that certain information has been provided before access to some elements is allowed; for example, logical design elements should be completed and placed under version control before physical elements are entered.

Access control

Data dictionaries generally provide access control features to prevent unauthorised access to system documentation. Passwords are commonly used and read or write access can be given at varying, appropriate levels from a single instance, through all instances of a type or named instances, to all contents. It is the data administrators job to ensure that these controls are used, so that individuals only have access to the information which they need.

The access control requirements for KBS applications should be the same as those for other systems. In fact, they may need to be more stringent, since 'expertise' which is possibly unique to the business and of great interest to competitors, will be documented. For example, the heuristics used to determine credit worthiness or the way in which the cost of insurance policies is derived would be of interest to many people. Some of the more powerful and sophisticated KBS tools have access control features, but why reinvent the wheel?

Maintenance and impact analysis

During the lifetime of a system, KBS or conventional, changes will have to be implemented. Some will be mercifully small and impact only on small, identifiable parts of a system. Others are likely to be more widespread, and the impact on the system as a whole may not be immediately apparent. For example, in a conventional system increasing the length of a field (attribute type) will affect all records (entity types) of which it is part and all programs which process those records. If such a system is documented in a data dictionary then enquiries can ascertain the impact of this change. If a KBS uses the changed field, but the KBS is not documented in the data dictionary, then only manual checks (which are error prone) can assess the impact.

Maintenance of existing systems requires a large resource, variously quoted as requiring between 50% and 70% of an IT department's time. Although maintenance of KBS does not loom so large at present, developers of KBS would be wise to use tools which facilitate this time consuming task. There are some KBS applications in live use and being maintained which are renowned as being huge. For example XCON, the DEC configurer, is claimed to contain hundreds, if not thousands, of rules and is maintained by several full–time staff. It is suggested that the system is being rewritten because of the large maintenance task. The maintenance of such applications is likely to be easier if they are documented in data dictionaries or similar repositories, so that the impact of changes can be assessed.

Standard notation

The development of KBS applications commonly involves:

*   writing down the expertise (rules and inferencing) in a notation which both the expert and the application builder understand;

*   translating this into a notation which a KBS tool can handle.

The former is application oriented; the latter is tool oriented; and the number of combinations of these two types of notation is enormous. The idea of having an independent notation, which fits between the two has been suggested and such a notation could be supported by a data dictionary.

5.1.4 Architecture

Most data dictionary systems, as they currently stand, cannot be used to support the development of KBS applications. Some data dictionaries have extensibility facilities that allow the user to define the type of information which he wants to hold in the dictionary, the validation checks to be associated with it and so on. It would be possible to use these facilities to incorporate new 'knowledge types' as discussed in section 4.5. Extraction programs could also be written to create application source. This idea is exploited in The Knowledge Dictionary described in 5.1.5 below.

The architecture of an integrated development system might look like that shown in figure 5.1.2. The data dictionary would hold all physical system design details. A database global view (schema) could be extracted to directly create a database as one operation; it is not uncommon with existing dictionary and database software to extract the schema definition into a file, then run a separate utility to create the database directory. KBS and application generator (AG) applications could be created directly from the dictionary.

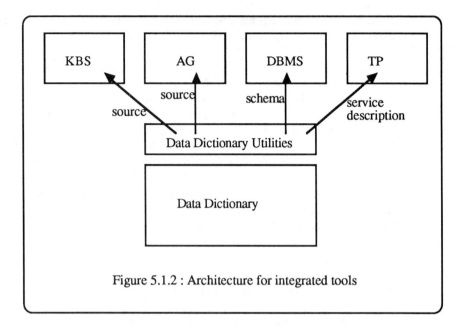

Figure 5.1.2 : Architecture for integrated tools

The following information for KBS could be held in a data dictionary:

- a model of the user's view of an application or system. This would encompass details of menus, questions, help text and mechanisms for retrieval, explanation, scope of the domain and tasks. Such information could be used to prototype the user interface;

- a model of the expert's knowledge or problem solving capability. This would include details such as facts, data, rules of thumb, inferences, limitations and so on. A graphical representation of this information would be needed so that the dictionary could be used to represent and reflect back knowledge gained during knowledge elicitation sessions with the expert;

- a specification of interfaces with conventional systems, which includes access to data;

- validation, where rules refer to data entities, attributes and relationships.

Other uses may well be identified if KBS tool vendors continue to pursue the possibilities of integration with conventional data processing.

5.1.5 Products and research

Predict and Natural Expert

Software AG has developed a fourth generation open integrated software architecture, part of which is shown in figure 5.1.3. The data dictionary, Predict, is tightly coupled with the DBMS Adabas, the fourth generation language Natural, and the KBS tool Natural Expert.

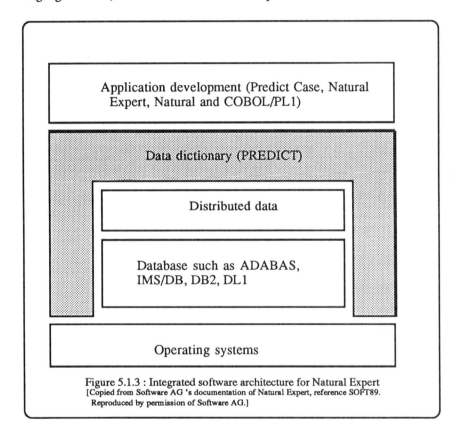

Figure 5.1.3 : Integrated software architecture for Natural Expert
[Copied from Software AG 's documentation of Natural Expert, reference SOFT89.
Reproduced by permission of Software AG.]

In Natural Expert domain knowledge is stored in an entity–relationship database called Entire. Not only does it hold the model definition, but also verifies model consistency whilst maintaining inter–rule relationships. Data from a wide range of database types can be accessed and updated in a way that guarantees transaction integrity and allows conventional applications to be integrated directly with KBS models. See figure 5.1.4.

Predict Case is Software AG's full life cycle support Case tool. It utilises Entire to maintain the complex structures and relationships required for conventional applications and KBS design and development. Integrated with all these tools is Predict, a data dictionary implementation which maintains definitions of data and modules used in applications. Meta–model information is held in Predict, which is based on the relational DBMS Adabas, and is referred to and updated by all the application development tools, including Natural.

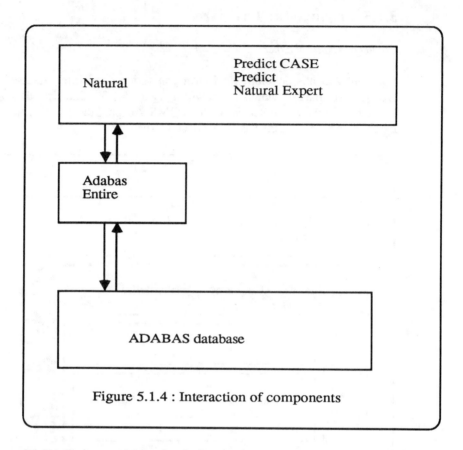

Figure 5.1.4 : Interaction of components

Adabas Entire provides a level of control over the Predict dictionary in that it takes care of version management including referential integrity across versions and it controls access.

The Knowledge Dictionary

The Knowledge Dictionary [JANS89] is a tool which is intended to facilitate the documentation and maintenance of KBS. It is based on the relational data model and stores heuristics as data rather than in an executable form. A prototype has been built using Prolog on a Macintosh machine.

It is suggested that the maintenance problem for integrated KBS and conventional database systems is complex because of the inter–relationships between data and knowledge. Tools will be necessary to aid in the control and understanding of such complex systems, for acquiring knowledge, performing efficient system design and performing maintenance and documentation tasks, in such a way that there are no inconsistencies, corruptions and logic errors.

The knowledge dictionary augments the functionality of data dictionaries for conventional systems by allowing:

- documentation of the knowledge–base;

- validation of the total system;

- browsing of the knowledge;

- processing of the rules using an inference engine;

- generation of a run–time knowledge–base in a variety of formalisms, including Prolog, frames and rules.

The Knowledge Dictionary is based on an entity–relationship model of object types and allowed relationships, but the model can be modified by the user to include new objects and relationships. A number of the objects and relationships are standard for conventional dictionaries, such as file, consists–of, record, system, collection–of, module, etc; rule, fact, task condition and others have been added. The knowledge–base details can be divided into a number of worlds or subsets, as is the case with conventional databases.

The conceptual model allows the knowledge to be treated as data so that standard data manipulation operations can be used to browse the knowledge. A number of functions have been made available to manipulate the data:

- occurrences of object types can be added and displayed;

- the usage function determines who uses what and how;

- add–rule and link–rule enable new rules to be input and use existing information in the dictionary;

- a forward chaining inferencing procedure allows rules to be executed and information to be output about rule usage.

Future enhancements are planned, including:

- knowledge–base checking, such as duplicate entries, pointers to non–existent entries, logic checking, etc;

- generation of run–time knowledge–bases;

- addition of other formalisms such as frames.

5.1.6 Use of existing CASE tools

Computer Assisted Software Engineering (CASE) tools are provided to facilitate the development of conventional systems. The functionality of these tools varies, depending upon the method and techniques which are supported and the extent to which the development life cycle is addressed. Some components of these tools may be used to support development of KBS, though complete support will be compromised since the tools are not provided for this purpose.

CASE tools may be used to develop KBS components as follows:

- some techniques such as data flow diagramming and entity modelling may be used to analyse and design KBS, particularly if KBS components are to be integrated with a conventional system. CASE tools which include diagramming, consistency checking and storage of such models can be used directly;

- a general diagramming tool may be used for KBS specific techniques, such as drawing of knowledge maps, semantic networks, inferencing hierarchies, etc. It may not be possible to validate the content of the diagrams, but it will be easier to maintain diagrams than if they were paper based;

- the underlying repository (dictionary) might be extensible so that new data types can be defined to store information;

- the user interface and some dialogue outlines can be documented in the same way as those of conventional systems.

Existing CASE tools, without modification, will not provide total support for KBS development. It is likely that new tools will emerge, perhaps linked to KBS tools, in the same way that Oracle CASE tools are marketed alongside the Oracle DBMS and application generator. The requirements of KBS CASE tools are likely to emerge from method development projects such as GEMINI.

5.1.7 AD/Cycle

AD/Cycle, as shown in figure 5.1.5, is a framework for the support of application development, including KBS, throughout the lifecycle. AD/Cycle comprises:

- a family of integrated tools that share development information;

- a platform that provides common services to these tools, such as a consistent interface for users of these tools and a common repository for development information.

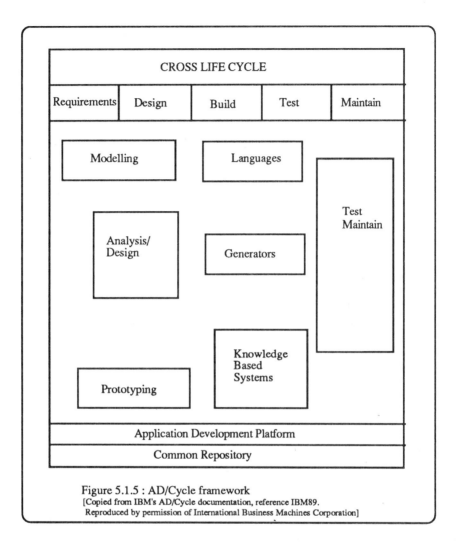

Figure 5.1.5 : AD/Cycle framework
[Copied from IBM's AD/Cycle documentation, reference IBM89.
Reproduced by permission of International Business Machines Corporation]

Knowledge–based systems are to be incorporated into the AD/Cycle framework to use the common services, including the repository. The analysis and design, and test and maintenance components, should also be usable with KBS components built using this framework.

AD/Cycle is intended to be an open framework so that new tools can be accommodated. The repository will be extensible so that new objects and methods can be included to support these tools. Some tools to be incorporated in AD/Cycle have been announced, such as DB2, SQL/DS, IMS, CICS, Excelerator, Cobol and Fortran. There have been no announcements so far about the KBS tools, but there is a wide choice on IBM platforms, not least ESE, Knowledgetool and KEE which are available from IBM.

5.2

Using conventional system building components

5.2.1 Introduction

An integrated development environment, such as the AD/Cycle framework described in section 5.1, would allow a number of development tools to be mixed and matched, so that the most appropriate tool could be used for building each function or process within a knowledge–based system (KBS), conventional system or a combination of the two types; see figure 5.2.1.

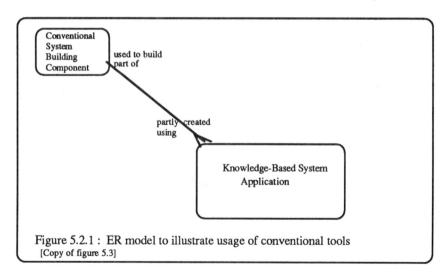

Figure 5.2.1 : ER model to illustrate usage of conventional tools
[Copy of figure 5.3]

Assuming that such an environment existed, it would be possible to use a whole range of tools alongside KBS tools, such as:

• fourth generation languages and application generators;

• report writers;

- graphic display tools and hypermedia;

- office automation facilities such as word processors and electronic mail;

- third generation languages;

- administration facilities.

This section looks at the potential for using such components; describes current product developments which use these ideas; and discusses the advantages and disadvantages of taking this approach.

5.2.2 Application generators

Screen and dialogue design

Most application generators include a screen painter, which allows the developer to design screen layouts and windows, and a dialogue specification mechanism so that screens can be linked together. For example, Ingres version 5 has Ingres/FORMS for screen design and Operation Specific Language (OSL) for coding logic to link the screens; version 6 of Ingres will allow windows to be defined and control logic to be directly associated with screens and windows; and Oracle SQL*FORMS is used for screen development and associated 'triggers' can cause other screens (forms) to be displayed.

Some uses of these components in building KBS are apparent:

- questions (inviting the user to input a value) and associated help and explanations (why the question is being asked and possible values which can be given) could be painted as a combination of screens and windows;

- menus could similarly be designed;

- screens of help text could be prepared and associated with a number of relevant screens or key words;

- a display mechanism for explanation about how a conclusion has been reached could be specified, providing that recursive elements are allowed to give increasing levels of detail.

Dialogue design for KBS applications may not be so detailed as that for conventional systems, because the logic which connects the screens need not be defined explicitly. In general and by default, KBS only attempt to obtain values for relevant facts; and screen layouts, windows or questions for deriving values from the end user can be associated with the facts. However, if the inference engine is allowed to determine the order in which all of the facts are instantiated, the dialogue (order of screen displays) could be confusing to the end user. Also, the number of combinations in which relevant screens could be displayed might be extremely large and difficult to test. Therefore, a combination of imposed ordering of screens and default display is likely to be used.

Consider a KBS application which emulates completion of a tax return form by an individual. The first screen is likely to be straightforward, requesting name, address, date of birth, marital status and so on. The sequence of the first two or three screens (which are likely to obtain values for commonly used facts) might be explicitly coded. But subsequent screens may be dependent upon fact values; for example if 'sex' is male and 'marital status' is single, then the system will not ask for details about his wife. Equally, if he declares that he has no investments the system will not ask for further details of the many possible types of investment, such as shares, building society accounts, etc. Hence the dialogue will be tailored to the individual and be dependent upon information supplied.

It is not suggested that existing KBS tool facilities for screen and dialogue design are in any way inadequate – in fact, in many cases they are superior to those of application generators; it is, however, suggested that the same tool can be used to create seamless dialogues for mixed conventional and KBS. Perhaps it might be more desirable to use KBS tools for screen and dialogue design in conventional applications.

Fourth generation languages

Fourth generation languages can be used to develop some procedural aspects of applications or evaluate complex expressions, instead of using a third generation language such as Cobol. They can be used to access and process data, before passing only the relevant data items, some of which may have been calculated, to a KBS application.

Products

It is likely that vendors of both application generators *and* KBS tools (rather than KBS *or* application generators) will lead in the development of integrated development tools. Information Builders, who market Level5 Object and Focus, plan to enable 'knowledge components' to be embedded within Focus applications. That is, the syntax of Focus would be extended. Software AG markets Natural (fourth generation language), Adabas (database) and Natural Expert (KBS tool); Natural and Natural Expert applications can be seamlessly integrated. Computer Power markets Today which is a fourth generation language and KBS combined. KBS can be built using Today development capabilities to create logic blocks, screens, reports, calculations and file handling.

5.2.3 Report writers

Report writing packages provide rich facilities for succinctly defining complex reports. Headers, footers, page layout, page break conditions, totalling lines, etc, can be defined more easily than in most other software packages, including

KBS. Many successful KBS applications have been built without the need for printing, but it is expected that there will be a requirement for report writers in large, integrated systems. It is desirable that existing software should be incorporated into KBS, rather than new facilities be developed which are specific to a KBS tool, and that a mechanism for passing bulk data to the report package be designed.

5.2.4 Graphic displays

Some machine environments provide graphics facilities, particularly those which use bit–mapped and high resolution screens. Not only can line graphs, scatter diagrams, bar and pie charts be produced but icons and images can be displayed. Drawing packages, such as MacDraw on Macintosh machines can be used to create complex diagrams and pictures. Those KBS tools which do not incorporate graphics facilities could provide better user interfaces through the use of graphic displays. Since many KBS applications are dependent on dialogues with the user, diagrams could provide an additional means of communication to text. They could be used to:

- present information in a summarised form;

- make the screens look more attractive;

- provide continuity in a dialogue. For example, an icon might be used to indicate how near is the end of the consultation, or images could be displayed while complex processing is taking place;

- request input in an imprecise form, such as asking for a response on a sliding scale (marking a point on a line or bar).

Sophisticated displays, such as dials which can be updated in real–time (active images) are available in some KBS tools, particularly the more sophisticated toolkits. These are particularly useful when building real–time systems, in that pressure gauges, thermometers, dials, clocks, etc, can be displayed with an indication of current readings. Integration of graphic display packages and KBS which do not have active images could make similar displays possible.

The use of KBS tools and hypertext at run–time is discussed in section 6.5. Hypermedia, including images and sound in addition to textual display, could be used to make KBS applications more attractive and interesting, particularly for the casual user of a system.

5.2.5 Office automation

Word processing

Sometimes word processing packages are used as general editors on source code; for example, WordStar can be used to create and amend SD–Prolog code.

However, word processors could be used, in conjunction with KBS tools as part of the application. For example, a Retirement Pension Forecasting and Analysis (RPFA) system has been developed by the Department of Social Security using ADS, the output being a letter to the customer giving details of their entitlement. A combination of standard paragraphs is used to produce a personalised, customised letter, and it has been claimed that no two letters are ever the same. ADS includes facilities for producing printed output, but such facilities are not so advanced in some other KBS tools.

There is also likely to be a reverse requirement; that is, to incorporate simple KBS applications in existing word processing packages. Grammatik IV, a grammar analyst and style checker which runs on personal computers, uses rules, backtracking and heuristics to analyse sentences in word processing documents.

Electronic mail

It does not require too much imagination to think of KBS applications which could produce a letter or memo, to be mailed electronically to a recipient in the organisation instead of printed output being produced. It is likely that in the future KBS tools or applications will be incorporated into office systems.

5.2.6 Third generation languages

A number of KBS tools, particularly those with rule induction facilities, are capable of exporting the contents of a knowledge–base as the source of a third generation language application. For example, XpertRule can export Pascal, Cobol, Basic, C and Fortran code. This may be particularly useful if:

- the performance of an application is critical and the code must be optimised;

- the KBS tool does not run on hardware on which the application must be delivered;

- the only resources available for maintenance of the application are those which support conventional applications;

- a KBS tool is used for prototyping conventional applications.

This may also be a solution to integration problems, since the exported code will be that used for conventional system development.

5.2.7 Administration

Administrative functions such as access control for security purposes, customisation to in–house standards, version control and housekeeping of files are generally provided as part of many software systems. Although such features are provided in some KBS tools, a unified mechanism might be preferred in an integrated development environment.

5.2.8 Advantages

This chapter is promoting the integration of software with the prime purpose of pointing out the advantages of an open approach to system development. One of the biggest gains from an integrated development environment for fourth generation languages is productivity; claims vary for the reduction in development effort from half to one tenth. The following advantages could be attributed to an integrated development environment for KBS application builders:

- reduction in the training overhead, if existing skills can be utilised;

- provision of a common tool set for all development, so that standards can be laid down, at organisation, national and international levels;

- construction of a seamless user interface for mixed conventional and KBS applications;

- the man years of effort put into AG tool development by vendors is capitalised upon, and as a consequence robust tools are available;

- building upon the philosophy of 'horses for courses'. That is, use KBS tools to build KBS applications, application generators for conventional processing, report packages for reporting, etc;

- realisation of the productivity gains from using development tools appropriately.

5.2.9 Disadvantages

It is perceived that the number of advantages far outweigh the disadvantages of having an integrated development environment, particularly when building open, integrated systems. Difficulties arise through the misuse of technology, that is, development tools are used for unsuitable components of applications. If, or rather when, it becomes possible to use a variety of tools for development of a system, the problem will change to that of *deciding* which tool is most appropriate for a particular task.

The mix and match of KBS and DBMS might be limited to fewer combinations, if application generators were included. However the move towards separating application generators and DBMS (as is happening with Ingres for example, such that the Ingres AG could be used to access an Oracle database in addition to an Ingres database) would overcome this problem. The greater the number of possible permutations of KBS tools, application generators and DBMS, the lower the potential for lock–in to a particular product supplier.

5.3

Generating rules from a database

5.3.1 Introduction

Most, if not all, central government departments have one or more databases, which may consist of separate files managed clerically or an integrated set of files managed by a database management system (DBMS). Whatever the make–up of the database, it is considered to be one of the major data processing assets which represents an investment for the department. Some marketing literature from Dataflex Services stated that:

> 'The two most valuable items in any business or organisation are intangible – the skills and expertise of its management and staff and the information contained within the organisational databases.' [†]

Although the data is stored to support current processing needs, there may be information 'hidden' in the data which would be useful to existing users or to management. Hidden information may be based on values derived from the data which is held, such as trends or classifications. This information may be revealed through the use of rule induction systems (see figure 5.3.1) and its potential then be explored. Such information need not necessarily be used to build a knowledge–based system (KBS) application, but may be viewed as analytical data. This information should be used with caution and action taken only with the approval of current users who understand the data, since the information may not be statistically correct.

The analysis of data using induction tools is different to statistical analysis, in that regularities in a given domain are discovered, without needing to know how they were derived. Very little expertise is required to use rule induction systems whereas statistical analysis, other than simple measures such as averages and standard deviations, is rarely carried out by non–statisticians. A statistician would know what techniques to use in an attempt to prove or disprove a data trend or relationship. Also, statistical calculations would use all of the data whereas inductive systems might choose to ignore some of the data records

---

[†] Reproduced by permission of Dataflex (Information Management) Services Ltd.

which do not follow general trends in most of the records. Although the algorithms used in inductive systems are usually mathematically based, the results may not be as objective as those produced by statistical methods.

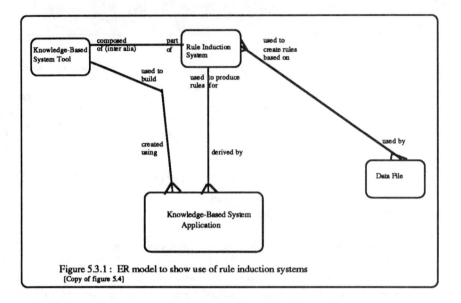

Figure 5.3.1 : ER model to show use of rule induction systems
[Copy of figure 5.4]

Databases are usually made up of a large number of records, possibly of different types. It must first be decided which data should be analysed, based on expert knowledge of the data. Induction systems are flexible with regard to processing, in that they will attempt to produce rules for any data set. Such analysis might or might not reveal hidden or implicit data in the database.

5.3.2 Further explanation of inductive systems

Induction systems produce a set of rules, based on a number of examples; that is they generalise from the particular. The example data includes a number of attributes which are thought to be considered in making a decision or determining an outcome. For example, all the attributes which a mechanic may use to diagnose a car fault and the outcome will be listed. Figure 5.3.2 shows a set of data (possibly incomplete) which might be used.

The rules which are generated are only as good as the samples of data. If the examples do not cover all possible or relevant permutations then the generated rules may not be universally applicable. The expert who understands the example data is invariably the only person who can decide whether the rules are realistic, valid and representative. The rules may not include some of the attributes specified in the examples. A well documented case exists where it was thought that 25 measurements were taken into account when an expert was making an analysis decision. An inductive system was used to identify the heuristics used by the expert when he made decisions based on these 25 measurements, using case histories. It was found that only four of the measurements were actually relevant to any one outcome.

Battery Status	Temperature of Engine	Noise Type	Steering Problem	State of Tyres	Oil Leak?	Verdict/ Diagnosis
x1	y1	z1	a1	m1	p1	q1
x2	y2	z2	a2	m2	p2	q2
x3	y3	z3	a3	m3	p3	q3
x4	y4	z4	a4	m4	p4	q4
'	'	'	'	'	'	'
'	'	'	'	'	'	'
xn	yn	zn	an	mn	pn	qn

Figure 5.3.2 : Sample data for input to an inductive system

An induction tool is often used in the knowledge elicitation process, whereby the knowledge engineer attempts to obtain information from the expert about the domain of interest. It has been found that some experts cannot articulate or express their knowledge or wisdom in a simple, intelligible manner to the knowledge engineer. This does not imply criticism to either party: they may not have a large enough common vocabulary which would enable them to discuss the domain; or the expert may not know *how* he uses his expertise. Figure 3.1.1 in section 3.1 shows how an inductive system could fit into the process of building KBS.

Whenever anyone tries to explain something, they frequently resort to giving examples. If an expert can give the knowledge engineer a sufficiently wide ranging, representative set of examples, an inductive system can be used to generate rules from those examples. The rules are then reflected back to the expert so that he can say whether they are true, false or between the two extremes. The expert may be able to offer direct modifications to the rules, such as including more qualifying conditions, or further examples which do not conform to the rules so that another set of rules can be generated through the induction process.

Many inductive systems use the same or similar algorithms for producing rules. ID3 (Iterative Dichotomizer Three) is the basic algorithm developed by Ross Quinlan of Australia on which others, such as ACLS and C4, are based. The processing is iterative and produces a decision tree structure. All the examples start at the root node. An attribute is chosen (based on Information Theory) on which to split the examples into two or more branches, and each of the examples are associated with the appropriate branch node. If all the examples at a node are of the same class (have the same outcome) then no further processing is needed. Otherwise, they are split on another attribute and lower level nodes are created. A rule set can be produced based on the decision tree and attribute values.

5.3.3 Applications

There are several well known examples of KBS applications which have been developed using induction systems, including:

- a system for tuning process control in a nuclear fuel refinery;

- evaluation of food tasting tests (trend identification) by a margarine manufacturer;

- diagnosing welding defects by a steel research group;

- a system to assist in performance assessment of engines;

- optimisation of off–shore gas–oil separation systems;

- a credit card application assessment system;

- systems to aid trouble–shooting or fault diagnosis;

- classification of glass fragments for forensic scientists.

In each of the above cases a database of examples was available holding attributes of real situations and the decisions or the outcome. Analysis of a database for trends or exceptions may not enable or warrant that a KBS application should be built, but implicit information may be found.

5.3.4 Requirements for database analysis

As already stated, inductive systems are often used in knowledge elicitation, that is, the process of extracting knowledge from the expert. A number of inductive tools require the user to input examples interactively via a terminal, which is not altogether surprising since knowledge elicitation is a 'people oriented' activity. This would be impossible though, when the examples consist of large volumes of data, such as that stored in a database. Some tools are able to read data from a formatted serial file, but very few products are thought to read data from a database. Today incorporates a fourth generation language which can be used to extract examples from databases controlled by Oracle, Informix, DB2 and Rdb. XpertRule can extract data from DataFlex files. And the Flex component of Prospect can access an Aspect database and the rule induction part of Prospect can use Aspect files.

Such a facility is desirable to provide tighter coupling if large numbers of records are to be analysed, although it may be possible to use a program to extract attributes into a serial file for use by an inductive system.

Attribute selection

It is unlikely that an inductive system could identify trends in a database containing a large number of record types and attributes, in a short time scale. The system would need to join all the records (on common attributes in a relational system) to form a single table, perhaps having a hundred or more attributes or columns per example. The user of a database is likely to know of a number of attributes which are irrelevant and he must decide which attributes should be input to the inductive system. If, for example, a database of customer sales were to be analysed, looking for conditions associated with customer spending, then attributes such as telephone number, customer name and order number may be irrelevant. Implied information could be relevant: for example, the telephone number gives an indication of geographical location if the customer address is not known. Attributes such as home town and age of customer, price, colour and date of purchases may be thought to be relevant, since the manufacturer can influence these factors through marketing. An inductive system cannot differentiate between relevant and irrelevant attributes and may identify nonsensical trends such as a correlation between order numbers and customer telephone numbers. Attributes introduced into databases to facilitate data access or to uniquely identify records are not likely to be input to an inductive system.

Occurrence selection

It is unlikely that all occurrences of the selected attributes held in a database need to be input to the inductive system. Duplicate records should be removed. Although duplicate records are rarely held in databases, this is often because unique access keys are added. For example 'order line' records will store the order number, so that order number and order line number together make a unique key. When this key is removed, there are likely to be many orders for the same quantity of an item from a variety of customers. It may be desirable to amalgamate these records, including a 'count' attribute to be used as a weighting factor.

There may be exceptional records which should be removed. For example, the managing director might receive exceptional discounts on his orders so they might be omitted. Also some information might be out of date, such as orders for items no longer in stock. Again, the data users would need to advise on which records should be removed. Erroneous data, that is invalid or missing values, would need to be removed from data samples.

Database and inductive system interface

The interface between an inductive system and a database could be based on a query language such as SQL, so that:

- only relevant attributes are retrieved (a projection);

- two or more records can be joined;

- only relevant records or tuples are selected;

- duplicates can be ignored.

Database extracts could be derived directly if inductive systems were extended to include standard SQL query facilities. However, the most likely method to be used at present is to extract data using a third or fourth generation language. A program could either create an intermediate extract file which was readable by an inductive system or pass records one at a time through an interface at run–time.

The database extraction program need not be concerned with read consistency levels, in that inconsistencies due to updates currently taking place are not likely to impact on the rules produced by the inductive analyser. Alternatively, it may be possible to use a back–up copy of the database so that live systems are not affected by the extra processing and database access. Since it is unlikely that this type of analysis could be applied to rapidly changing data, the fact that the data is out of date will not matter.

If the data does change dramatically over a short time period then the problem is likely to be too unstable to investigate, unless retrospective analysis is worthwhile. An example of this might be analysis of changes in the stock market, such that factors which caused a major change are identified and can in future be monitored; that is, existing systems would be modified in accordance with past experience.

5.3.5 Method of working

Inductive systems can be used in a number of ways to generate rules, two of which are described below.

Varying data occurrences

The first step is to take a set of example data and pass it through the inductive system to produce a decision tree or a set of rules, with which the data user may or may not agree. If he can refute or reject some of the rules, they should be amended or deleted, and new ones inserted if necessary. The initial data set should be run against the new rules and information about the 'closeness of fit' of the rules to the data should be output. This may cause the user to modify the rules again making this an iterative process.

The final 'hypothesis' or rule set can then be tested by running different sets of data against it. Old data or other examples, if only a subset from the database was used to produce the initial rules, may be used. Information about data which does not conform to the rules should enable the user to refine the rules.

Varying the attributes

In this case, all the relevant data occurrences are used on each pass through the inductive system, but on the first pass only a small proportion of the attributes, perhaps those which are most significant, are submitted and the rules are placed on one side. On a second pass further attributes are added and a new set of rules generated which can be compared with the first set. This process can be repeated a number of times, adding new attributes and perhaps removing some which do not have a significant effect on the rules. The user can then select and use the rule set which he believes to be correct.

Points to watch

Since induction systems were not specifically designed to analyse data in the way that has been suggested here, the user should bear in mind the following:

- many inductive systems can only cope with low volumes of data, that is a few hundred example records and tens of attributes. This may be insufficient to produce meaningful results for some problems;

- inductive systems are unable to determine which attributes are relevant or irrelevant. They will attempt to identify similarities and differences across example data which may be purely coincidental;

- the user may not be able to give weightings to attributes. Perhaps the second method of using inductive systems should be used if some attributes are known to be more important than others;

- not all inductive systems inform the user that some example records have been ignored when they do not fit identified trends;

- it is unlikely that missing values (NULL or unknown) can be handled.

5.3.6 Use of generated results

Rules or decision trees produced by induction systems as part of knowledge elicitation would normally be used as a basis for building a KBS application. The results from analysing a database using an inductive tool need not necessarily be used in this way. It is envisaged that they could be useful to management or existing users of the data. For example:

- a company about to undergo major expansion might analyse labour costs, skill profiles, etc;

- a sales manager would be interested in an analysis of a customer sales database;

- a store manager would use results from an inventory and stock control database;

- a personnel manager may use rules generated from a database holding staff details such as turnover of staff, pay levels, qualifications, etc.

The types of information which can be generated fall into a number of categories which are discussed below.

Simulation based on known facts

A well known company produces a model of sales patterns for the following year based upon contracts taken out in the current year and modified for predicted business, using a Prolog based KBS tool. The model is used to try out 'what–if' queries on predicted business for the next year. Such a model could be built using an inductive tool. The 'what–if's could be investigated by changing the data and investigating the changes in the generated rules.

Trends and summaries

Rules can be used to express generalisations about data, which do not necessarily hold true for all data instances. Generalisations such as 'Scandinavians have blonde hair' (or the equivalent rule would be 'if nationality = Scandinavian then hair–colour = blonde'), 'IT staff earn a lot of money' and 'anyone who overeats will put on weight' are commonly made, but there are always exceptions to these rules. However, such rules help us to make judgements, even if they are sometimes wrong or inaccurate.

Database users may not know what trends the data follows. An individual salesman is likely to know the trends which his own customers exhibit, but the area sales manager may wish to know the general trends of all the customers in a given region. Examination of customer sales by region using an induction system may reveal general trends which do not hold true for customers of any individual salesman. Rules generated by an induction system could be validated by subsequent statistical analysis, for example testing whether a correlation between attributes is significant.

The rules can be viewed as a 'first–cut' at identifying related attributes. This would be particularly useful if the user has no idea how the attributes may be related. For example, the results of a questionnaire or survey could be analysed without prejudice, bias or preconceptions.

Classifications

Rules can classify information, in that they specify general conditions which hold true for a number of instances. For example, books are commonly classified by subject matter: if book_subject = biology, then book_class = science. A librarian may be able to classify books in several useful ways, for example books could be grouped according to the number of loans per year, using a book loans database. The classification may be dependent upon such attributes as age of book, subject matter, weight of book, number of pictures and pages, and author. This would be an artificial classification but it could be used to identify books which should only be allowed out for short loan periods or be easily accessible. Analysis of the same database could classify books and lenders on a whole range of subjects, which may or may not be useful.

The rule induction system Beagle was used in a forensic science classification application [EVET87] and it was found that the induction system performed 'as well as if not better than conventional statistical methods at the chosen task'. The statistical methods compared were nearest neighbour and discriminant analysis.

Exceptions

An induction system may identify a rule to which only one instance of data conforms. Some induction systems report on exceptional examples of data which have been ignored or should be removed from the induction analysis, since they do not conform to the general trends exhibited by the other data. It is unlikely that these exceptions could be identified visually or by statistical analysis. These exceptions may be significant, in that they could identify errors, peculiarities or loop–holes in the system. The owner of the data may choose to take action as a result of finding these exceptions. For example, a combination of circumstances may give an individual rights which were not intended, or error routines in a validation suite may not be catering for rare situations. Perhaps an induction system could be used as a database integrity checking tool, though this may prove to be a sledgehammer to crack a nut.

Complex relationships

An induction system may be able to identify subtle or complex relationships between attributes which would be impossible or time consuming to pursue using statistical analysis packages. These are the types of relationships which may be of interest to management since decisions often have to take into account a number of tenuously linked factors which are not immediately supported by facts. The relationships identified between attributes may require interpretation, but could provide back–up to what is a hunch or idea based on experience or instinct.

Probabilistic analysis

It has been suggested that induction systems can help with probabilistic analysis [MCCA89], to predict likely outcomes, rather than just whether or not it will occur. For example, a rule induction system could be applied to credit card data in an attempt to predict how good or bad a risk a potential new customer will be. Dr Al–Attar suggests that there are about 30 factors which could be used, and that it is easy to find the very good and the very bad risks. Some companies are thought to be identifying only 55 percent of the good and bad applicants, which is only marginally better than random. After the use of XpertRule, a decision yield of up to 70 percent is claimed.

5.3.7 Rule induction tools

About twenty induction systems were identified by a study conducted within CCTA [CONW88]. An induction system is generally an optionally used part of, or front–end to, deductive KBS tools, enabling development of an initial knowledge–base. Add–on induction system components are now being marketed with some deductive KBS shells, which have been available for some time. For example, Xi Rule has been added to XiPlus and the Crystal Induction System has been added to Crystal.

A number of the induction systems are small, frequently running on micros. This may limit the analysis of large databases held on minis or mainframes. Some tools can only deal with a relatively small number of example cases (up to a few hundred) from which to generate rules. Nevertheless the small products are relatively cheap, costing in the region of £150, and may be useful for experimentation in this area.

Beagle

Beagle (Bionic Evolutionary Algorithm Generating Logical Expressions) is marketed by Warm Boot Ltd and is described as a 'novel analysis system'. It uses an evolutionary induction strategy to devise rules for testing. Two types of output are produced: a set of decision rules for human consumption and subprograms in Pascal, Basic, C or Fortran.

There are 6 main modules in the system which can read data in comma–delimited, ASCII format, as dumped by a number of databases. The modules are:

- SEED (Selectively Extracts Example Data) which puts external data into a suitable format;

- ROOT (Rule Oriented Optimization Tester) which tests an initial set of user–suggested rules;

- HERB (Heuristic Evolutionary Rule Breeder) generates decision rules by naturalistic selection;

- STEM (Signature Table Evaluation Module) makes a signature table from the rules produced by HERB;

- LEAF (Logical Evaluator And Forecaster) uses the above output to produce forecasts and classifications;

- PLUM (Procedural Language Utility Maker) converts a Beagle rule–file into languages such as Pascal and Fortran.

A version is available to run on IBM micros and compatibles, Data General and VAX machines and has been used for weather forecasting, medical diagnosis and forensic identification.

Expert–ease

Expert–ease runs on micro machines, is written in Pascal and produces rules in Pascal. A spreadsheet format is used for supplying up to 255 examples which may have up to 31 attributes. Lists or columns of attributes are specified, the last column being the decision or outcome. A classification rule is derived in the form of a decision tree. Further examples can be added after rules have been induced and if they refute any of the rules a restructuring of the rule–base can be requested. Rules become more sophisticated as more examples are given and the user is informed about contradictory or identical rules.

Extran7

Extran can take examples from the screen using a spreadsheet interface or from a file with a defined format. Extran7 is coded in Fortran–77 and rules are generated as Fortran code, hence the rule subroutines can be incorporated into existing or new Fortran systems.

It runs on many machines including IBM mainframes, VAX, microVAX, UNIX workstations, IBM micros and compatibles. The price depends upon the machine environment but examples are in the region of £29 000 for the IBM mainframe version and about £2000 for a micro version. The former could potentially be used for analysing DB2 databases.

RuleMaster

RuleMaster has an inductive element (RuleMaker) and a rule language (Radial) so that rules can be coded directly. It is claimed to generate uncertainty, can use fuzzy attributes and be used for heuristic and deep models. The inductive system is based on finite state automata. RuleMaster is written in C and can generate rules in C. It runs on VAX, UNIX workstations and IBM micros.

Today

Example data can be derived from databases such as Oracle and Informix via applications written in the fourth generation language Today. It generates decision trees which can optionally be converted into rule sets. The user can also specify rules directly.

The C4 algorithm is used in the induction process to produce the decision tree. Pruning and rationalisation techniques are included: pruning ensures that redundant rules are removed; and rationalisation combines rules, where appropriate, removing redundant conditions. Pruning involves user confidence levels to prune branches caused by 'noisy' examples; a manual override of attributes chosen by C4 is available, which typically results in a tree of greater depth. Today can transform trees into sets of rules, during which further checking is done to remove redundant conditions from rules and combine rules where appropriate.

Today offers support for using real case history data, as opposed to example data constructed by experts. It supports 'don't know' and 'don't care' categories, example weighting, tests for statistical independence and random selection of C4 training data from very large case histories. In the latter case, 1000 examples may be selected from 100 000 case histories. Three types of example set are supported: a training set for producing the tree; a test set for validating the tree; and a critical example set(produced by the system) which contains the minimum set of examples needed to reproduce the tree.

Attributes are driven from the Today active dictionary and can have continuous, enumerated or ordered enumerated values. Decision trees and rule sets are limited to 255 attributes each, but they can be nested into a hierarchy of arbitrary depth.

The knowledge engineer can generate reports which reflect the progress of the induction system: a tree generator conflicts report lists examples which have conflicting decisions; a test set of examples can be run against the generated rules, and examples which are not classified correctly are listed with a percentage measurement of accuracy.

XpertRule

Up to 2000 examples can be input using a spreadsheet–like interface or imported from an ASCII file. The choice of attributes can be automated or manual. The induction process can be truth preserving (non generalising) if a full set of examples is given or if a subset of examples is given as exceptions to a default rule. Irrelevant factors will be removed and missing factors are highlighted.

XpertRule represents knowledge using decision trees; up to 64 chained decision trees are allowed per application, and up to 32 attributes and 32 outcomes per decision tree. There is a decision tree pruning algorithm to enable probabilistic rules to be produced from noisy example data. An automatic verifier checks the accuracy of current rules, by comparing a training example set with a second test set. The rules can be converted and exported as DataFlex command language or single decision trees can be converted to C code.

XpertRule is written in Turbo Pascal and runs on IBM personal computers or compatibles.

Integration of tools at run–time

Purpose

This chapter looks at the integration of tools at run–time. It is not always possible to just consider how a knowledge–based system (KBS) tool can access a database, without thinking about the surrounding software environment, within which both of these tools operate. Each of the sections within this chapter consider different aspects within the context illustrated in figure 6.1.

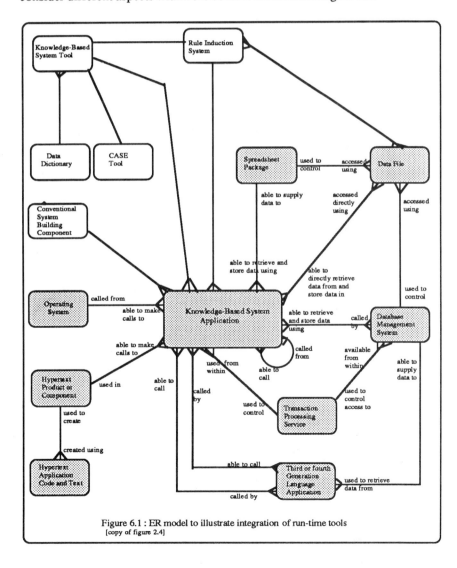

Figure 6.1 : ER model to illustrate integration of run-time tools
[copy of figure 2.4]

Section 6.1

Section 6.1 contains the 'meat' of the chapter, in that it describes how KBS tools and databases may be linked, reading data from the database for use in inferencing and storing data generated by inferencing in the database, as shown in figure 6.2. The basic capability of interfacing these tools is fundamental.

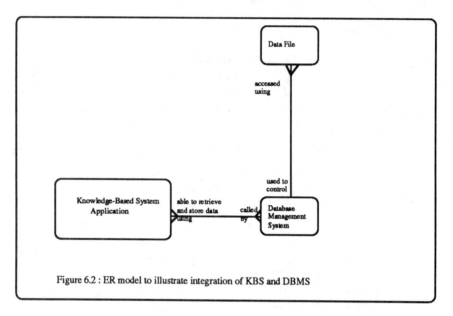

Figure 6.2 : ER model to illustrate integration of KBS and DBMS

Section 6.2

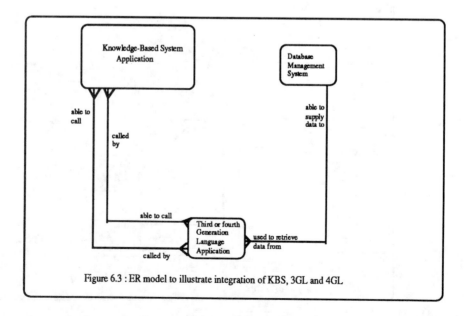

Figure 6.3 : ER model to illustrate integration of KBS, 3GL and 4GL

Section 6.2 looks at the coupling of KBS with third and fourth generation languages, as depicted in figure 6.3. The concept of using them to indirectly access a DBMS is introduced in section 6.1, but interfacing KBS tools and languages presents opportunities beyond accessing data.

Section 6.3

Section 6.3 describes how some databases which are controlled by a transaction processing (TP) service can be accessed by KBS, as illustrated in figure 6.4. This is particularly relevant to tools which run on mainframes, when KBS applications are required to be integrated with large, existing, on–line systems.

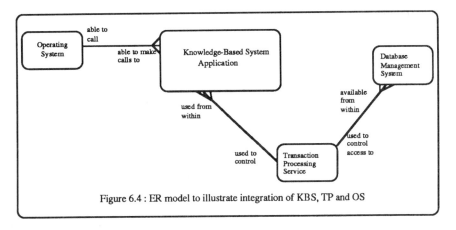

Figure 6.4 : ER model to illustrate integration of KBS, TP and OS

This section also considers the communication link between KBS and operating systems. Such links widen the potential for accessing any database or file, which may be held locally or on another hardware platform. This is particularly relevant to those KBS applications which are delivered on specialised workstations. The fundamental aims are to use TP and operating systems to provide seamless connectivity, the ability to use services in an open system manner and to have a data interchange capability.

Section 6.4

Section 6.4 considers the integration of KBS tools and spreadsheets, as shown in figure 6.5. A number of ways of integrating DBMS, spreadsheets and KBS tools are discussed including the use of KBS to link DBMS and spreadsheets, and use of KBS in calculating cell values.

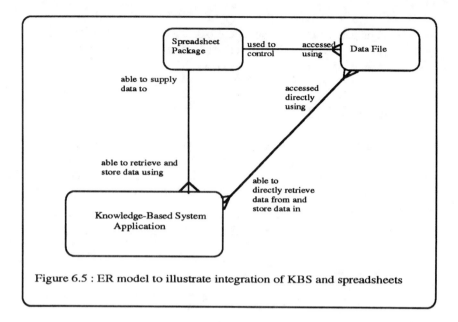

Figure 6.5 : ER model to illustrate integration of KBS and spreadsheets

Section 6.5

This section is concerned with incorporating hypertext systems within KBS applications; see figure 6.6. A hypertext system can, broadly speaking, be considered as a combination of a programming capability, a small scale data storage and a presentation vehicle. Exploitation of the latter is considered in conjunction with KBS.

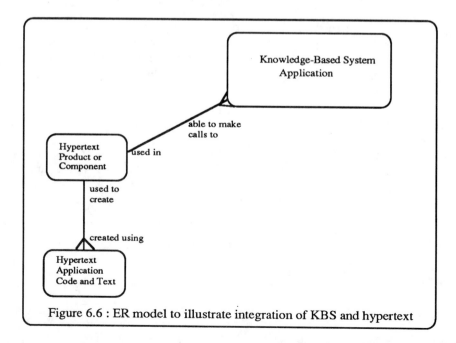

Figure 6.6 : ER model to illustrate integration of KBS and hypertext

Section 6.6

Section 6.6 rounds off this chapter by investigating links between two or more KBS applications which have been built using the same or different KBS tools. This is depicted in figure 6.7 as a recursive relationship. This topic is not directly relevant to linking KBS and database management systems, but is necessary if totally integrated information systems are to be built.

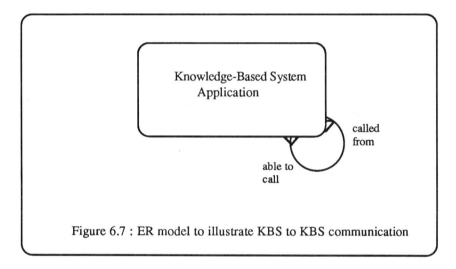

Figure 6.7 : ER model to illustrate KBS to KBS communication

6.1

Extracting data from, and storing data in, databases

6.1.1 Requirement

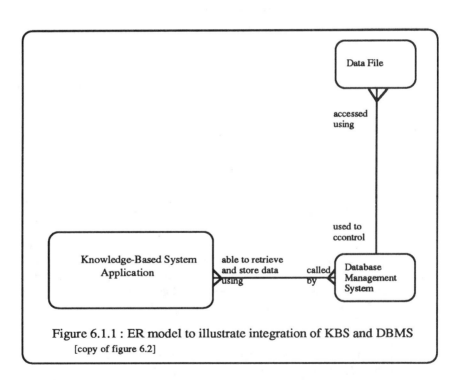

Figure 6.1.1 : ER model to illustrate integration of KBS and DBMS
[copy of figure 6.2]

There are several reasons why it is desirable that a knowledge–based system (KBS) tool should provide the application builder with facilities to access database management systems (DBMS) as illustrated in figure 6.1.1:

- a KBS application may need some data which has already been collected and stored in a database by existing, conventional systems. It is generally considered bad practice to expect users to input the same data more than once within a computing environment and it would also mean that the integrity of the data must be re–checked. If large volumes of data are required, for example a CAD/CAM application might use gigabytes of data, then it would be impossible to manually input the data. Therefore a KBS application needs to be able to read data from a database;

- there may be a requirement to share persistent data between many users of the same or different KBS applications. For example, a KBS which diagnoses machine faults may need to refer to a log (database) of case histories, where the results of applying corrective actions for faults are kept. Such logs will grow with time and are best stored independently of the KBS application, otherwise the source of the latter will need to be frequently updated with case histories;

- an application may need to write to an existing database, inserting, deleting and amending records. A KBS application might obtain useful information during a consultation which can be stored on a central database for use by the same application in a future consultation or by other systems. This upholds the concept that data should only be captured once;

- some KBS applications may themselves have an internal data storage requirement, the data not necessarily being used by other systems. For example, look–up tables might be used as part of a coding and decoding mechanism. Storage of a lot of data in main memory, rather than on backing store, can cause performance problems. Also the structure of such data may be complex, justifying the use of a DBMS rather than flat files for data storage.

6.1.2 Definition of KBS and DBMS data

The representations of data in KBS and DBMS may be different and therefore some problems may occur in mapping data definitions from one to the other. However, this is not a new problem introduced by KBS technology since mismatches occur between conventional languages such as Cobol and Fortran. The following section explores mapping problems with respect to existing KBS tools.

Section 3.2 describes three views of a database: external, global and internal views. The external view is of most concern here, since a KBS will access data, directly or indirectly, using this view, and the DBMS will take care of the mapping of physical data on to it. A DBMS might require separate external views to be defined for use by applications generated using different tools; for example ICL's DBMS, IDMS, requires separate subschemas (external views) for Fortran and Cobol programs. It is unlikely that DBMS vendors will develop external view definitions specifically for KBS tools, therefore they must be able to use views which are already available, or databases must be accessed indirectly via an external system which can use existing views.

KBS data

Items of data in KBS tools are often referred to as facts, though other names
such as variables, predicates and parameters are used. [The term fact is used here
to differentiate between KBS data and DBMS data.] Facts roughly equate to
variables in conventional programming languages such as Cobol, which are used
to store values at run–time. However, there are some differences. A variable in
Cobol has a name (such as *NI–number*) and a value (which may be rubbish left
in store if not initialised or a value assigned to the variable by the program). A
KBS fact also has a name and a value, but in addition there is an internal
indicator which shows whether or not the fact has been instantiated. So, if a
Cobol program is running and an instruction 'WRITE NI–number' is executed
then the value of NI–number will be written to a file. If a KBS application was
about to execute a 'DISPLAY NI–number' instruction, the inference engine
would check whether or not NI–number had been instantiated; if it had not, then
a mechanism for obtaining a value would be triggered before attempting to
display the value of NI–number.

There may be other differences: for example some KBS, by default, only cause
facts to be evaluated once during a single consultation, whereas variables in a
Cobol program may hold a series of values during a single run, derived through
calculations, reading of input files, etc. Extra information may also be
associated with facts: for example a fact in ICL–Adviser can have an associated
default value, such that if the application fails to find a value using other means
such as by asking the user or by derivation from other facts, then the fact will be
instantiated with the default value.

There are different types of facts which, to a large extent, depend upon the type
of tool. Most KBS tools allow single integers, real (or floating point) numbers
and strings to be declared (simple facts). For example, the KBS tools BIM
Prolog, ICL–Adviser and Expert Systems Environment (ESE) all use these three
basic types. Some tools also use fact types which are rarely, if ever, stored in
databases: for example 'condition' used in Savoir can have a value of true, false
or unknown; a boolean parameter in ESE can take the values true and false; an
'assertion' in ICL–Adviser can be used as a boolean, to hold the values true or
false, or to store a numeric representation of degrees of truth. 'Conditions',
booleans and 'assertions' provide similar functionality but may be implemented
differently in different products.

Most KBS tools allow structured facts to be defined, that is groups of logically
associated facts as well as single facts, possibly made up of different fact types.
ICL–Adviser uses arrays and records: an array consists of repeating facts of the
same type (such as integer) and records are logical groupings of many facts of
different or mixed types. Complex representations can be defined since arrays
can contain records and records can contain arrays. Classes in KEE can be
mapped on to one or more relational tables, which are made up of mixed data
types. Natural Expert has a rich selection of fact types such as constructed types
(lists) and tuple types, and additionally the developer can define his own new
types. An ESE parameter can have multiple values which can be ordered. All

versions of Prolog (BIM Prolog, Quintus Prolog, MVS/Prolog, etc) and Lisp include the concept of a list, which is an ordered sequence of facts, rather like a record.

Object orientated tools provide yet another method for specifying facts. A *class* can be thought of as the equivalent of a record type or structured fact and an *object*, an instance of a class, equates to a record instance. Some tools use different terms which can be confusing, for example, KEE calls both classes and members of classes units. Associated with each class is a *frame*, made up of a number of *slots*, which allows enumeration of the component attributes or facts. A slot, like a relational database column, can be used to store a single value such as a string or number, but in addition a slot may be a more complex data type, such as an array or list. The frame of a class will consist of all slots inherited from parent classes as well as those declared for that particular class. Slots can be instantiated at both the class and object level.

DBMS data

The entity–relationship (ER) model is commonly used as a means of deriving the data structures and descriptions needed to support applications. The technique is applicable regardless of the type of database management system (network, relational, etc) which is targeted. Data is logically represented by:

- entity types, which map on to collections of items such as orders, people, customers, books, cars, etc;

- attributes, which are properties associated with entity types, for example a car will have a registration number, colour, manufacturer, model, date of first sale, etc;

- relationships, which are ephemeral, logical connections between entity types, for example customers place orders, *place* being the relationship between the two entity types.

The physical storage of the above logical structures depends upon the type of DBMS. In network, hierarchic and relational databases an entity type is stored as a record type or table, made up of a number of data items (fields or columns) which map on to attributes. Network and hierarchic DBMS store relationships as pointers (physical addresses of records) on records, whereas relational DBMS represent a relationship between two entity types by the presence of an attribute (column) of one entity(table), in another entity (table) as a foreign key. An application program need not be concerned with the physical data storage though, since access will always take place via an external, logical view.

Attributes can be of various types: integer, real and string (character, text, alphanumeric) types are common to all DBMS. Some DBMS provide types (or domains) such as date and time (for example Ingres, Sybase and Oracle), money or amount (for example Ingres, Sybase and Unify) and group fields (for example Unify and IDMS). Non–relational databases commonly allow repeating groups (arrays) to be stored.

Text retrieval databases such as Status use different mechanisms for describing data. A text retrieval database can be considered as a hierarchy of chapters, articles, sections, paragraphs and words if traversing the hierarchy from top to bottom. Chapters can be indexed on words which can be numeric, date or string types.

Object oriented database management systems are beginning to emerge from research and development work. For example, G–Base, a French product, is marketed by Scientific Computers Ltd. Objects (classes) or entities are defined in terms of properties: terminal properties contain local values; structural properties express a link or relationship. Classes (generic objects) and specific objects (instances) are managed in the same way by G–Base.

6.1.3 Mapping of facts and data

In the past, KBS have tended to use a large variety of facts, for which there may be a small population. That is, the data tends to be 'wide', requiring many different facts to be declared, and 'shallow', having very few occurrences (sometimes only one) of the same fact. DBMS are, on the other hand, particularly useful for the storage and control of wide, complex data structures which are 'deep', having many occurrences of each logical grouping. However, this does not mean that there is no common ground: knowledge–based systems may select just a few record occurrences, of a few or many types, for processing; or, as is the case with some more recent KBS which interface with DBMS, they may inference over large volumes of data.

As explained above, facts are declared differently across KBS tools and external views of data vary across many DBMS. Therefore, not surprisingly, there can be no simple, generic mapping of facts in all KBS tools to data in all types of databases. The transfer of data will be dependent upon compatibility of pairs of KBS tools and DBMS external view definitions.

Low level mappings

At the lowest level, there is a degree of correlation, in that both KBS and DBMS tools use integers, real numbers and character strings. There may still be problems however, since the storage representation of integers and real numbers varies across software tools. For example, Quintus Prolog uses 29 bits to store an integer, whereas Unify uses up to 32; the three most significant bits of a large integer could be lost when reading data from a database. Also the same products use 20 and 24 bits respectively to store the mantissa of a real number, which may cause loss of precision in the KBS application. Providing that the developers of applications are aware of this and write code to protect values outside compatible boundaries this mismatch is not a problem. However, details such as this are often not clearly documented and mismatches could cause corruption of a database.

Some data types in databases cannot be transferred to some KBS tools. For example, binary data items in a Unify database are not supported by Quintus Prolog. Sybase 'datetime' data types are not directly supported by BIM Prolog, but there is a translation mechanism. A 'datetime' item is represented by two long integers in C, and the Sybase BIM Prolog interface converts these to a string or 'atom'.

Conversely, it may not be possible to move data in the opposite direction; for example, facts of type probability and condition in Savoir are not directly supported in a database such as dBASE III, although redefinition of such facts in terms of dBASE III data types may be possible. Language specific data types are known to cause problems when building systems using several tools. For example, Fortran programs can store complex numbers which are not supported in any other language. Natural Expert, which is based upon a functional language, has an extensive set of data types, but some, including structured types, unbounded lists and nested tuples, cannot be passed as parameters to Natural applications for storage in a database.

A further potential problem arises from the values which may be held in relational databases and KBS. For example, a column (data item) in a table controlled by a relational DBMS can be declared to allow NULL values to be stored. It is usual for a NULL value to be stored when the column does not have a value for an instance (tuple) in that table. Some databases such as SIR allow multiple null states to be declared so that it is possible to differentiate between concepts such as not evaluated and not relevant. The proposed ISO SQL3 standard includes syntax for specifying multiple null states.

There is no equivalent to NULL in KBS, except that some facts may be in an unevaluated state if they have not been used. The product ESE translates a NULL value in DB2 into a single space in a string, with a certainty of 0 (in the range −1 to +1). KBMS treats NULL values in SQL/DS as 'not available' values.

A fact in a KBS application may be set to the value 'UNKNOWN' regardless of type, which means that the application has attempted to evaluate the fact but has failed. There is no direct equivalent in relational databases unless a null state is defined in the external view for this purpose. A developer of an application needs to be aware of how the interface of a given tool deals with the conversion of unknown values, if attempting to use or store them. The documentation for Natural Expert explicitly outlines how to mimic the use of UNKNOWN values in Natural programs which are used to indirectly retrieve or store data.

A minority of KBS tools are limited to passing single or simple facts to and from DBMS; for example Savoir does not allow structured facts to be declared.

High level mappings

The mapping of structured data (arrays, records, lists and objects) depends upon how the external (logical) and internal (physical) views are reconciled. Fortran programs store arrays by columns, so the array in figure 6.1.2 would be stored

as 11111RRRRR22... Cobol programs store arrays by rows so the same array
would be stored as 1R2T1R2T... The logical views in such programs must be
reconciled with the physical storage of data and hence the requirement for ICL's
DBMS, IDMS, to have separate subschemas for Cobol and Fortran programs.

```
01  ARRAY.
     03  A OCCURS 5.
          05 B PIC 9.        (all occurrences set to the value 1)
          05 C PIC X.        (all occurrences set to the value R)
          05 D PIC 9.        (all occurrences set to the value 2)
          05 E PIC X.        (all occurrences set to the value T)
```

Figure 6.1.2 : COBOL array definition

A KBS tool needs to support and interpret complex structures in the same way
that the DBMS stores and retrieves them; that is, a consistent group
representation is needed. A number of DBMS interfaces provided with KBS tools
can deal with structured facts: for example, Reveal can read records from a serial
file; ESE, KBMS, ADS and CA–DB:Expert can read and update records or
tables from compatible databases; Nexpert Object provides a one–to–one
mapping between tables, records and fields in databases and classes, objects and
properties in knowledge–bases respectively; and the mapping of data items to
Knowledgetool variables is included in the code of the knowledge–base.

Quintus Prolog allows the coder to define views of the database, therefore new
logical groupings consisting of data items from one or more record types can be
declared. The developer of a KEE knowledge–base can specify the mapping
between tables and columns in databases and classes and slots in
knowledge–bases. It is possible to map multiple tables on to a single class; map
one table on to multiple classes; map multiple columns of a table or tables on
to values of a single slot; and map one column to multiple slots. This is quite a
powerful mechanism in that more complex, or more simplified, structures than
those declared in an external view associated with the DBMS can be used.

Multiple facts

The 'width' of data which can be read on a single call to the DBMS is discussed
above. All tools mentioned in this book can pass at least a single data item,
remembering that not all KBS tools can access external data. The 'depth' of the
data, that is the number of record occurrences, which can be retrieved on a single
database access varies, although most interfaces pass only one record at a time.
A number of the tool interfaces described in annex D are based on SQL, and it is
usual for SQL to operate at table level and return the set of records which satisfy
a query rather than a single record. However, SQL tends to be treated as it would
be in a Cobol program, such that the first record is returned on the first call, the
second on the next and so on, until all records have been returned.

The 'single record retrieval' mechanism works, in general, as follows. A cursor, which can hold the address of a record and act as a pointer, can be defined in an external view to be used with a specified table in a database. A cursor is opened before the required data (a set of records) are retrieved and placed in working store allocated to the DBMS. When records have been read the cursor will be pointing to the first record or row in the retrieved data table. This record can be read into the program and processed. Statements which retrieve data from this intermediate table cause the cursor to move through the rows of the table. A value in a 'code' data item associated with the cursor will identify when all the records have been read and processing should terminate. At this point the cursor should be closed.

Knowledgetool and CA–DB:Expert use the above mechanism to retrieve data from DB2 and SQL/DS databases. Implementations of Prolog also use this mechanism and are well described in LUCA88 and GRAY 88(1).

Some tools can accept a number of values for a fact on a single call to the DBMS. For example, parameters in ESE applications can be declared as multi–valued, allowing all values which satisfy a query to be returned together. KBMS maps relational tables from DB2 on to objects, the objects being multivalued since a single object can represent all the tuples in a single table. KEE has multi–valued slots which can be used to store a number of retrieved records.

6.1.4 Summary on data mapping

A general problem is that many of the available DBMS do not have an effective external view mechanism. If they did, it would be possible to define the mappings for the data required by an arbitrary KBS (or any other programming tool for that matter), together with appropriate error messages if significant data would be lost or could not be represented. A practical solution at present is to:

- use the highest level mappings available between compatible KBS and DBMS tools;

- use traditional (conventional) solutions for complex data access, where multiple records of complex, mixed types are required but not supported by the KBS and DBMS interface, by exploiting an interface to an external sub–routine (see 6.1.6, indirect coupling).

6.1.5 Functionality of data manipulation language

This sub–section is concerned with the data manipulation language (DML) provided as part of the DBMS interface, the main issues being reading from and writing to a database, sharing data, security and accessing schema information. The database interfaces of several KBS tools are described in annex D.

Read and write access

A minority of tools can only read data from a database. For example, Spices can only retrieve documents from Status databases and Inference ART can only read data from databases such as Oracle. The majority of KBS tools can not only read, but can update the database, where update means inserting new records, deleting and amending existing records. CA–DB:Expert, for example, can update or delete a number of records (rows) through one SQL command and single records can be inserted on an SQL call. Quintus Prolog has two 'delete' predicates: one for single record deletes, the other for multiple deletes.

Some control information is available within a KBS application so that the success or otherwise of database accesses can be monitored. For example, MVS/Prolog SQL commands can use a 'return code' to indicate if the SQL call was successful (value 0), and if not an error code (value non–zero) is provided. ESE uses a 'status' parameter, which can be tested and cause subsequent database access commands, which would normally be actioned through forward chaining, to be ignored if an error is found. Interfaces which use cursors for reading records one at a time must provide indicators to show when all the data has been read, as is the case with Knowledgetool. It is important that database access error codes are monitored, just as they would be in conventional applications, to ensure that the application executes correctly.

Shared data and transactions

If data in a database is to be updated and shared, that is used by more than one person at the same time, then a transaction locking mechanism is required. This is generally provided by the DBMS, but applications must be able to use the appropriate DML to start and finish transactions and specify when locks should be applied. A number of tools have facilities to specify the start and end of a transaction, including Quintus Prolog when accessing Oracle databases, CA–DB:Expert and MVS/Prolog. At any time, updates which have been executed can be committed to the database or abandoned.

The number of databases (that is, physically, separately controlled databases) which can be used concurrently is controlled by the KBS. Quintus Prolog can have a number of Unify databases open at any one time. A KEE application can have access to a number of databases running on an IBM mainframe, controlled by different DBMS (such as Adabas and DB2) at the same time. In the case of most KBS tools though, only one DBMS and one database will be used at any one time when a KBS application is running, particularly when updating.

Security and integrity

The DBMS controls access to data and KBS applications will need to be given authorised access in an appropriate mode (read or update) to relevant data by the database controller (commonly called the database administrator). There are potential problems with maintaining data integrity when KBS are able to update data, especially if some of the database integrity constraints are encoded in programs rather than in the DBMS (see section 4.1 for more about integrity constraints). A subset of constraints is usually implemented through the DBMS global view, such as range checks, completion of non–NULL fields, duplicate keys disallowed, mandatory relationships and so on. More complex constraints such as 'customers must not order goods of a value which exceeds their credit limit' are usually implemented in the programs which update the relevant record types, since DBMS often do not have the necessary facilities to express complex requirements. Developers of KBS applications which change customer orders in the above scenario must ensure that they include the integrity checks which are encoded in existing programs. Therefore, there is a requirement for expressing data validation in KBS code, but this is not likely to be difficult in rule–based systems.

The proposed ISO SQL2 standard allows more complex integrity constraints to be specified for DBMS control. Triggered actions may be used, for example when deleting records which contain attributes used as foreign keys in a relational database or which are owners of sets of records in a network database. Association of integrity constraints with the DBMS may alleviate the problem of encoding validation in programs, including KBS applications, for those DBMS which conform to ISO standards.

Global view (schema) access

Some tools can retrieve information about the global view of a database and housekeeping details. For example, Savoir can request a display of the dBASE III file structure and list files which are open. Crystal can obtain a description of a dBASE III field. Since ESE can issue any SQL command, all table descriptions and associated details can be obtained.

Facilities to amend the database global view are available in some tools. Many SQL implementations allow dynamic global view manipulation, but it is unlikely that the database administrator (DBA) will allow KBS applications to amend those for databases which support other processing requirements. BIM Prolog has a 'create' predicate which can be used to define a new table in an Ingres database. ESE has full access to all SQL commands for manipulating DB2 or SQL/DS databases. Quintus Prolog has two predicates, 'db_create_table' and 'db_drop_table', which are used to create and remove tables respectively from an Oracle database. Savoir allows the index files of dBASE III to be manipulated.

Summary on DML

The level of access to a database required by a KBS tool will depend upon the application being considered. However, the richer the functionality the more versatile the tool is likely to be. Many KBS tools allow multi–user access to applications. When databases are shared it is essential that transactions and error logging is provided if operational databases are to be accessed. The database administrator (DBA) is unlikely to authorise users to access the database unless they can demonstrate that the database will remain valid and consistent. All the DML facilities provided for database access by conventional tools should be looked for in KBS tools.

6.1.6 Methods of access

The methods used to link KBS tools to databases can be considered to fall into three categories:

• indirect coupling;

• direct coupling;

• coupling via a controlling third party.

These methods are illustrated in figure 6.1.3. Each of these categories will be described below with example products where appropriate. In all cases, the DBMS remains in control of the data in the database. The different methods are concerned with how control is passed to the DBMS for accessing data.

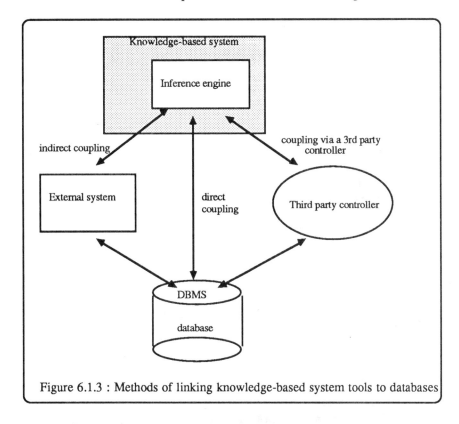

Figure 6.1.3 : Methods of linking knowledge-based system tools to databases

Many academic papers written on the subject of database access from KBS refer to loose and tight coupling; these concepts are orthogonal and complementary to direct and indirect coupling. Loose coupling generally implies that at the start of a consultation with a KBS application all the required data is loaded into store from the database and no dynamic access takes place. Alternatively if the database is to be updated, access will occur at the end of the KBS consultation, prohibiting incremental update. Tight coupling refers to on–line, dynamic access to a database, such that KBS inferencing is interleaved with DBMS usage. This section of the book is primarily concerned with tight coupling. All three methods described here (direct, indirect and via a third party) could, however, be used for loose or tight coupling, but in the case of loose coupling all data 'reads' would be executed at the beginning of a consultation and all data 'updates' would occur when the KBS application consultation was complete. GRAY88(1) includes a discussion about loose and tight coupling.

Indirect coupling

The term 'indirect coupling' is used here to describe a linkage between a KBS and a DBMS using external software, commonly written in a third generation language such as Cobol, Fortran, Pascal, Algol or C. The KBS application calls a sub–routine, passing appropriate parameters such as selection criteria if reading data or values to be stored. The sub–routine in turn accesses the database in a conventional manner for that language. It then returns control and possibly data to the KBS application. The sub–routines are sometimes provided by the vendor for specific DBMS products, for example routines are provided with Savoir for accessing dBASE III databases. See section 6.2 for more information about indirect coupling.

There may be considerable advantages to be gained in using indirect coupling, such as:

- flexibility, in that almost any database can be accessed, limited only by environmental constraints;

- the KBS application code does not become cluttered with database control statements, such as opening and closing of files. Most KBS tools claim to use a declarative rather than a procedural specification of what is required but some of the DML which controls data access does not adhere to a declarative approach;

- existing programming expertise can be used in writing sub–routines;

- a database expert would provide the DBMS calls (for a programmer) in a conventional format, which from experience he knows will work;

- solving complex fact/data mapping problems which cannot be handled directly;

- providing a 'fire–wall' between the KBS applications and the DBMS, so that the DBMS does not lose control of shared data.

Direct coupling

Tools which use direct coupling have a well packaged interface, and as far as the coder is concerned it provides a similar kind of access to databases as other data processing tools, such as third generation languages and application generators.

There is no need to write code in another language; instead, DML can be embedded in the knowledge–base of an application. The inference engine will pass control directly to the DBMS when the DML is executed for data retrieval and storage. Most of the direct interfaces in KBS tools described in annex D rely on SQL or a similar declarative language.

There are a number of advantages in using SQL:

- if standard SQL is used, in theory it should be relatively easy to connect to any DBMS which conforms to the ISO standard or the vendor should be able to provide such an interface at a low cost. For example, if Ingres was to be ported to IBM mainframes, then ESE may only require small changes to be able to access Ingres databases. [Binding of ESE to a DBMS is only provided for IBM DB2 and SQL/DS at present];

- if a KBS tool or application is ported to a number of hardware environments (SUN workstations, VAX equipment and any number of manufacturers's mainframes, for example), then a standard interface increases the number of potential DBMS which it can access;

- standardisation on SQL can be interpreted as a commitment by vendors to portability and open system interconnection;

- database programmers do not need to learn new DML if a DBMS with an SQL interface is already in use;

- better performance in data access is likely to be achieved through use of SQL query optimisers.

Most of the tools described in annex D which run on IBM mainframes and access either DB2 or SQL/DS, use SQL commands to access data. This includes ESE, ADS, CA–DB:Expert, Knowledgetool, MVS/Prolog, IBM Prolog for 370 and KBMS. Quintus Prolog running on SUN workstations and VAX machines uses a query language which offers similar facilities to SQL.

Coupling via a third party

In the above two methods, control of execution is effectively with the KBS and is briefly passed to the DBMS while accessing data. There are suggestions [ALZO87] that control could reside with third party software, such as an active or dynamic data dictionary or an on–line transaction processing (TP) system. Section 6.3 describes some KBS which can be used within TP systems; in brief, the TP system routes database accesses to the DBMS which is available from within the service and returns data to the run–time system which requested it.

A non–trivial problem associated with coupling via a third party is that existing software must be modified, a new system be written or both. It is conceivable that a KBS application could operate in an heterogeneous environment; that is, the third party software could link a number of KBS applications (possibly built using different tools) with a number of DBMS. Software to manage sharing of data, and hence transaction handling and recovery, would need to be embedded in the third party controller. Departments which have a complex mix of applications and DBMS may consider writing a control system but this approach does not conform with current trends of some well known products. However, it may encourage a move towards an open architecture, which is desirable and perhaps the way ahead in the long term (see chapter 7).

Szuprowicz [SZUP89][†] suggests that sooner or later KBS applications will require permanent and seamless connectivity with a variety of databases operating on different platforms throughout a company. He suggests that networking, through intelligent database networks, is one of the obvious solutions, see figure 6.1.4. This could not only connect KBS and DBMS but could provide access to real–time information and value added networks if the corporate databases did not hold the required information.

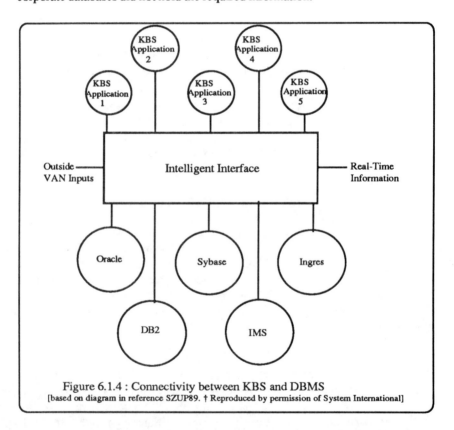

Figure 6.1.4 : Connectivity between KBS and DBMS
[based on diagram in reference SZUP89. † Reproduced by permission of System International]

KADBASE is a prototype product, described as a knowledge–aided DBMS prototype, which has been developed so that multiple KBS, multiple DBMS and multiple databases can communicate as independent components within a loosely coupled distributed engineering computer system [HOWA87, HOWA89]. Each KBS and DBMS is linked only to the interface, therefore new applications

---

[†] Bohdan Szuprowicz is director of Touche Ross Management Consultants' Knowledge–Based Systems Centre in New Jersey, US. Article first published in the UK in Systems International, July/August 1989.

and databases can easily be added to the integrating environment. KADBASE consolidates information contained in the global views of individual engineering databases into a single global schema based on a semantic database model. A request for data issued by a KBS is translated from the DML and data structure of the requesting component into a global syntax referencing the global schema. The interface processor identifies target databases containing information required to answer the query and generates subqueries to those databases. The appropriate DBMS are invoked to process the subqueries. Inverse mappings return results to the requesting components.

KADBASE is divided into three components, see figure 6.1.5:

- the Knowledge–Based System Interface formulates the queries and updates to be sent to the Network Data Access Manager (NDAM) and processes the subsequent replies;

- the Knowledge–Based Database Interface acts as an intelligent front–end for DBMS, accepting queries and updates from the NDAM and returning appropriate replies;

- the NDAM receives requests, locates sources of the referenced data and decomposes each request into a set of subqueries or updates to individual databases. The subrequests are processed by the database interfaces, the replies are combined by the network manager and returned to the system interface.

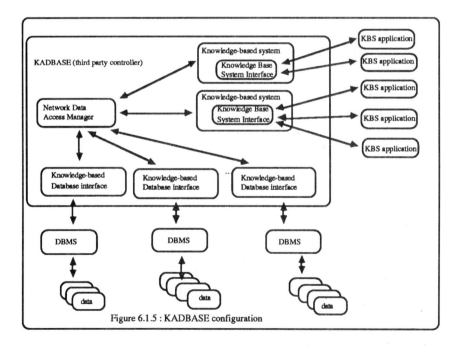

Figure 6.1.5 : KADBASE configuration

The KADBASE prototype has been tested in conjunction with two application systems: HICOST, a cost estimator for detailed building designs; and SPEX a structural component design system. HICOST accesses multiple databases

including a building design database, a project management database and a library
database of unit costs. Lisp was the principal programming language and the
sample databases were supported by the Ingres database management system.
Figure 6.1.6 shows the distributed environment for the two applications and four
databases.

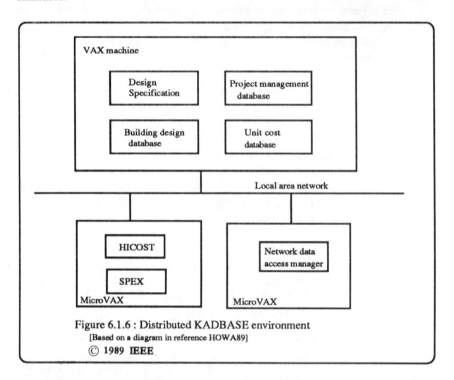

Figure 6.1.6 : Distributed KADBASE environment
[Based on a diagram in reference HOWA89]
© 1989 IEEE

An architecture which appears to be similar to that of KADBASE may be
adopted in Level5 Object. Database interface modules containing all the reading
and writing access capabilities for all the supported databases for the current
hardware platform will be delivered as a system component, in a separate library.
Level5 Object will have a consistent internal representation of an ideal database
into which all 'real world' databases are mapped.

Summary for methods of access

The key aim in linking KBS applications to databases is an open system
architecture. By using standard, tried and tested approaches, such as SQL, 4GL
or Cobol interfaces, or interfacing to extensible third party systems, KBS can be
embedded within, or added on, to existing systems which already use databases.
The trend of new KBS tools is moving towards integrated open systems and it is
likely that new releases of older products will begin to conform.

6.1.7 Specification of access

This sub–section describes the amount of effort which the coder of the knowledge–base has to put into defining the database access mechanism. As a rough guide, the effort required is directly proportional to the closeness of coupling. An article [POPO88] suggested that 'a number of factors must be analysed before deciding which vendor's method [of linking KBS and databases] is appropriate for a given application'. Two critical questions must be asked. 'How much original code do we want to write every time we need to embed a KBS?' and 'at what level of complexity do we want to write that code?'.

Explicit coding

In many cases the coder explicitly writes DML calls to the DBMS or to the intermediate sub–routine as part of the KBS application which is held in the knowledge–base. This may be standard SQL in the case of CA–DB:Expert or 'open database' and 'read' statements in Reveal. The interface between some tools is more complicated as illustrated by the details given for XiPlus and ICL–Adviser in annex D. In short, an ICL–Adviser application declares a function which must be executed to call a Cobol sub–routine; the latter accepts data, accesses the database and returns each individual field to the ICL–Adviser application as separate actions. XiPlus uses external files to hold the database query and to store the retrieved data temporarily. The knowledge–base holds the names of these files and mechanisms to cause data to be accessed.

The interfaces to XiPlus and ICL–Adviser probably appear complex, but they follow a standard pattern which can be copied from examples given in manuals or code provided by the vendor. Nevertheless, considerably more effort is required in coding such interfaces than when SQL statements can be used.

Implicit access

Implicit access can only be applied to reading data, and not updating except on completion of a transaction, since access is triggered by a requirement to process the data. The general idea is that the coder does not need to explicitly state 'go and read a record', but instead writes DML in association with fact declarations. When the inference engine attempts to instantiate a fact it causes the database to be accessed. This is one of the ways in which ESE can operate. When a parameter (fact) is defined, it can be specified that it should be retrieved from a particular column in a database table, under given conditions. Therefore when such a parameter is a goal or subgoal an SQL query is generated by the inference engine and the parameter evaluated. There may be a number of goals which can be evaluated at the same time, in which case the inference engine will attempt to produce a single SQL query if the conditions are compatible, or a series of SQL queries may be produced and executed in series. Complex SQL queries which involve joining tables may be produced. KBMS operates in a similar way, whereby objects are associated with tables and SQL is generated by the system to access the appropriate table.

KEE connection (see annex D) also provides implicit data retrieval. The developer of an application specifies how tables and columns are to be mapped on to classes and slots, using a sophisticated window interface. The system is flexible in that multiple tables can map on to a single class, one table can map on to multiple classes and data values can be transformed and computed on retrieval. KEE connection generates the SQL necessary for retrieval of data and controls network processing for accessing remote databases.

Implicit access complements declarative languages, where the user states what is required and not how to achieve it. The conditions under which data should be retrieved from the database (the equivalent of integrity constraints) are also associated with the facts and not the processing. A possible disadvantage of implicit data access is that the database may be accessed more frequently than is necessary and by non–optimal access methods. If trace information can be obtained about the generated queries while testing the application, then this can be investigated.

6.1.8 Existing combinations of KBS and DBMS

Annex C includes a matrix showing some of the combinations of compatible KBS tools and database management systems. The matrix is illustrative and not necessarily comprehensive, since vendors of KBS tools continually enhance their products to provide new interfaces. A collection of papers edited by Gray and Lucas [GRAY88(1)] describes at least five Prolog interfaces to relational databases.

Early releases of KBS tools could only access DBMS on the machines on which they ran; but there is an ever increasing number of exceptions these days. For example KEE running on an Explorer terminal can access a Mapper database running on a Unisys machine, via a network link. Also Inference ART running on a Symbolics machine can access Oracle on a DEC VAX and IBM mainframe DBMS via a communication link and software written for this purpose by Ferranti. This is the only way in which applications developed on specialised machines or terminals (Lisp machines for example) are likely to access existing databases (unless the applications are portable across machines) until communication software allowing electronic data interchange (EDI) becomes more widespread in use. Improvements in communications and a move towards open systems will facilitate the interworking of systems across machines beyond what is described here (see chapter 7).

A second dimension to communicating systems running on different hardware is added through distributed databases. Oracle, for example, offers reasonable location transparency for read access of data. Therefore, a KBS application able to communicate with a VAX machine for example, could request data believed to reside on the VAX, but which the DBMS actually retrieves from another machine, such as an IBM mainframe. Sybase offers similar facilities.

A third dimension to communicating systems is added by KBS tools which run on a number of hardware platforms and provide the software to link distributed KBS applications. For example, Top–One can run on an IBM personal computer (pc), IBM mainframes and ICL mainframes. An application running on a pc can communicate with another application running on a mainframe, and data can be passed between them. Therefore ICL IDMS data can be made available to a pc Top–One application. ADS provides the same functionality for linking pc applications to IBM mainframe DBMS such as DB2, and KEE connection includes a communications module which can access data from databases held on remote machines.

A number of tools which access databases on the same machine are:

- MVS/Prolog which accesses DB2 and VM/Prolog (superseded by IBM Prolog for 370 from January 90) accesses SQL/DS;

- Crystal accesses dBASE III;

- BIM Prolog accesses Ingres and SunUnify database on Sun workstations;

- Reveal, ICL–Adviser and Top–One access VME files and IDMS databases.

If a third generation language is used to interface KBS and DBMS, then there is potential for more flexibility. This is dependent upon portability and connectability of applications and conformance to OSI standards (see chapter 7). A lot of work is being done in this area and DBMS connectability may well be extended when standards in this area are implemented.

Those people who are interested in purchasing a KBS tool to access existing databases should look beyond those tools which run on the same hardware as the DBMS. However, users of IBM mainframes and DB2 or SQL/DS have a wide choice of software for that environment including CA–DB:Expert, ADS, KEE, Expert Systems Environment, Knowledgetool and KBMS, plus implementations of Prolog. Users of ICL mainframes and IDMS databases currently have the choice of ICL–Adviser, Reveal and Top–One, though KES, Egeria (June 90) and XiPlus are likely to become available in the near future. Unisys has chosen KEE and KES as their strategic products. DEC have developed OPS5 which may be able to access Rdb and other databases on VAX machines. KBS tools which have been integrated with 4GLs, such as Natural Expert (with Natural), Level5 Object (with Focus) and Today (4GL and KBS combined), can run on a number of different machines and access several DBMS.

Most KBS tools which run on IBM pcs, such as Crystal, Savoir and XiPlus, have interfaces to dBASE III. There are many more KBS tools which fall into this category which have not been included in this report. The largest range of KBS tools and DBMS are likely to be available on UNIX machines in the future. For example, DBMS available on Sun workstations include Oracle, Ingres, Sybase, Informix, Empress and SIR; KBS tools running on the same machines include many dialects of Prolog and Lisp, Knowledgecraft, OPS5, Inference ART, KEE and S1. Although all combinations of these tools are not available, potential is maximised by them running in a common environment.

Over the past two years a number of tools have been extended to provide an interface to databases and programming languages and there are likely to be more developments in this area. Newer products, such as KBMS from AI Corp and Level5 Object from Information Builders offered DBMS interfaces at the start; in fact one of the major marketing points made by AI Corp is that KBMS can be integrated with existing systems. In future, KBS tools are likely to have better interfaces which can be used for integration with a number of DBMS, especially when the tool runs on hardware such as DEC VAX machines and Sun workstations, where many proprietary DBMS are available.

6.1.9 Rules for integration

The following rules for integration have been drawn together from a number of sources including Peter Mossack of Software AG, Germany, HOWA89 and the information provided in this section. Potential purchasers of KBS software can use these rules for assessing competing products.

1 Environment

The KBS tool should be able to run within a conventional data processing environment, using existing hardware and software. That is, the user of the tool should not be expected to buy a totally new system to run the tool, although he might be expected to extend his configuration. For some people it will be essential that the KBS can run on a mainframe under a particular transaction processing monitor; others might need a KBS to run on a network of minis and personal computers.

2 Multi–user

A single user tool in a personal computer environment might suit the needs of a small group of users, but a strategically chosen KBS, for use throughout an organisation, must provide multi–user capabilities. This includes multi–tasking so that many people using the tool to build and execute knowledge–bases at the same time can use the same copy of the tool which is publicly loaded, the code being re–entrant. The knowledge–base of all applications should also be re–entrant (perhaps after compilation) so that only one copy of the code need be available to all concurrent users.

3 Comparable performance

The tool must provide performance levels which are comparable with those of existing development and run–time environments. This might be high speed in the case of an engine control system taking real–time information from measuring devices, or medium speed in the case of a system which maximises space utilisation in an airline booking system. Database access should not be allowed to slow down the system.

4 Clean interfaces

A clean interface should be provided to existing data processing languages, such as SQL, C, Cobol, PL/1 or whatever is normally used. Developers should not be expected to learn C if they normally use Cobol, for example. The interface should be 'clean', particularly where database access is concerned, to ensure that the DBMS maintains control over the data and the application can monitor the success or otherwise of database accesses.

5 Database update

Facilities to update a database, in addition to retrieval mechanisms, should be provided; that is, the ability to insert new records, amend existing records and delete existing records.

6 Transaction integrity

A system which allows users to concurrently update a database must provide for transaction integrity. It must be possible to specify the start and end of a transaction. At the end of a transaction the user of an application must have the choice of committing the changes to the database and invoking integrity checks, or rolling back to forget the data changes made in the transaction. The system must also use the data locking mechanisms provided by the DBMS to prevent concurrent users from updating logically associated records at the same time.

7 Non–ambiguity

Applications built using the KBS tool must be totally predictable: there should be no loss of data because of unspecified incompatibilities between data items and knowledge–base variables; the effect of values such as NULL and UNKNOWN should be documented; the database access mechanism should be fully specified with facilities to handle errors.

8 Minimal re–invention

The KBS tool should use those facilities which are already provided with the DBMS for database access, and the developer should not be expected to write large and complex data access modules. The KBS should use the DBMS access control facilities, data integrity checks and recovery procedures.

9 High level data mappings

The KBS tool should be able to handle data at the record or object level, rather than having to deal with individual data items. It should only be necessary to specify the mappings between database data items and KBS data items once for each application. Direct usage of external views provided by the DBMS is desirable.

10 Multiple DBMS

It may be desirable to be able to use: more than one database through a single
DBMS; more than one DBMS, such as both Ingres and Sybase; and more than
one type of data model (hierarchical, network and relational), through DBMS
such as IDMS and Oracle. Ideally these complexities should be hidden from the
KBS application developer, such that a data item can be requested in terms of the
KBS internal data model, without knowing where and how it will be found.

11 Multiple KBS

A DBMS interface should support independent KBS applications, possibly built
using different KBS tools, which share common data, and cooperating KBS
components that work together in problem solving tasks.

12 Heterogeneous KBS tools

Different KBS tools are suited to different types of tasks or problem domain. It
should be possible to pass data between cooperating applications which may
have been built using different KBS tools. This is covered in more detail in
section 6.6.

It is unlikely that any existing KBS tools can satisfy all twelve rules. Readers
are encouraged to assess the tools which they know against this yardstick.

Communications with third and fourth generation languages

6.2.1 Introduction

Accessing a database via a third generation language is briefly discussed in section 6.1 and is termed *indirect coupling*. Some advantages of taking this approach are also mentioned in section 6.1 for comparison with other types of coupling. This section is intended to look at some of the detail of linking knowledge–based system (KBS) applications with third and fourth generation languages and to expand on the use of such integration.

6.2.2 Architecture

Two fundamental architectures for integrating KBS and third and fourth generation languages are represented in figure 6.2.1.

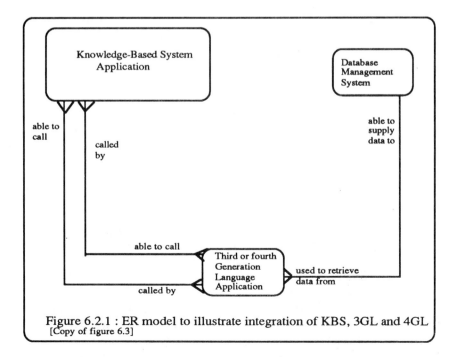

Figure 6.2.1 : ER model to illustrate integration of KBS, 3GL and 4GL
[Copy of figure 6.3]

In the first case, the application written in the third or fourth generation language is in control, and is able to call one or more KBS applications. This architecture is likely to be implemented when knowledge–based components are added to existing systems. Any data which is required by the KBS application can be passed as part of the calling mechanism. Some KBS tools cannot be used to build applications to be called in this way, since they can only be called directly from the operating system.

In the second case, a KBS application is in control, and can call one or more third or fourth generation language (3GL and 4GL) applications. This design is likely to be used when the 3GL or 4GL is used to perform functions best suited to languages or which cannot be coded in the KBS application.

A hybrid design might be used, such that there is no controlling or dominant application. In this case, the designer must ensure that all processing terminates correctly, particularly if a component expects control to be returned after calling another component, as would be the case with a Cobol module. Any component which opens a database must close it when processing is complete.

Since many KBS tools can interface with several 3GLs (see 6.2.4) there is no reason why a KBS application should not call Cobol modules, and Pascal modules, and C modules and so on. In fact, the most appropriate language should be used for the processing requirements. In many cases, however, a single language is likely to be used which will be Cobol for many government administrative applications.

When a 3GL or 4GL program is used for indirect coupling to a database, the program is effectively the 'glue' in a client/server architecture (see section 3.2): the KBS application is the client component with which the user interacts; the database management system (DBMS) is the server, providing data; and the 3GL or 4GL program is the link, in the same way that SQL links application generator code to relational DBMS.

6.2.3 Requirement

The prime requirement for linking KBS applications with third and fourth generation languages, as far as this book is concerned, is to facilitate access to databases. However, looking at integration in a broader context, such links can fulfil other requirements.

3GL and 4GL programs can provide facilities which KBS tools lack or functionality which is not best performed by KBS. Two examples are calculations or number manipulations and procedural processing. Third generation languages invariably, but not without exception, can perform these functions more easily than KBS tools.

The converse is also true: KBS can provide new facilities to a 3GL or 4GL environment. For example, it might be desirable to include a rule processing module in an existing batch or on–line system.

As mentioned in section 6.1, when a 3GL or 4GL component is used to access data, the data can be sorted, restructured, converted to suitable formats and generally manipulated before being passed to the calling KBS application. The 3GL or 4GL program need only pass the essential data in a format which can be handled by the KBS. Additionally, third generation languages are generally able to access a wider range of DBMS so they may provide the only possible link in a specific KBS and DBMS combination.

6.2.4 Use of fourth generation languages

There are no well known combinations of KBS and fourth generation languages at present, but the release of at least three combinations is expected in 1990: Software AG has developed Natural Expert to link with Natural; Information Builders are working on a new release of Level5 Object which will integrate with Focus; and Computer Power Europe Ltd are expected to release Today which is a fourth generation tool and KBS combined. All of the fourth generation tools mentioned here (Natural, Focus and Today) can access a number of DBMS. Perhaps some of the relational DBMS vendors, such as Ingres, Sybase and Oracle, will consider releasing KBS products to sit alongside their application generator software.

Natural Expert

Software AG has developed an integrated software architecture (see figure 5.1.1) which is based upon existing products such as the DBMS Adabas, the fourth generation language Natural, the data dictionary Predict and the CASE tool Predict–Case. Natural Expert is part of the architecture.

Gateway functions are provided in the syntax of Natural Expert to enable execution of Natural subprograms directly from a KBS model at run–time. When the types (Natural Expert is a strongly typed, functional language) of input and output data (text, range, integer, etc) have been specified the knowledge processing environment is capable of generating the data parameter which must be coded at the beginning of a Natural program. Thus, a framework for a Natural program is generated for the gateway and the developer needs to edit this framework to include the data access mechanism.

6.2.5 Use of third generation languages

Many KBS provide a general, indirect interface, in addition to specific, direct interfaces, to databases. For example, CA–DB:Expert can call Cobol sub–routines; BIM Prolog has an external language interface to C, Pascal, Fortran and Assembler; Quintus Prolog can call sub–routines written in C, Fortran or Pascal; a specific interface to C is provided for KEE; and an interface to Oracle from XiPlus has been developed by AEA Technology using Microsoft C. However, all of these KBS tools also have facilities for directly accessing DBMS.

Some KBS tools which appear to provide a direct interface to DBMS actually access data via 3GL components, but the parameter driven components are provided with the KBS software. Commonly, these components are written in C, perhaps because many KBS tools are written in C to make them highly portable.

For some KBS, indirect access to DBMS via a 3GL is the only mechanism provided. ICL–Adviser can call sub–routines written in Pascal, Cobol and Fortran, although only sub–routines written in Cobol and Fortran can directly access an IDMS database. Reveal has an internal database, but access to external data must be via a sub–routine or using serial files for data input and output.

The matrix in annex C includes many examples of KBS and third generation language combinations; this is by no means comprehensive. The most commonly used third generation languages are C, Cobol, Fortran and Pascal. A number of tools can communicate with Assembler and PL/1, though this is perhaps indicative of the large number of tools which run on IBM mainframes. Two KBS tools can use Basic, but they are inductive systems which can generate Basic code. Two tools, Nexpert Object and Reveal, can access Ada and Algol respectively. It is likely that more tools will communicate with Ada in the future, when there is an increased requirement for KBS applications to be embedded in operational or real–time systems.

6.2.6   Open systems interfaces

The term 'interoperability' has been coined by Open Systems pundits to cover two large domains. Firstly, Open Systems Interconnection (OSI) standards facilitate one form of interoperability by providing protocols that permit conformant software on *different* hardware to communicate. This is discussed in section 6.3. Secondly, the interworking of different software tools on the *same* hardware has been termed interoperability and this is of interest here. Unfortunately, this type of interoperability is less advanced in the standards world, although there are a number of initiatives which attempt to address this problem.

SQL1 (ISO 9075) has been established as a standard language for relational DBMS and offers a degree of interoperability between RDBMS products. However, in practice, the extent of the interworking is diminished because vendors provide product unique features, some of which are advanced features and variants on syntax in the SQL2 and SQL3 proposals. The SQL standard is unlikely to provide a suitable standard for the interoperability of KBS and third or fourth generation languages.

The Information Resource Dictionary System (IRDS) standard is intended to address the problems of interworking application development tools in the field of data management, which should include KBS and languages. However the ISO IRDS is unlikely to deliver standards until late 1990 or 1991.

The Portable Common Tools Environment (PCTE) standards work is developing a Portable Tools Interface which has a UNIX base. The theory is that any software developed on PCTE will have sufficient commonality to permit interworking or interoperability. There appears to be some potential conflict and overlap between the concepts employed in PCTE and ISO IRDS and therefore short term solutions are unlikely to emerge.

In short, there appear to be no open systems standards on which to base a generic interface to alleviate the problem of software developers producing specific, bilateral interfaces between products. And because KBS tool vendors are keen to include interfaces in their products now, in response to user demands, it is unlikely that they will all conform to a standard generic interface, if one is ever developed.

Annex D includes some descriptions of bilateral implementations of an interface between KBS tools and third generation languages for ICL–Adviser, Inference ART, Savoir and XiPlus. Some of the generic features for linking are described below.

Specification of 'call'

A mechanism for 'calling' third generation language programs is required. This might be an option for obtaining data, instead of deriving data by inference, directly calling a DBMS or requesting information from the user via the screen. Execution may be triggered by the need for a value (backward chaining), a possible method of evaluating more facts (forward chaining) or by an explicit instruction (watch–dog or demon).

The specification of the 'call' might be simple, such as 'CALL program–x WITH parameters–y', such that program–x is recognised as an external sub–routine and parameters–y are instances of data types within the KBS, the values of which will be passed to the called sub–routine. Alternatively, more sophisticated and complex interfaces might be required, so that separate sending and receiving data buffers could be specified, with an area for diagnostics, such as in Top–One.

Obviously the parameters to the 'call' statement must correspond with those specified in the third generation language module, so that data is not lost. This will be dependent upon the syntax of the language for specifying linkages to other sub–routines.

Parameters

The types and volume of data which can be passed will depend upon the types supported by the KBS tool and the 3GL; this is discussed in depth in section 6.1. In summary, integers, decimals and strings are likely to be supported by most tool combinations; the accuracy of some real numbers might be lost; if structured data types, such as arrays or matrices are supported, then larger volumes of data can be passed.

Without exception, it must be possible to pass data in both directions; that is, to the 3GL sub–routine from the KBS application (for example selection criteria and names of record types) and in reverse to return data and error or success codes.

Error checking

A mechanism for monitoring the status of the called sub–routine and the success or failure on termination are desirable. A continuous status monitoring system will give the KBS application an indication of how quickly the sub–routine is performing, and in turn, messages might be output to the screen to reassure the end user that the system is still working, if there is a poor response time. Some KBS tools allow inferencing to continue, while awaiting a reply from a called sub–routine (giving the impression of multi–processing).

Diagnostics should be returned to the KBS application to indicate whether the sub–routine has terminated successfully (these will need to be coded into the 3GL routine). The KBS application, like all conventional systems, should be capable of 'graceful' termination and restart, in the event of errors or problems.

Database update

If a database is being accessed in update mode via a third generation language, then the sub–routine must take care of committing data to the database or rolling back to undo changes which have been executed. If a consultation with the KBS application is aborted then the 3GL routine must be called to close down the database and generally leave the system in a tidy state, as would be the case if the routine had been called from within a transaction processing service.

6.3

Use of TP and operating systems

6.3.1 Introduction

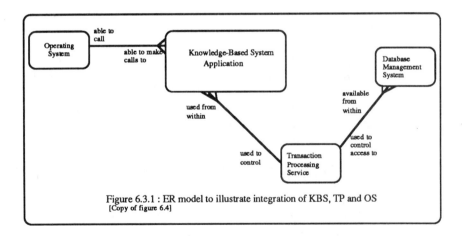

Figure 6.3.1 : ER model to illustrate integration of KBS, TP and OS
[Copy of figure 6.4]

Figure 6.3.1 illustrates the types of integration which are considered in this section. The main reasons for wanting to embed knowledge–based systems (KBS) into both transaction processing (TP) and operating system environments are to provide seamless connectivity, the ability to use services in an open system manner and to have a data interchange capability.

Firstly transaction processing: many on–line, mainframe computer systems have been built such that overall control resides with a TP monitor. If KBS components are to be embedded within these systems, then KBS must be capable of being called from within a TP service. Additionally, one of the fundamental reasons for using a TP monitor is to provide, for end users, a seamless interface to a number of services or systems. There is no reason why this architecture and software should not be used to provide a similar service to users, where the service consists of a number of multi–user, KBS applications.

Not only does a TP monitor control applications, but it will control access to databases used by those applications. Therefore, KBS applications which access such databases must be embedded in the TP service, or the database be used when the TP service is closed down.

Secondly, operating systems: it may be desirable to link applications, both KBS and conventional systems, without the use of a TP monitor. This might be because small machines such as microcomputers are being used and TP systems are either unavailable or too resource hungry; alternatively, systems on different machines need to be linked and a TP system might not provide the necessary functionality. Whatever the scenario, the operating system(s) should be able to provide the connectivity and data interchange capability. Additionally, the operating system can be used for a number of other reasons, if it can be called from a KBS, not least to create and allocate files.

The need for connectivity has been recognised by other people; for example the following quote is from reference POPO89:

> 'With the increasing acceptance of knowledge–based system technology as a valuable adjunct to corporate information processing, users and developers must confront the issues of integrating this technology into existing system, management and organisational structures. They also must assess the impact that this integration will, in turn, have on the technology itself. In particular, corporations are looking to embed the inference capabilities of today's expert system shells within mainframe transaction processing environments like CICS and IMS/DC... The ability to reside within, and invoke the resources of, a transaction processing environment, is overriding.'

The following quote from Bohdan Szuprowicz was printed in July 1989 [SZUP89][†] :

> 'What is most likely to happen during the next few years is a proliferation of expert system applications often originated by end user groups to support their specific business objectives. Sooner or later these expert systems will require permanent and seamless connectivity with a variety of databases operating on different platforms throughout the corporation. Networking is one of the obvious solutions already well underway in many instances but this will not be enough in itself to make strategic expert systems as effective as they should be.'

[†] Bohdan Szuprowicz is director of Touche Ross Management Consultants' Knowledge–Based Systems Centre in New Jersey, US. Article first published in the UK in Systems International, July/August 1989.

Many developers of knowledge–based system applications are aware of the need for connectivity and data interchange, not least because they are experiencing problems in integrating conventional applications. Some companies are avoiding the integration problem with KBS by, for example, making the decision to only use KBS tools which run on existing hardware and/or interface with software already in use within the company. Others commission tool vendors to develop software which will connect KBS tools to given software. The solutions to the problem of connectivity should be, and in the future are likely to be, provided by the software vendors.

6.3.2 Requirements for TP

If applications built using KBS tools are to be used within a transaction processing environment, then together they must exhibit some of the following features:

- a KBS tool can act as a server to a TP monitor, in the same way that a DBMS serves to control data;

- the KBS tool is capable of multi–tasking;

- the application code must be re–entrant, so that the same code can be accessed concurrently by more than one user in an efficient manner. That is, one copy of the application is loaded into memory and only the run–time data is stored for each user. This is essential for some highly tuned systems which run 24 hours per day, such as airline booking systems;

- performance (response time as far as the end user is concerned) should be as good as that of conventionally built software, with which the KBS application is integrated. This might mean that the knowledge–base should be compiled into object code to improve central processing unit (CPU) speed and to reduce the memory requirement;

- provision of enhanced scheduling requirements, so that TP monitors re–schedule on waiting for input and output from terminals. It may be necessary to time–slice to ensure that KBS do not monopolise the system resources;

- the TP system should take care of storing intermediate results for the KBS for multi–phase transactions, just as it does for existing applications in a TP service. It may be desirable to minimise the size of the data set which has to be stored;

- the TP system should control the display of screens and return of results input through the screen to the application.

Potential purchasers of KBS tools for use in a TP environment should press vendors for details on the above topics in order that the suitability of products can be assessed, and the adequacy of facilities compared. Many KBS vendors are enhancing their products to address these requirements and up–to–date information should be sought.

6.3.3 KBS and TP links

A number of mainframe KBS tools, particularly those which run on IBM mainframes, can operate in a TP environment (see annex C for examples). Two products have been chosen to illustrate this section, Top–One and ADS; this choice does not imply that these products are better than, or representative of, other tools; readers must judge this for themselves.

Top–One

Top–One on the mainframe (both ICL and IBM) is a multi–user system which provides two methods of development: Flex, which has English–like rule syntax and is object oriented; and Prolog. The system may be integrated with TP systems such as IBM CICS and IMS, and ICL TPS, Quickbuild and TPMS.

The mainframe implementation is multi–user in that it is a fully re–entrant, multi–threading program, allowing and processing multiple, concurrent consultations, on the same knowledge–base, with full capability for each consultation to run in a safe and controlled way. In an on–line TP environment, the system is both resilient and recoverable; in the event of a complete system failure or the failure of a single thread, all affected consultations are rolled back to the start of consultation or end of last successful message pair, whichever is more recent, by the 'warm start' or message abort processing (this includes the co–ordination of recovery of database, conventional file and knowledge–base updates). There is also a 'retry after rollback' option.

Top–One is well suited to delivery of applications where:

- the delivery hardware is mainframe or mainframe/workstation network;

- data is accessed from the knowledge–base or from databases in real–time;

- there are many potential users and high transaction volumes;

- knowledge–based systems may be embedded behind 'ordinary' transactions;

- intelligent front– and back–ends may be developed for databases.

ADS

The Aion Development System (ADS) offers support for building, integrating and delivering large–scale production KBS applications on IBM mainframe and personal computers. ADS can be used to build knowledge–based systems for integration into existing systems.

Applications can run in a wide range of IBM operating environments including MVS/TSO, MVS/CICS, MVS/IMS and VM/CMS. File management and screen interaction control is handled by transaction processors, allowing ADS applications to function as 'proper' CICS and IMS programs. Applications are fully re–entrant for multi–tasking support.

Figure 6.3.2 illustrates the architecture of an MVS/CICS configuration. The Aion region contains the multi–tasking monitor, which controls multiple concurrent sessions of knowledge–base development and execution. All knowledge–base processing occurs in the Aion region to minimise impact in the CICS region. The Aion transaction is a CICS pseudo–conversational transaction that runs under the control of CICS.

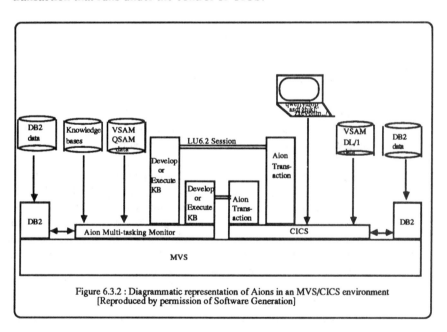

Figure 6.3.2 : Diagrammatic representation of Aions in an MVS/CICS environment
[Reproduced by permission of Software Generation]

The Aion region and the CICS region communicate using VTAM LU6.2 services. When the Aion transaction is invoked, it allocates a VTAM session and exchanges information with the Aion multi–tasking monitor. All screen interaction is handled by CICS through the requests generated by the Aion transaction.

DB2, VSAM and DL/1 data that exist under the control of CICS are accessed through requests generated by the Aion transaction, so data integrity remains under the control of CICS. Data that exists outside of CICS can be accessed directly from the Aion address space.

The high performance of ADS applications is achieved by use of:

- VTAM services which allow placement of knowledge–base processing on a separate machine for installation–wide load balancing;

- a High Performance Option (HPO) which allows compilation of performance critical applications into object code (through Pascal source code) and thereby optimises processing speed. It is claimed that record input and output is two to three times faster. The multi–tasking monitor controls execution of compiled and standard knowledge–bases;

- a re–entrant execution system which reduces memory requirements under the multi–tasking region. It is suggested that memory requirements for both object data structures and application data storage, when compiled using HPO, are two to four times smaller than with the standard Aion Execution System. Since the load modules are re–entrant, they can also be shared between multiple concurrent users, reducing the amount of memory required.

6.3.4 Requirements for operating system access

If a KBS application is required to access a database for which an interface is not provided, or if the KBS and the database reside on different hardware platforms, then perhaps the only method of communication is via the operating system(s).

It is not uncommon for a KBS application to be delivered on a different machine to that which supports corporate databases. Many KBS applications run on microcomputers or high performance machines such as Symbolics workstations. Some vendors of KBS tools have developed software to allow such machines to communicate with mainframes, which invariably depends upon operating system functions. Some examples are given in 6.3.5 below. Such links increase the number and types of database which can be accessed from a KBS application.

The use of distributed databases should not be forgotten within this context. Some proprietary distributed database management systems (DBMS), such as Oracle, can provide invisible, cross machine links to data controlled by that DBMS within a single schema. For example, if a database can be distributed across IBM personal computers, IBM mainframes and UNIX workstations, and the data can be controlled by a DBMS which resides on all of these hardware platforms, then theoretically KBS applications on any one of the hardware platforms should be able to access the data on all of the hardware platforms. Some DBMS also provide gateways to other DBMS controlled data. For example, the Open Server of Sybase allows access to other DBMS such as Oracle and Ingres.

Some early releases of microcomputer KBS tools could access ASCII format, serial files, but not databases. Therefore, it was possible to run a data extraction program to produce an ASCII file. This program could be run before the KBS consultation started, or if the operating system could be called dynamically, the program could be run when necessary.

More sophisticated communications can be developed, depending upon the operating system. For example, if an event system is provided by the operating system for developers' use, then it can be used to trigger and halt processing in co–operating KBS and conventional applications. It may also be possible to pass data, such as strings, without using intermediate files.

Calls to the operating system can be used for other purposes, in addition to data retrieval, for example:

- triggering other processes, such as running of programs, production of reports, office automation facilities including preparation of word processor text and diary interrogation, etc;

- alerting operators to bring on–line special hardware or to warn them that a special job is about to begin;

- assigning, creating and deleting files;

- sorting data files;

- starting a shared database service;

- listing directories and libraries;

- producing graphic displays;

- obtaining the current date and time from the machine clock.

6.3.5 Existing links

The number of tools which can communicate directly with the operating system rapidly increased in the late 1980s and more development in this area is expected in the future. The following examples are intended to illustrate what can be done.

ADS

Aion Development System (ADS) on microcomputers includes the Cooperative Processing Option (CPO) to provide access from Aion applications on a micro to data residing on IBM mainframes. VSAM, DB2 and DL/1 databases under CICS control can be accessed.

Ferranti Inference ART connections

Ferranti have, in the past, provided a link to enable Inference ART running on a Symbolics workstation to be connected to an IBM mainframe in order to access a resident database. Ferranti have also written specific interface software for customers requiring access to an Oracle database.

KEE connection

KEE connection is marketed by Intellicorp to build bridges between KEE applications and SQL relational databases. A data communications module performs all network processing required to access remote databases. In a typical operation, KEE connection sends an SQL request through the network; the communications software on the remote machine receives the request and passes it to the DBMS. The reply takes the reverse path. The communications module can detect crashes and unavailability of the DBMS. Faulty connections are also reopened automatically.

Level5 Object

The architecture of Level5 Object has been designed to isolate major areas of functionality into libraries and modules. The control layer handles the dispatch of event processing to appropriate modules. The application layer consists of the inference engine and developers' tools. The utilities layer provides a number of services which are system dependent. Included in this utilities layer are: system service utilities which access functions such as time and date, sorts, hashing and program activation; file management utilities for file reads, writes, opens, closes, deletes and file locking; and window management utilities that control all the interfaces to the user via the keyboard, mouse, displays and printers.

Level5 Object will support the Dynamic Data Exchange (DDE) format for intertask communications and data exchange. This will enable Level5 Object models to be embedded into other programs and for process monitoring and control applications.

Quintec Prolog

A general interface to the host operating system (UNIX, VMS, ULTRIX or OS/2) is provided. A command string may be issued to the operating system from Prolog or the environment shell for immediate execution. This allows access to all operating system functions including deleting, creating and renaming of files, listing of directories and invoking sub–processes.

Top–One

Top–One systems can connect to more or less anything indirectly, by writing interface code and utilising whatever communication facilities are available, such as IBM LU6.2, ICL IPA and communications boards. Telecomputing report that new, direct connections (that is direct from the knowledge–base source statements) are continually being incorporated into the product in response to user requests.

Top–One applications which run on micros can access databases held on remote mainframes without the developer writing the communication routines. Top–One/Connect will simulate the logon to a TP system, provide the necessary passwords, request the use of an application which can retrieve the required data and return the data to the micro–based application. The communication between machines is invisible as far as the user of the application is concerned.

Unisys KS/A

Unisys market a software link (KS/A) enabling KEE and Lisp applications running on an Explorer workstation to access databases such as Adabas and DB2 which are resident on an IBM mainframe, via Answer/DB software on the mainframe. The operating system on the mainframe may be MVS or DOS/VSE, and both IMS/DC and CICS environments are accessible. This link is described more fully in annex D.

6.3.6   Future

Szoprowicz [SZOP89] suggests that the answer to the connectivity problem probably lies in the development of intelligent database networks (IDBNs) that will provide seamless connectivity between knowledge–based systems and any database operating anywhere within the corporate structure (see figure 6.1.4 in section 6.1).   The open systems database standards, SQL in particular, have made a significant move in this direction. Intelligent interfaces will, however, not only connect knowledge–based systems with databases, but will also suggest and provide alternative access to real–time information and outside value added networks (VANs) if specific knowledge is not available within the corporate database structures.

6.4

Use of spreadsheets

6.4.1 Introduction

Section 6.1 is concerned with knowledge–based system (KBS) applications accessing large databases, which are managed by, in the main, sophisticated database management systems (DBMS) as part of large administrative systems. This section is concerned with accessing small 'databases' (where the term is used more loosely to mean a collection of data) managed by spreadsheet software, which may be part of a management information system (MIS) or a decision support system (DSS). See figure 6.4.1. Generally speaking, spreadsheet databases are created and used by individuals rather than groups of people.

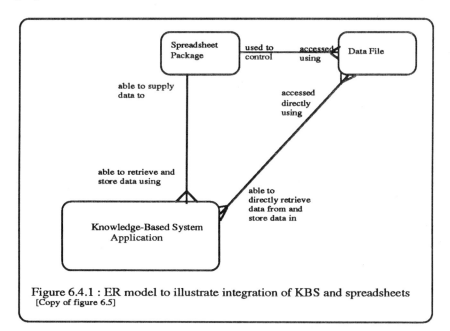

Figure 6.4.1 : ER model to illustrate integration of KBS and spreadsheets
[Copy of figure 6.5]

6.4.2   Usage

Four requirements for accessing large databases from KBS are outlined in section 6.1:

- to read existing data, which has been captured by another system;

- to save data captured by a KBS application, for use by other systems;

- to update existing data, which has been captured by another system;

- to save data captured by a KBS application, for use in further consultations.

These requirements also apply to data managed by spreadsheet software. Illustrating point two, data may be captured or created through inferencing in a KBS application, which is stored in a spreadsheet database, possibly combined with other data, for future use. In particular, the user might want to investigate a number of 'what–if' queries when some spreadsheet cell values are changed.

Illustrating point three, it may be possible to invoke a KBS application from a spreadsheet cell formula, such that the value of that cell is derived by KBS inferencing using values in other cells. In this scenario, the KBS tool would need to be tightly integrated with, or be part of, the spreadsheet software.

KBS can be used to combine large databases and spreadsheets as part of a decision support system, effectively acting as the link in a client (spreadsheet)/server (DBMS) architecture. Lucas, University of Aberdeen, has produced a prototype whereby a spreadsheet is used to provide a flexible user interface to a DBMS. The end user can specify column names, formulae which include column names and values within cells; a Prolog link produces SQL for retrieving the appropriate data from a database (via a DBMS such as Oracle) and returns values to the spreadsheet. The displayed values can be manipulated through the spreadsheet and any new values which are generated may be stored in the database.

The combination of knowledge–based systems, spreadsheets and DBMS could facilitate better usage of corporate data. Many managers can use spreadsheets, but they do not have time to learn SQL or other means of accessing large databases. Using a combination of tools they could manipulate data using familiar tools, perhaps having access to more than one database, where each database could possibly be managed by different proprietary DBMS.

6.4.3 Linking KBS tools and spreadsheets

The types of data held in a spreadsheet database are the usual types of text, number, date, etc, and these are generally compatible with those provided by most KBS tools. It might be useful if a new data type of 'rule' could be made available in spreadsheet software, such that formulae could be made up of rules. Very simple 'knowledge' or rules–of–thumb could then be built into spreadsheet software without the need for integration with more elaborate KBS tools.

The ability to handle arrays in KBS is desirable, so that extracts of large spreadsheets can be retrieved and manipulated. It is important that the mechanisms for specifying columns and rows are well described in tool documentation, so that there is no confusion between them.

The problems of shared and concurrent access are not relevant to spreadsheet databases, unlike large databases, since a spreadsheet database will only be used by one person at any time. The choice of loose or tight coupling between the spreadsheet software and the KBS is likely to be dependent upon the type of application: it might be desirable to pre–load small databases into KBS applications so that all the data is in memory for quick access; alternatively, selective, dynamic access to spreadsheet data files might be preferred if the database is large and only a limited number of cell values is required. If a workstation allows multi–tasking, such that a user could switch between running a KBS application and using the spreadsheet directly, then all of the data should ideally be loaded into main memory.

The method of access should always be direct (as defined in section 6.1) in order to make the interface simple and efficient; that is, the code which causes the spreadsheet database to be accessed should be included in the KBS application.

Functionality

The interface between Crystal and Lotus–123 is briefly described in annex D as an example of interfacing a KBS tool and a spreadsheet. The interface functions provided by Crystal are comprehensive: not only can existing files be opened (and loaded) and closed (after data has been saved), but new files can be created and defined. This would be useful where a KBS application supports the user in a first attempt at creating a spreadsheet; for example, a project planning application might propose a number of criteria to be considered and costed. Alternatively, a database might be created on a user's first consultation with a KBS, saving data for future consultations by that user. Individual cells and ranges (sub–arrays) can be read into and written from Crystal applications, as dates, text or numerics.

6.4.4   Tools

Most micro–based KBS tools can access spreadsheets, including Crystal, XiPlus and Leonardo. Some tools which run on a wide range of hardware, including personal computers, can also access spreadsheets, such as ADS, KES, Top–One, Guru and Nexpert Object. Annex C identifies a number of other tools which can access Lotus–123 spreadsheet databases. The interfacing software is often a separately purchased package since the market for these tools is very competitive and low prices are maintained.

It is likely that many KBS tool vendors developed interfaces to spreadsheets as a first move towards integration. Having solved some of the basic problems of interfacing, they went on to develop interfaces to small database management systems such as dBASE III and then more sophisticated products such as DB2, Oracle and Ingres.

The following information is by no means comprehensive, but will give the reader a flavour of some of the features included in a number of KBS products.

Guru

Spreadsheet processing is an integral component of Guru and the inference engine always has access to the value of all cells in the currently loaded spreadsheet. A 'lookup' command can be associated with a description of a variable in Guru, specifying the cell coordinates of values to be retrieved. Spreadsheet cells can also be referred to in rule premises and conclusions so that data can be accessed and updated.

Guru allows the user to define a cell of a spreadsheet as a KBS consultation; when the user re–evaluates the spreadsheet, the value of that cell is determined by the result of a Guru consultation.

KES

A KES application has been used by a German management consultancy to collect and analyse customer information, reducing the amount of time consultants spend with clients. The requirement for the system specified, among other things, a spreadsheet for gathering and analysing numeric data; an on–line database to store supply industry independent information; and an expert system to analyse spreadsheet and database data, asking the user for further relevant details and producing advice on how to increase turnover. Early prototypes used Lotus–123 but Excel was used in the final system. Clipper programs were used to retrieve data from dBASE files.

Lotus HAL

Lotus has produced an English language add–on package (a KBS application) to Lotus–123 called Lotus HAL. It is intended to increase productivity by making complex commands easier to formulate. It has a customisable vocabulary of 2000 words that allows users to specify command words instead of cell addresses. The interface works with database querying features and allows search–and–replace anywhere in a worksheet.

Nexpert Object

Nexpert Object on IBM micros can access two data formats commonly used by spreadsheet programs. The SYLK format is used by Excel, for example, and spreadsheet files can be interpreted as data files by Nexpert; tables of rows and columns represent objects and properties (SYLKDB type), or individual cells may be named after Nexpert variables (SYLK type). The WKS format is used by Lotus–123 for example, using the same mappings as for SYLK but using WK1 type and WKS type respectively.

Parys

Parys is described in advertising literature as an expert system application environment, designed for human resource managers, as a set of tools for customising applications, such as job design and vacancy management to organisational needs. Parys software can be integrated with word processing systems, spreadsheets and personnel records systems.

6.5

Use of hypertext

6.5.1 Introduction

This section is concerned with using a combination of knowledge–based and hypertext systems. A hypertext system can be considered to consist of: a programming capability; some small scale data storage and management; and a presentation vehicle. In theory, it should be possible to substitute a knowledge–based system (KBS) tool for the programming capability, perhaps with some added features, and a proprietary database management system (DBMS) for data storage and management. The presentation vehicle from a hypertext system would continue to be used. In practice, there are no tools at present which allow this. Therefore, the only type of integration of hypertext and KBS considered here is concerned with interfacing both types of application; see figure 6.5.1.

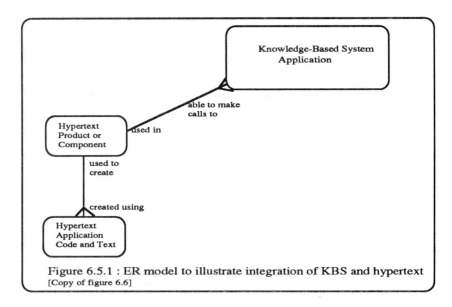

Figure 6.5.1 : ER model to illustrate integration of KBS and hypertext
[Copy of figure 6.6]

6.5.2 Usage

Morrison suggests that hypertext systems can be used as an alternative, rather than in addition, to KBS tools for some applications, when the need for a flexible presentation of information outweighs the requirement for automated inference capabilities [MORR89]. If it is desirable to make implementation of a system as simple as possible by only using one tool, then a choice of hypermedia or KBS may be necessary. However, now that technology has advanced (latter half of 1989 onwards) such that both types of tool can be integrated, the best of both types of tool can be exploited. Brian Robins, manager of Neuron Data Europe, was quoted in JONE89(2) as saying 'You need expert systems technology to use hypermedia meaningfully'.

User interface

A hypertext system could be used to enhance the presentation of information and increase the flexibility of what information can be accessed. A hypertext system may be used to develop the entire user interface, possibly incorporating all the help and explanation information. A hypermedia system, which incorporates images and sound, can provide facilities which are not available in most KBS tools at present.

Hypertext systems offer flexibility in that a variable amount of information can be supplied, in accordance with an end user's response. Typically, a KBS tool will allow one or two levels of explanation for an outcome or request for input data. A hypertext system can cater for users with different levels of experience, providing low level explanations for novices, but only on request.

A hypertext user interface might also be desirable if the KBS application is an add–on to an existing hypertext system, so that the user interface remains consistent across the entire system.

Access to knowledge

More flexible access to knowledge (facts, rules, etc) stored in a knowledge–base of a KBS application might be provided if a hypertext application could use the knowledge–base as the data source. For example, hypertext could:

- provide a *variety of structured access paths* to the knowledge;

- allow the end user to *control access paths* when viewing parts of the knowledge–base, particularly explanatory text. That is, the line of enquiry might be different, depending upon the experience of the end user;

- make a system amenable to users of differing levels of experience, by providing a *flexible number of levels* of help and explanation.

In many KBS applications, the user's access to knowledge is restricted to those parts which the KBS developer provides as advice and explanation; and in many cases, this is sufficient. However, when an expert is allowed to update the knowledge, or is required to maintain the body of knowledge, then better browsing facilities are required. Ideally, KBS tools could include hypertext facilities for the knowledge engineer to use when developing applications; for example, indexes and routes could be automatically built to provide debugging facilities, such as a display of all rules which use a given fact and a context sensitive editor.

Control

KBS do not, in general, give the user full control over an application. That is, the system leads the consultation, asking the end user questions and inferencing in accordance with the answers given. Hypertext systems which focus on displaying information work differently; that is, user responses, rather than designers of the system, control paths taken allowing users to traverse complex networks built on top of the data source. A combination of the two technologies may bring implementors closer to better user communication by allowing a balance of end user and system control.

6.5.3 Applications

A number of concept demonstrators and some real systems have been produced to show that there is a requirement for integrating KBS and hypertext tools.

A feasibility study was carried out by Logica on behalf of CCTA for a Computer Based Method Exposition Tool (COMET project) to facilitate the development of methods. A HyperCard (Apple Macintosh hypertext product described in section 3.7) demonstration was built to show how to capture and structure elements of a method model and to link this to the text of the method. A separate demonstrator was built using KEE to show the potential for hypothetical reasoning in such a system. These two demonstrations were not linked, not least because the HyperCard and KEE prototypes ran on different hardware, but here is an obvious requirement for integrating these types of tools if a real system was to be built.

A system is being developed in Leicester [AHME89] which integrates 'techniques from AI and relational database management, as well as the concept of hypertext'. A palliation (relief of symptoms of illness, without attempting to cure the underlying disease process) support system will allow enquiries by clinicians on symptoms and therapies, to assist in making complex treatment decisions, as an educational and patient management tool. A relational database holds core information on symptoms and their causes, drugs and non–drug treatment, interactions, etc. Hypertext is being used to incorporate intelligently–linked text screens to increase the value of the system as an educational tool. The system is being developed on a microcomputer so that it can be delivered as an active decision support tool for use by doctors and nurses.

Glowinski and others [GLOW89] have developed a generic framework in an attempt to meet the growing needs for sophisticated information systems in primary care; it shows the versatility required to provide varying levels of information retrieval, data management and decision support facilities required by medical practitioners. A prototype implementation incorporates a version of this framework. Facts may be considered to embody a network, the object and value fields corresponding to nodes and the attributes to links, as may be found in some hypertext systems. However, in this prototype the facts can also be used in inferencing to make decisions.

Robins [JONE89(2)] reported on some other applications: a handbook for running a factory has been developed using Nexpert Object and HyperCard; and retail and aerospace developments are also taking place.

6.5.4 Products and interfaces

In early 1989 it would have been difficult to suggest any combinations of hypertext and KBS tools. The situation is moving rapidly and integrated technology in this area is very likely to improve over the next few years.

Concordia and Genera

Symbolics provides a hypermedia–type interface development environment called Concordia as an extension to its KBS software environment Genera. An on–line maintenance manual for a rolling mill has been developed in the United States [JONE89(2)]. The system comprises about 30 000 pages of documentation with text and graphics, including engineering drawings.

Symbolics offers a board for Macintosh machines, providing them with the Genera environment which includes support for Concordia.

HyperCard

External commands and functions are extensions of the HyperTalk built–in command and function set. External commands and functions are executable Macintosh code resources, written in a Macintosh programming language which are attached to a HyperCard application or a stack with a resource editor. They are called from HyperTalk in more or less the same way as user defined message and function handlers are called. These links could potentially provide access to KBS, perhaps via a language such as C or Pascal.

KnowledgePro

KnowledgePro from Intellisoft Ltd combines hypertext and KBS technologies in a high level language which uses 'topics'. A topic is a 'chunk of knowledge' containing rules, calculations, commands, text or graphics.

Williamson describes some features of KnowledgePro [WILL88] and suggests that the user interface is consistent and well thought out. Function keys play a major role and can be activated through the keyboard or a mouse. A source file can be created using any text editor; and explanatory hypertext paragraphs can be embedded where required.

MacProlog and HyperCard

MacProlog, marketed by Logic Programming Associates, integrates Prolog with the Macintosh philosophy of mice, menus and icons, in a multi–window management system. There are primitives (clauses) which generate dialogues, install user defined menus, track the mouse or draw and manipulate complex graphical objects. These can be used to produce hypertext–like facilities. MacProlog also has access to resources ('files' created by other Macintosh packages), therefore HyperCard applications can be executed from within a MacProlog application. There are also C and Pascal interfaces which could potentially link to separate hypertext systems.

Natural Expert

Natural Expert from Software AG features an integrated hypertext based knowledge acquisition tool, which stores textual information items and the relationships between these in the Adabas Entire database. A direct link to any part of the knowledge–base is provided, which may be exploited during development of an application as an advanced mechanism for comments, or for structuring the informal knowledge of a domain expert, as well as during inferencing, since the hypertext information may be retrieved from the database via a gateway program. This possibility has already been used to provide a user–coded explanation component, and could potentially be applied to dynamically create or update hypertextual information.

Nexpert Object and HyperCard; AI Vision

A bridge has been built between Nexpert Object and HyperCard to allow Nexpert Object to access information stored in HyperCard stacks and to use HyperCard as the front end to a KBS application. Non–linear and dynamic links are allowed between cards in the stacks when those links are generated with Nexpert Object rules.

Neuron Data is adding a hypermedia type front end to Nexpert Object. AI Vision adds graphical interfaces (images in the form of windows or pictorial figures) to Nexpert Object applications and has been described as 'HyperCard–like', its object oriented script language being similar to HyperTalk. AI Vision can trap questions during inferencing and replace them with graphical displays. The user can then return answers by clicking on predefined buttons.

6.5.5 Problems

Glowinski spoke at the Fifth International Expert Systems Conference in 1989 [GLOW89], about integrating KBS and hypertext. He perceives that the current generation of hypermedia systems suffers from a number of faults that will prevent large or complex applications being built or used. For example:

- there is no explicit model of what information is held nor an explanation of how it may be used;

- the way in which information is to be used is fixed by the author;

- it is not possible to express a context for a query, to be able to retrieve different types of information in different circumstances other than by explicitly creating a new node for each combination of circumstances. That is, the hypertext system cannot interpret dynamic control information. He gives the example that in medicine, treatments differ in the context of the patient's age. Morrison suggests that users can add their own links to cards in a stack by creating extra buttons.

It is possible to create large, complex networks of interconnected information and it will be difficult to test that all the required connections and no unnecessary connections have been made. Maintenance of such networks may be difficult and users may experience difficulty in using them. Discipline is required in the design and creation of hypertext systems.

Hypertext systems have the capability to increase the flexibility of user interfaces beyond the existing capabilities of the average KBS tool. Unless and until end users can learn to use KBS development tools, they will have to work within the constraints of pre–built networks. Alternatively, end users will need to learn how to build their own networks, based upon the types of information they need.

6.6

KBS to KBS communication

6.6.1 Introduction

Earlier sections in this chapter have been concerned with interfacing different software types with knowledge–based systems (KBS); that is, KBS and database management systems (DBMS), KBS and 4GL, etc. This section discusses how KBS applications can interface with other KBS applications.

There are two possibilities: the two KBS applications may have been built using:

- the same KBS tool, in which case they can be considered to be modules of an application; or

- different KBS tools, which is the equivalent of interfacing Fortran and Cobol programs, or Oracle and Natural processes.

There are also two ways of looking at the relationship in both of the above scenarios:

- a KBS application *may call* another KBS application;

- a KBS application *may be called by* another KBS application.

These are the inverse relationships shown in figure 6.6.1. Some KBS applications may only be able to call, or be called; others can deal with both.

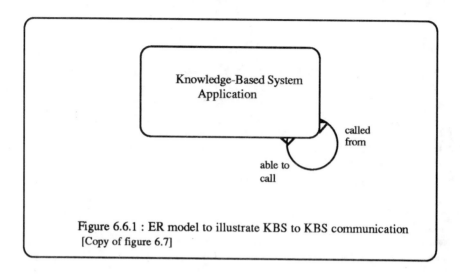

Figure 6.6.1 : ER model to illustrate KBS to KBS communication
[Copy of figure 6.7]

6.6.2 Reasons for requirement

Modularisation

There are a number of reasons for wanting to modularise KBS applications:

- large knowledge–bases can become unwieldy, and difficult to document, understand and maintain. It is desirable that each module should have a particular goal or intent, with some modules providing control and forming the glue between the functional modules;

- a problem (requirement) can be broken down into manageable chunks so that more than one person can implement the system. It is very difficult for more than one person to work on the same knowledge–base (file);

- parts of a KBS system may need to be run on different hardware platforms. For example, there may be a requirement for some local working on a workstation, linked to central processing on a mainframe;

- there might be a requirement to share code or parts of knowledge–bases, just as common routines are written for Cobol applications. The common processing should be separated out from applications rather than duplicated across applications;

- the performance of a KBS application may be degraded as the size of the knowledge–base increases, since more rules, facts, etc, will need to be searched.

Communication

There are also a number of reasons for wanting KBS applications, built using different tools, to communicate:

- in order to integrate historically, disparate system development. When developers are allowed to choose the most appropriate tools for developing different systems, invariably a number of tool will be used within an organisation. Then, at some time in the future, it might be decided that the systems should use common information or have a common interface. It is preferable to be able to link existing systems rather than rewrite them;

- some KBS tools are directed at particular types of application or have strengths in different areas; for example, one tool might have rich knowledge representation features, while another provides better user interface building functions. Therefore, implementors might choose to use more than one tool to build a large system. Ideally, developers should be able to mix and match applications regardless of the development tools used;

- if local and centralised working is required (cooperative processing), but the same KBS tool does not run on all the hardware platforms required, it may be necessary to build different parts of a system using different tools. There are many tools available on UNIX workstations and IBM personal computers for example, but the same tools might not run on mainframes. Although many KBS tools are written in C and are portable across a number of platforms, they may not run on all components of existing architectures used by departments.

6.6.3 Distributed knowledge–bases

There are very few documented cases of the development of large knowledge–bases, where the size is concomitant to that of may government conventional administrative systems. This comes as no surprise, since many organisations are still experimenting with KBS. However, in the future, when the use of KBS becomes more commonplace, there will be a requirement to build and control large knowledge–bases. Feigenbaum mentions the idea of a giant 'encyclopaedia of knowledge' for use in the next generation of KBS [FEIG88]. The Japanese Fifth Generation project has spun off a company to create a large knowledge–base for use in tasks of language understanding and translation.

It is not too difficult to extrapolate such developments to government. Large scale development could provide:

- public information, such as advice about which benefits are available from the department of social security, or interpretation of tax laws and regulations so that individuals understand what they are required to pay;

- public information on a limited basis, perhaps through subscription, so that some advice can be made available which is now provided by lawyers or medical practitioners, for example;

- limited scope information. For example organisation–wide information, such as civil service pay and regulations, could be made more widely available and accessible within the organisation through the use of KBS.

These large KBS are not going to be built tomorrow, or even in the next two years. However, with the increased uptake of computing, and extrapolations that suggest most homes will possess a computer in the next century, then government departments should be considering how they will deliver their services using this technology, as part of their strategic planning process. It is not a fantasy that large knowledge–bases will be required: rather, it is a question of when they will be economically possible and if they will be socially acceptable.

6.6.4 Tools

A number of tools offer the facility of modularisation. The response to the need for open KBS systems (different KBS to KBS communication) is expected to be slow while vendors continue to protect their own markets. DBMS vendors have been slow to produce fourth generation tools which allow cross linking of DBMS and are perhaps only doing so, in response to pressure from users of the tools. There is no reason to assume that the KBS market will be different.

Some of the KBS to KBS communication facilities provided by a few example tools are given below to illustrate what can be achieved.

Aion Development System (ADS)

ADS allows 'states' to be developed, where a state is a relatively self–contained part of a knowledge–base. The main or root state is at the top of a hierarchy and leaf states occur on branches. A branch includes all of the states between the main state and a leaf state. The 'scope' controls which states the inference engine can use to determine values for parameters. The scope of the inference engine is limited to the current state and those above it in the branch.

ADS provides a Cooperative Processing Option (see annex D) which allows an ADS application on a personal computer to communicate with another ADS application on an IBM mainframe. Local and central processing can therefore be provided using a single tool.

CA–DB:Expert

A CA–DB:Expert knowledge–based system can be called by an external program or any tool which supports calls to external routines. Knowledge–bases may be constructed to participate in cooperative processing applications. Knowledge–bases can also be chained together, so that an application can be modularised.

Level5 Object

The architecture of Level5 Object has been designed to isolate major areas of functionality into libraries of modules. A control layer contains the root of the program as a shell, which is the main event processor. It handles the dispatch of event processing to appropriate modules.

Since it is assumed that knowledge–based applications will be modular, a project control facility is provided in RuleTalk, the interactive knowledge–base editor. A project tree may be displayed to show how knowledge–bases, subroutines, external programs and files can be navigated. It also provides for shared fact blackboards (see 6.6.5) and configuration management support.

The developer can create blackboard files to allow facts to be shared across knowledge–bases. The file holds information on shared facts and which knowledge–bases may reference them.

Quintec Prolog

Quintec Prolog provides support for modularised development, such that modules can be incrementally linked together. Each module has a unique name and defines a number of objects which may be exported for public access. Each module also defines which external objects are to be imported for internal use. All non–public objects defined in a module are private and invisible to other modules.

Programmers can therefore develop modules in isolation without concern for name clashes, though agreement on conventions would be desirable. Each member of a development team need only be aware of the interface specifications between modules, which define the public communication channels.

Today

Communication links between Today (the fourth generation language and KBS combined) and a co–resident task, which may be another Today application, are allowed. It is thought that in principle, Today can call a 3GL program, which in turn can call a KBS built using a different KBS tool; however it is not known whether this mechanism has been tested.

Top–One

Top–One provides an environment for the development of cooperative micro–mainframe linked applications. That is, an application can be implemented locally, centrally or both. In all cases, the application can be modularised.

6.6.5   Availability of data

In the above information about tools, some mechanisms for sharing data were mentioned, such as blackboarding and scoping. The following gives a brief overview of these useful mechanisms.

Blackboard approach

The blackboard approach was first developed in the context of a speech understanding project. The intention is that the system is made up of a number of independent modules that contain specific knowledge and a blackboard, which is a shared data structure to which all the modules have access.

When a module is activated knowledge is applied to the blackboard contents, such that new data may be added to the blackboard, or existing data be updated. It is possible, given this architecture, to have asynchronous or parallel execution of knowledge–bases.

The important feature to note with this approach is that data is explicitly defined as being shared or specific to a knowledge–base. As a result it is not necessary to specify data to be passed between modules.

Variable scoping

As the term implies, the access to data variables can be scoped, such that only certain modules may access the data. In the blackboard approach, data is either globally available to all modules or private to a single module. Scoping allows more controlled access, depending upon the implementation.

A hierarchic approach to modularisation could be implemented such that:

- the root module has access only to its own data;

- a leaf module will have access to all data in that branch, including the root and all intermediate nodes;

- intermediate node modules will have access to data in that module and those above it in the hierarchy. Data declared in lower modules is not available.

Alternatively, a network approach might be possible: for example, it might be possible to specify a level of access when a datum is declared, such that all modules with that level of access may use it. Such a system would be flexible but applications might be difficult to maintain, unless a compiler could rationalise and list all data items and accessibility.

6.6.6 Future developments

As can be seen from the above, a number of mechanisms for communicating between KBS modules have already been implemented. The ideas behind the blackboard approach and scoping could be developed into standard export and import facilities, not just for KBS, but for processing in general. If this were to happen, the potential for communication between applications built using different tools would be greater.

7

Open systems

7.1 Introduction

An 'Open Systems Environment' is a concept in which interconnection and interworking of different hardware and software products (which are components of the Environment) is achievable by the use of common interface definitions based on accepted, formal standards. The majority of the IT industry accepts that Open Systems is the direction their customers wish to take; industry's commitment to open systems is demonstrated by the resources given to support the evolution of open system standards.

A Framework for Open Systems (FOS) is being developed by CCTA [FOLL89]. Five domains of interest have been defined:

- management disciplines to handle development, infrastructure administration and security, to provide a coherent approach to the management of information systems;

- user interface support for the delivery of services;

- system interfaces to tools and services;

- information definition and organisation;

- communications to cover external communication services and transfer syntax.

Management, user interface and communications standards which are being defined for computer systems in general, should be usable by knowledge–based systems (KBS). It will be necessary to define system interface standards between KBS and other tools, which correspond to the application layer in the seven layer OSI Reference Model (IS 7498), and information definition and organisation standards for KBS.

Interoperability

The Basic Reference Model for Open System Interconnection (OSI) facilitates communication between software on different hardware platforms by providing protocols for connectivity. Generalised standards for the interworking of software on the same hardware platform (system interfaces in the above list) are less advanced and depend upon the emerging Information Resource Dictionary System (IRDS) or Portable Common Tools Environment (PCTE) standards. The structured query language (SQL) standard facilitates the interworking of database management systems (DBMS) and application programs, including some KBS.

Portability

Portable software can be transferred from one machine to another and be used without amendment. The aim of initiatives such as X/OPEN is to provide a Common Applications Environment (CAE) across a wide range of hardware, so that tools can be developed to run in this single environment. X/OPEN uses the UNIX operating system as a basis for CAE. The Portable Operating System Interface for Computer Environments (POSIX) standard is being developed. The POSIX initiative has the same UNIX base, but is an attempt to develop a more generalised architecture across operating systems.

For practical purposes, portable systems are commonly written in C to run under the UNIX operating system. Due to the proliferation of proprietary operating systems on many different hardware platforms, vendors choosing to develop software to run on a number of these hardware platforms must produce a variant for each environment.

7.2 Why open systems?

The standard specification of IT system components and methods, which forms the basis of open systems, is an important part of IT policy because it:

- enhances the general level of system availability and life time of a system;

- achieves a common user view of IT services;

- facilitates application portability and maintenance;

- promotes a common pool of reusable skills;

- improves the quality of system design;

- promotes the interworking between separately procured systems.

The last point provides the purchaser with a competitive choice for the selection of system components which leads to reduced cost in procurement. Vendors can compete on equitable terms and purchasers do not tie themselves to any single supplier.

7.3 Standards

Standards underpin open systems, since it is necessary to document the common parts of information systems, such as interfaces and communication protocols.

Data Management

A Reference Model for Data Management is being specified by the International Standards Organisation (ISO), which provides a framework for existing and future standards work in data management [ISO89]. The standard defines a number of terms commonly used in data management. There is a need for this standardisation since different implementors use different terms to specify similar functions, and some implementors use the same term to describe different functions.

Four broad categories of data management standards are described:

- interface standards, which define the kind of services which are provided at an interface. Between processing elements this might be a procedure call with parameters (as in Cobol), and between a processing element and a DBMS it may be SQL;

- data content standards, concerned with representation;

- interchange standards for communication between different types of systems;

- functional standards, which assemble other standards to be used together.

Two specific data management standards, SQL and IRDS, have been mentioned in other chapters of this book. A Remote Database Access (RDA) standard is also being developed.

Knowledge–based systems

Very little standards work has been done for KBS in comparison to data management; this is not surprising, due to the relative immaturity of KBS. The British Standards Institute (BSI) is currently working on standards for Lisp and Prolog syntax. There may be other standards being worked on by other bodies such as ISO and ANSI.

CCTA is carrying out some work to produce a generic model for KBS tools, which will include a description of all the logical components and variations of these components. Sections 4.5 and 5.1 mention some researchers in the UK, USA and Australia, who are working to produce a similar model for KBS applications which have been implemented. These models could be put together to produce a KBS Reference Model.

Timing

It is worthwhile considering the development of a KBS Reference Model for future KBS standards work, bearing in mind the following dilemmas outlined in LUCA89, which hold true for all standards work:

- defining a standard is one issue; implementing it in a consistent fashion is entirely different;

- standards take a long time to specify and be agreed; it takes even longer for them to be implemented in a significant selection of products from different vendors;

- there is often variation in the detail of implementations, which can give rise to incompatibilities. Detailed specification of a standard and conformance testing of products against that standard are important processes;

- a standard cannot usually be established in advance of some product implementations. Thus, there is a time lag between a market or technical opportunity first appearing, and a standard being agreed. Vendors are unlikely to delay development until the standard is agreed, therefore products will invariably be ahead of standards and may not be 'retrofitted';

- if a standard is developed too early it restricts progress, yet if it is developed too late, it is worthless. It has to be done at the right time to avoid being either a straight–jacket or a dead letter.

The standards bodies, such as BSI, ISO, ANSI, AFNOR, IEEE and CCITT, will no doubt decide when the time is right for developing KBS standards, but there is plenty of grist for the mill available now.

7.4 KBS open system architecture

A number of features discussed in this book contribute to an open systems architecture for KBS. Section 4.5 proposes a new architecture for KBS based on storing the knowledge–base in a database, as illustrated in figure 4.5.6. Sections 5.1 and 5.2 consider the use of an integrated system development environment, so that appropriate tools can be used to build integrated components. Section 6.1 investigates the various interfaces which have been developed between KBS and database management system (DBMS) products. Section 6.2 describes an interface between KBS and third and fourth generation languages. Section 6.3 looks at how KBS tools can be integrated with the machine environment, and section 6.6 considers how applications built using different KBS tools might communicate.

Japanese fifth generation computers

The architecture of the fifth generation computer systems [FAVA87], as illustrated in figure 7.1 could be described as 'open'. The human interface has been separated out, so that windows, printers, mouse devices and keyboards which conform to a specified standard can be used. An 'intelligent interface software' component is included for interfacing with other system components. It is interesting to note that a DBMS has been included and depicted as a hardware component, as have some inferencing mechanisms. It is likely that inferencing micro–chips will become available for plugging into machines, at some time in the future.

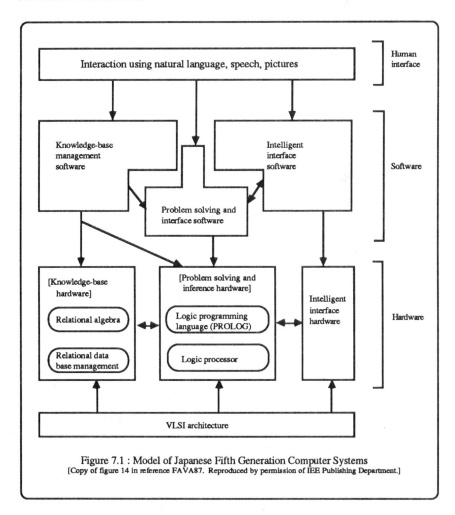

Figure 7.1 : Model of Japanese Fifth Generation Computer Systems
[Copy of figure 14 in reference FAVA87. Reproduced by permission of IEE Publishing Department.]

Level5 Object

The architecture of Level5 Object is moving towards an open system architecture, as shown in figure 7.2. Major areas of functionality have been separated out into libraries of modules, isolating as much code (written in C) as possible from hardware and software dependencies.

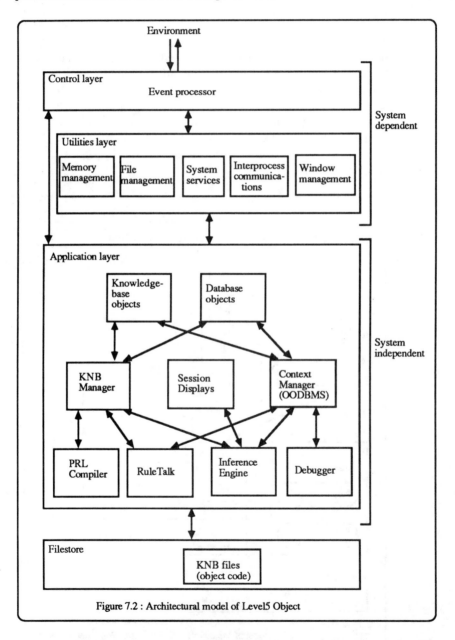

Figure 7.2 : Architectural model of Level5 Object

The control layer is the main event processor which dispatches events to appropriate modules. It is system dependent; under windowing environments, some of the work is done by the environment.

The utilities layer is also system dependent and insulates the application layer from the environment. The file management utilities are used for all file access, such as read, write, open, close and file locking operations. If a standard interface could be provided, possibly based on SQL, there may be no need for this component.

The system service utilities are used to access various system dependent functions, and again a standard interface could make this component redundant. The Dynamic Data Exchange (DDE) format for inter–task communication and data exchange is supported, so that Level5 Object can be embedded in other programs. The window management utilities control all user interfaces. Microsoft Windows used by Level5 Object conforms to IBM's System Application Architecture (SAA); the latter defines how window based user interfaces are to be ported to non–window based mainframe environments.

The application layer is portable and independent of the environment. Again, the system has been modularised, separating out various functions. The inference engine could, conceivably, be partly implemented as a hardware component without having to re–write the system. There appears to be a separation of the object code and knowledge–base object descriptions; it seems that the KNB management could be replaced by a DBMS.

7.5 KBS interfaces

A number of types of interface have been mentioned throughout this book, between KBS and:

- database management systems;

- third and fourth generation languages;

- the environment, consisting of TP monitors and operating systems;

- spreadsheet software;

- hypertext systems;

- other KBS applications;

- office automation systems;

- user interface software.

It would seem superfluous to define separate standards for all of these types of interface, although it is unlikely that one would be sufficient due to the different types of information to be passed across these interfaces. Where standards already exist, such as the SQL standard for interfacing with a DBMS, they should be used. It may be necessary to add new facilities to enable KBS to use these standards. It is suggested that standards should be developed so that KBS can be included in an open system environment, in a similar way to DBMS servers (in a client/server system). A KBS system could be called to carry out some knowledge processing, just as a DBMS is called to access some data.

7.6 Knowledge representation and manipulation standards

There is a breadth of knowledge representation formalisms used by KBS. There are many variations on the production rule (if... then...); some are based on mathematical formalisms such as predicate calculus; there are many flavours of Prolog and Lisp, although Edinburgh Prolog seems to be almost a *de facto* standard; there are various implementations which are object oriented; and there may be others. The richness of this variation provides the developer with an excellent choice, but also presents a dilemma about which one should be used for any given application.

The *flex* toolkit has become established as an extension to Prolog systems. It was first implemented with LPA's Prolog Professional tool on IBM micros, which is now also available on Macintosh hardware. Since then, a number of companies have incorporated flex into their KBS products. Telecomputing has included flex in Top–One which runs on IBM and ICL mainframes. Quintec uses it in association with Quintec Prolog on Sun and VAX workstations. Lateral Systems have an implementation on micros in the Prospect system. BIM include it with BIM Prolog on Sun workstations. Quintus market Proflex on Sun, Apollo, VAX and NCR machines, and ISL market Poplog flex on UNIX and VMS based machines. Flex code is portable across platforms, although user–defined Prolog routines may need to be changed. It seems that flex could become a *de facto* standard extension to Prolog.

There is a breadth of logical knowledge representation techniques, used during the analysis and design of KBS applications. Some conventional techniques, such as entity modelling and data flow diagramming are used in analysis to represent facts and ordering of tasks respectively. But other techniques are used to describe the knowledge and fact manipulation, such as knowledge maps, semantic nets, object hierarchies and many home–grown techniques which do not have sufficiently well developed names. The choice of logical techniques may be driven by the type of application under development and the skills of the expert whose domain is being analysed.

A standard for knowledge representation will need to be sufficiently flexible to encompass the breadths of both logical and physical representation which are available, while being sufficiently rich to include all the underlying concepts. Such a notation should be supported by information repositories and contribute to the IRDS standard. It is intended that a standard notation such as this should be produced as part of the GEMINI project.

7.7 KBS methodology

In the framework for open systems, mentioned in 7.1 above, the information definition and organisation stream will include methodologies for analysis and design, such as SSADM. There is a proliferation of analysis and design methods and, so far, there are no standards for methods.

The GEMINI project will be developing a methodology for the analysis, design and implementation of knowledge–based systems, over the next two years. It is destined to become the *de facto* standard for KBS methodologies.

8

Conclusions

8.1 Summary

The purposes of this book, as specified in the introduction (chapter 1), are to:

- increase the awareness of administrative computer systems implementors of the potential for integrating knowledge–based systems (KBS) technology with their existing and future computer systems;

- stimulate vendors to address the problems associated with integrating KBS and other technology.

This book is believed to have achieved the above by:

- identifying and documenting the various ways in which KBS and other software can be integrated, in both development and run–time environments. Chapters 5 and 6, and annexes C and D address this topic;

- identifying KBS tools for data processing departments which have a large investment in data and information systems. Sections 3.1, 6.1, 6.2 and 6.3, and annexes B, C and D address this topic;

- commenting on the relative merits of methods of coupling KBS and database software. Section 6.1 specifically addresses this topic;

- describing some integrated system architectures which may be used. Chapters 4 and 7 address this topic.

The rest of this chapter summarises the conclusions reached on a number of issues in these topics.

8.2 Postulated open system architecture of KBS tools

Figure 8.1 presents a new architecture for KBS tools, based upon information given in section 3.1, chapter 4, section 5.1 and chapter 7.

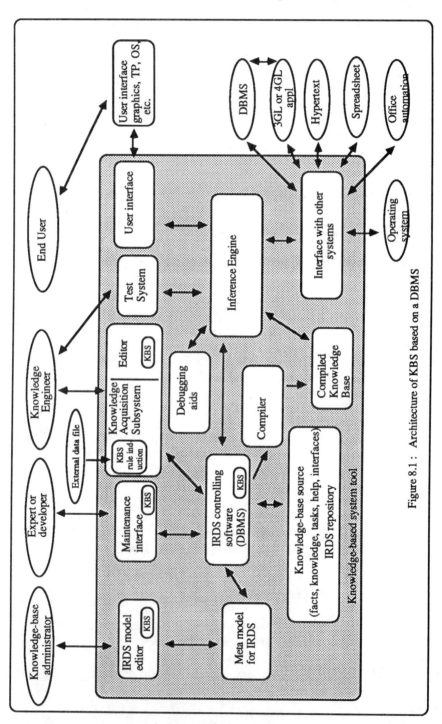

Figure 8.1 : Architecture of KBS based on a DBMS

Knowledge–base storage control

Sections 4.5 and 5.1 discuss the use of a database and a data dictionary respectively for storing the knowledge–base of a number of KBS applications. The repository which stores dictionary information is a specialised database. It is suggested that some controlling software, based upon information resource dictionary system (IRDS) principles, should manage knowledge stored in a database. The description for the knowledge–database (the schema, or meta–model for IRDS in figure 8.1) should be held in an accessible file, so that a knowledge–base administrator (KBA, equivalent to the database administrator) can amend it, using the IRDS model editor. The KBA may choose to modify the generalised knowledge description so that the dictionary can be tailored, for example to conform with organisational standards, or to suit a particular implementation tool.

If the IRDS repository was to be built upon existing database management (DBMS) software, then it is likely that a relational DBMS would be used. However, in the future an object oriented DBMS could provide a suitable vehicle. The IRDS repository would not only store knowledge, but would hold details of conventional applications too, if the knowledge–based system (KBS) tool was to be incorporated into a computer assisted software engineering (CASE) tool.

The IRDS controlling software might use KBS techniques and applications for such functions as, optimisation of queries, access control and maintaining integrity of knowledge–base information.

The meta–model for IRDS would be stored in a database, managed by the IRDS controlling software. The meta–model would describe all the types of data, facts, knowledge, processing, etc, which could possibly be stored in the IRDS repository. Standards are required for the definition of knowledge and its manipulation, and interfaces to other systems.

The IRDS model editor would be DBMS software for interrogating and updating the meta–model for IRDS. This could be a natural language or any other query interface; KBS components may be incorporated into this software.

Knowledge database

Many of the benefits associated with databases would apply when a knowledge–base is stored in a database, bearing in mind that some of these features are already provided by some KBS tools:

- integrity constraints could be enforced by the DBMS;

- access control mechanisms would be applied by the DBMS;

- recovery facilities are available;

- concurrent access to knowledge–bases is allowed;

- distributed knowledge–bases can be created;

- knowledge can be shared or reused by applications;

- standards can be enforced.

A knowledge–base management system would generally increase and improve the flexibility and versatility of knowledge–bases, as part of a move towards open systems.

Many existing KBS applications are relatively small, compared to conventional administrative systems. However, it is anticipated that in the future large knowledge–bases will be developed; control over the knowledge–base, modularisation, reuse and distribution will be important factors in the successful implementation of such systems.

Development of knowledge–bases

It is likely that development facilities for building KBS applications will be incorporated into CASE tools, as exemplified by the proposed architecture for IBM's AD/Cycle. In this scenario, the editor used for creating and amending the knowledge–base would be a general editor for all the contents of the IRDS. It would provide a high level interface, including graphic displays of diagrams; the external view (subschema) would hide the storage mechanisms of IRDS, presenting the developer with rules, object hierarchies, etc.

A knowledge acquisition subsystem, based upon rule induction, could be included in the developers' toolset. This would be able to read external data files to generate information in the IRDS knowledge–base.

The testing and debugging facilities would be similar to those already provided with KBS tools. They may be identified as separate components within the KBS architecture to facilitate re–use as part of a generalised CASE tool and to demonstrate a move towards an open systems architecture.

It is envisaged that a compiled version of each knowledge–base would be produced for use by the inference engine at run–time. The IRDS controlling software would be able to identify the extent of changes to knowledge–bases when edited, so that incremental compilation could be carried out.

The maintenance interface is intended for non–technical staff, having a different interface to that provided with the editor for knowledge engineers. Information in the knowledge–base must be presented in a format suited to the end user. An embedded KBS application could be used to tailor this interface for individuals.

Run–time interfaces

In order to move towards an open systems architecture, standard interfaces should be defined for the user interface and interfaces with other processes, such as hypertext and Cobol systems. There is a move towards using graphic and window–based interfaces provided with the hardware platform, for presentation of the user interface. A standard interface to this software is usually specified. The user interface, as generated by the inference engine, would need to be compatible with this interface.

The SQL standard has been developed for interfacing DBMS and application software and a similar standard for interfacing KBS applications with other software is needed. This could potentially be based upon SQL, since a number of KBS tool vendors have developed SQL DBMS interfaces. It is desirable that interface standards build upon existing standards for data processing and management.

KBS tools implementations

The architecture shown in figure 8.1 is based upon a number of theoretically possible ideas, some research and the architectures of existing and proposed future tools, in particular Natural Expert, Level5 Object and AD/Cycle. Natural Expert embodies the idea of storing the knowledge–base in a database; Level5 Object has been broken down into discrete components, so that system independent functions can be delivered on a number of hardware platforms; and AD/Cycle will incorporate KBS within a framework for total system development.

Software vendors recognise the need for an open systems architecture, so that customers can procure discrete system components and be guaranteed that the components can be linked together on a number of hardware platforms. KBS vendors seem to be addressing this requirement, just as quickly as vendors of DBMS and other system software. Unfortunately, the KBS industry is hampered by the lack of standards for system interfaces and knowledge representation formalisms. It is hoped that the GEMINI project will address this issue over the next two years.

Client/server architecture

A client/server architecture has been implemented in some DBMS, such that the user interface software (client) and the data storage and access mechanisms (server) are logically separate, and may be physically separated by being installed on different, communicating machines. Such an architecture may be suitable for KBS, in that the user interface questions, displays, explanation mechanisms, etc, could be separated out into the 'client' and the inference engine and knowledge–base would become the 'server'. A KBS architecture, such as that presented in figure 8.1, consisting of interfacing components, could be implemented as a client/server architecture.

There are suggestions that some parts of DBMS and inferencing mechanisms will be implemented as hardware in the future, as depicted by the Japanese fifth generation computer systems (see chapter 7). In order to implement some inferencing functions as hardware, the functions will need to be isolated from the general KBS architecture.

8.3 Object orientation and standards

Object orientation could provide the logical model for integrating DBMS and KBS, not least because it is a common feature of both types of software. Some non–research object oriented DBMS are available. It is possible to map relational, hierarchic and network models on to object models. A number of KBS tools offer object orientation as an optional development model.

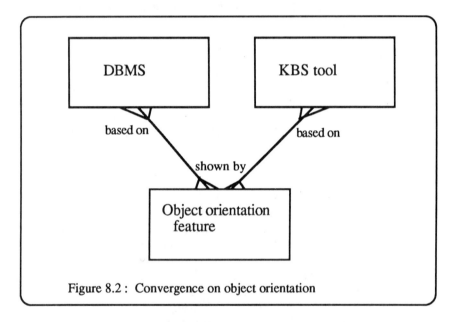

Figure 8.2 : Convergence on object orientation

Object orientation could be used as a basis for developing KBS standards, such as a KBS Reference Model, although existing data management standards, such as SQL, cannot be ignored. A KBS Reference Model could provide standard definitions for commonly used terms. There is a need for this standardisation since different implementors use different terms to specify similar functions, and some implementors use the same term to describe different functions.

KBS interface standards are needed to define the kinds of service that are provided at the interface. For example, a KBS–DBMS interface would specify the different types of function, such as read, write, update, etc, the parameters which are to be passed from KBS to DBMS and vice versa, the types of error checking, etc. Since many tools already use SQL, it would be possible to build a standard based upon the existing SQL standard.

There are a number of benefits to be gained from using a KBS tool which conforms to the ISO SQL standard, including the following:

- SQL is part of the open systems initiative and a number of DBMS software vendors are committed to it;

- substantial resources have been, are being and will be expended on development of the SQL standard;

- compatibility with a number of relational databases, providing flexibility;

- there is only one data manipulation language to learn for DBMS access;

- essential facilities for data manipulation will be provided.

There are also potential problems with standardising on SQL, such as:

- it cannot be used to access most network and hierarchic databases;

- it cannot be used to access flat files;

- SQL is difficult to learn, write and understand.

Standard interfaces are also needed for KBS communication with graphics and windowing packages for the user interface, and other applications built using third and fourth generation languages, hypermedia, spreadsheets and so on.

A standard for knowledge representation and manipulation is required which: is domain and implementation tool independent; is compatible with the many logical representations used in analysis; and can be the source for translation into the representations used by KBS tools. CCTA is working on a generic model which could form the basis of such a standard.

8.4 KBS interfaces

The number of KBS tools which can communicate with DBMS, third generation languages and spreadsheet packages has rapidly increased over the last two years. Annex C is purely illustrative, but some of the identified KBS tools can access more than five DBMS, and a single DBMS can be accessed by more than six KBS tools, on average. More than ten KBS tools can access Oracle or Ingres, which are two of the most popular DBMS. It is estimated that at least twelve different KBS tools can interface with Cobol, C, Fortran and Pascal applications. Over fifteen KBS tools have been identified which can access Lotus–123 spreadsheets. This progress in the development of interfaces to other software is very encouraging, in that vendors of KBS tools seem to regard communication with other software as a very important feature. It is unfortunate that many KBS tool vendors are implementing interfaces in various ways, emphasising the need for a standard.

Incompatibilities have always existed between data types in different software tools, for example Cobol and Fortran are not fully compatible. Not surprisingly, there are some incompatibilities between data types stored in DBMS and fact types declared in knowledge–based systems. All KBS which can access databases should make a clear statement about the conversion of data when retrieved and stored, and the types of data which cannot be handled.

Ideally, KBS should access data at the record level (groups of data items) and even at set level (many occurrences of records) since the latter is concomitant with declarative processing. Many KBS tools can deal with simple structures at record level. If record level data handling is not implemented, or if there are many fact–data incompatibilities, then it may be preferable to access data via a subroutine, written in a third or fourth generation language (3GL or 4GL), on the assumption that records could be passed across this interface and that there is a high degree of compatibility between a 3GL or 4GL and the DBMS.

8.5 Rules for integration

Twelve rules for the integration of KBS and DBMS have been drawn together from a number of sources including Software AG, HOWA89 and the information provided in this book. Potential purchasers of KBS software can use these rules for assessing competing products.

1 Environment

The KBS tool should be able to run within a conventional data processing environment, using existing hardware and software. That is, the user of the tool should not be expected to buy a totally new system to run the tool, although he might be expected to extend his configuration. For some people, it will be essential that the KBS can run on a mainframe under a particular transaction processing monitor; others might need a KBS to run on a network of minis and personal computers.

2 Multi–user

A single user tool in a personal computer environment might suit the needs of a small group of users, but a strategically chosen KBS for use throughout an organisation must provide multi–user capabilities. This includes multi–tasking so that many people using the tool to build and execute knowledge–bases at the same time can use the same copy of the tool which is publicly loaded, the code being re–entrant. The knowledge–base of all applications should also be re–entrant (perhaps after compilation) so that only one copy of the code is available to all concurrent users.

3 Comparable performance

The tool must provide performance levels which are comparable with those of existing development and run–time environments. This might be high speed in the case of an engine control system taking real–time information from measuring devices, or medium speed in the case of a system which maximises space utilisation in an airline booking system. Database access should not be allowed to slow down the system.

4 Clean interfaces

A clean interface should be provided to existing data processing languages, such as SQL, C, Cobol, PL/1 or whatever is normally used. Developers should not be expected to learn C if they normally use Cobol, for example. The interface should be 'clean', particularly where database access is concerned, to ensure that the DBMS maintains control over the data and the application can monitor the success or otherwise of database accesses.

5 Database update

Facilities to update a database, in addition to retrieval mechanisms, should be provided; that is, the ability to insert new records, amend existing records and delete existing records.

6 Transaction integrity

A system which allows users to concurrently update a database must provide for transaction integrity. It must be possible to specify the start and end of a transaction. At the end of a transaction the user of an application must have the choice of committing the changes to the database and invoking integrity checks, or rolling back to forget the data changes made in the transaction. The system must also use the data locking mechanisms provided by the DBMS to prevent concurrent users from updating logically associated records at the same time.

7 Non–ambiguity

Applications built using the KBS tool must be totally predictable: there should be no loss of data because of unspecified incompatibilities between data items and knowledge–base variables; the effect of values such as NULL and UNKNOWN should be documented; the database access mechanism should be fully specified with facilities to handle errors.

8 Minimal re–invention

The KBS tool should use those facilities which are already provided with the DBMS for database access, and the developer should not be expected to write large and complex data access modules. The KBS should use the DBMS access control facilities, data integrity checks and recovery procedures.

9 High level data mappings

The KBS tool should be able to handle data at the record or object level, rather than having to deal with individual data items. It should only be necessary to specify the mappings between database data items and KBS data items once for each application. Direct usage of external views provided by the DBMS is desirable.

10 Multiple DBMS

It may be desirable to be able to use: more than one database through a single DBMS; more than one DBMS, such as both Ingres and Sybase; and more than one type of data model (hierarchical, network and relational), through DBMS such as IDMS and Oracle. Ideally, these complexities should be hidden from the KBS application developer, such that a data item can be requested in terms of the KBS internal data model, without needing to know where and how it will be found.

11 Multiple KBS

DBMS interfaces should support independent KBS applications, possibly built using different KBS tools, which share common data and cooperating KBS components that work together in problem solving tasks.

12 Heterogeneous KBS tools

Different KBS tools are suited to different types of tasks or problem domain. It should be possible to pass data between cooperating applications which may have been built using different KBS tools.

It is unlikely that any existing KBS tools can satisfy all twelve rules. Readers are encouraged to assess the tools which they know against this yardstick.

8.6 KBS in CASE tools

In 8.2, above the architecture of KBS tools, in the context of CASE tools for development work, is mentioned. KBS applications can also be used to *build functions* within CASE tools as illustrated in figure 8.3. Several vendors of CASE tools on the market suggest that KBS have been used to semi–automate conversion of a logical data design to a physical data design for a particular DBMS, and for reverse engineering.

A KBS application has been built by a well known KBS tool vendor to facilitate conversion of Cobol source to run on different hardware. Some researchers have also looked at the generation of metrics for MASCOT. There are some other prime candidate applications which may, or may not, have been considered by CASE tool vendors, including: integrity checking of data flow diagrams, entity models and entity life history diagrams; giving advice on how to use techniques such as data flow diagramming; automatic system generation, that is producing source code for an implementation tool from a design specification; and configuration management of design information.

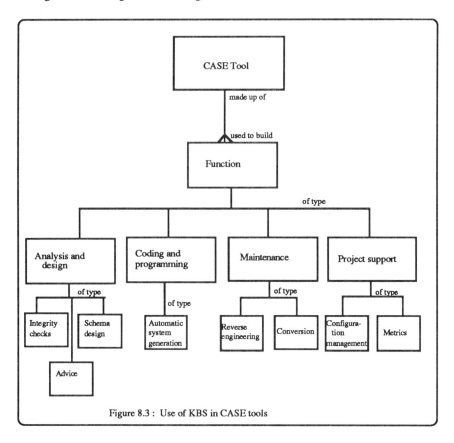

Figure 8.3 : Use of KBS in CASE tools

Most CASE tools support a single method, such as SSADM, or a collection of analysis and design techniques, such as data flow diagramming and entity modelling. In the future, when IRDS can be implemented, CASE shells may become available, so that organisations can 'plug in' their own method rules or a purchasable rule set for a method, or a combination of 'standard' and organisational rules.

8.7 Convergence of KBS and DBMS

Sections 4.1, 4.2 and 4.3 discuss some DBMS functions which can be implemented using KBS technology, which are summarised in figure 8.4.

Integrity constraints and actions for maintaining integrity are possible candidates. Some DBMS, such as Sybase, have implemented trigger mechanisms for maintaining integrity. It is suggested that a rule format (if... then...) could be used for specifying the constraints and actions, and inferencing mechanisms such as forward chaining and firing of demons could be used in the implementation of them.

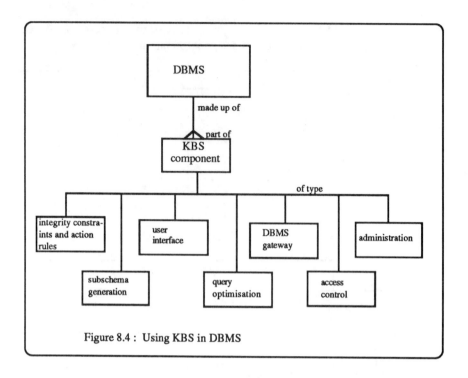

Figure 8.4 : Using KBS in DBMS

Transformation and inference rules, which decode and generate data, could be used to implement subschema mechanisms. The data held in accordance with the storage schema (or internal view) must be reorganised and new data calculated according to an external view being used by a processing system.

Better user interfaces than those provided by computer language oriented query systems have been developed using KBS, including some natural languages and front–ends to SQL. These are particularly important for casual database users who do not have time to learn and remember the syntax of some query languages. Interfaces to text databases have been developed which can increase the likelihood of retrieving information which the user requires.

KBS may be used in the query optimisation process. Rules may guide the choice of query transformation rules and identify detachable sub–queries. Query evaluation strategies may also be generated by rules, so that evaluation costs based on knowledge about storage structures and database statistics can be compared. Ingres Ltd use an AI-based query optimiser and it is likely that other DBMS vendors are investigating the use of KBS for query optimisation.

DBMS vendors are developing gateways between DBMS, so that a user of one proprietary DBMS can access a database which is controlled by another DBMS. A potential application of KBS is an 'intelligent' gateway, which can locate and access data held in other databases, possibly held on other machines.

Ingres Ltd market the Knowledge Management Extension to Ingres which allows the developer to input rules which control database access. The entire access control mechanism could be a KBS application, which processes access control rules, that the DBA could update as required.

A number of database administration functions could be provided to support the DBA. For example, rule induction systems which run against indexes and file access information could provide the DBA with information to enable him to tune the database.

8.8 Rule induction

The ability to induce rules from data, that is, to create generalisations from examples, is interesting and exciting, but it is important that inductive tools are used wisely and that the results are viewed with caution. It is possible to see how results which lack credence could be produced by having insufficient example data. Interpretation of these results by people who do not understand the input data could lead them to false conclusions.

It would be possible to put a lot of effort into inducing rules and achieve nothing of value. But equally, there are some well known cases which have resulted in large savings in expenditure. Some small scale, representative experiments should be conducted first to test the feasibility of using inductive tools to analyse large bodies of data.

8.9 The future for KBS integration

The development of an open systems architecture and standards for interfacing with other software is imperative for the successful exploitation of KBS by large organisations. Without these it will be difficult to build, manage and maintain large, integrated knowledge–based systems, which may be modularised and distributed across a network.

KBS tools will become optional components within CASE tools, programmers workbenches, integrated project support environments and development frameworks, in general. Knowledge–based systems will become integral components in an information systems architecture, placed alongside data management components.

Annex A

Contacts

A large number of people who work for software and hardware companies have helped me in compiling this book by providing up-to-date information, answering telephone enquiries, and reviewing the book contents to ensure that my interpretation of material is sound. I hope that the individuals concerned will identify with the organisations listed below.

AEA Technology	Intelligent Environments Ltd
AI Corp	Intellisoft (UK) Ltd
Apple Computer Inc	Keylink Computers Ltd
Artificial Intelligence Ltd	Knowledgelink
Attar Software Ltd	Lateral Systems Ltd
Ashton-Tate (UK) Ltd	Logic Programming Associates Ltd
BIM	MDBS International Ltd
Carnegie (UK) Ltd	Oracle UK
Chemical Design Ltd	Parsoft
Cognitive Applications	Quintec Systems Ltd
Computer Associates Ltd	Radian Corporation
Computer Power Europe Ltd	Relational Technology Inc (Ingres Ltd)
Creative Logic Ltd	Roolan International

Cullinet

Deductive Systems Ltd

Electronic Facilities Design Ltd

Expertech

Expert Systems International

Ferranti Computer Systems Ltd

Grafton Software Ltd

Graphael

IBM

ICL

Information Builders (UK) Ltd

Ingres Ltd (RTI)

Intellicorp Ltd

Scientific Computers Ltd

SD-SCICON

Software Architecture and Engineering

Software AG

Software Generation

Software Sciences

Sybase

SystemStar Ltd

Telecomputing plc

Texas Instruments Ltd

UKAEA

Unibit

UNISYS

Warm Boot Ltd

Annex B

KBS Tool Overviews

A short overview of the majority of the KBS tools mentioned in this book has been compiled. This is intended to provide readers with a broader view of the tools and a reference for obtaining further information. The following are included:

Advisor–2	Knowledgetool
Aion Development System (ADS)	Leonardo
Beagle	Level5 Object
BIM Prolog	LPA Prolog
CA–DB:Expert	Mac Prolog
Crystal	MVS/Prolog
Db–Edge	Natural Expert
Expert–ease	Nexpert Object
Expert Systems Environment (ESE)	Parys
Extran	Personal Consultant Series
G–BASE	Prospect
Generis	Quintec Prolog
Goldworks	Quintus Prolog
Guru	Reveal
IBM Prolog for 370	Rulemaster
ICL–Adviser	Savoir
Inference ART	SD–Adviser
Intellect	Spices
KBMS	Today
KEE	Top–One
KES	VM/Prolog
Knowledgecraft	XiPlus
KnowledgePro	XpertRule

NAME OF PRODUCT   *Advisor—2*

OTHER NAMES (previous names etc)   *ESP–Advisor*

NAME OF VENDOR   *Chemical Design Ltd*

CONTACT PERSON   *Elizabeth Wilkins*

ADDRESS OF VENDOR   *Unit 12, 7 West Way, Oxford OX2 0JB*

Telephone Nº.   *0865–251483*

Names of other vendors/supporters/collaborators
NONE

Telephone Nº. of other vendors

ENVIRONMENT FOR RUNNING PRODUCT

Machine   *IBM PC XT/AT or compatible with minimum 512K RAM*

Operating System   *PCDOS v 2.0 or later*

Other required software

PRICE   *£495*   MAINTENANCE CHARGE   *15% p.a.*

CURRENT RELEASE: *1.05*

COMMENTS
Menu and function key driven expert system shell. Has its own language KRL, uses IBM PC colour and graphics. Can interface to Lotus–123, dBASE III, Gem Graphics, Prolog-2, C, Fortran, Pascal and Assembler. Can call DOS from within applications. Written in Prolog-2.

NAME OF PRODUCT *Aion Development System*

OTHER NAMES (previous names etc) *ADS*

NAME OF VENDOR *Software Generation*

CONTACT PERSON *Christine Bennett*

ADDRESS OF VENDOR *Software Generation, Portmill House, Portmill Lane, Hitchin, Herts, SG5 1DJ*

Telephone Nº. *0462 422525*

Names of other vendors/supporters/collaborators *Aion Corporation*

Telephone Nº. of other vendors *(USA)*

ENVIRONMENT FOR RUNNING PRODUCT

Machine *IBM mainframe and pcs*

Operating System *MVS, VM, MS-DOS, OS/2*

Other required software

PRICE | MAINTENANCE CHARGE

CURRENT RELEASE:

COMMENTS

ADS can run in a variety of teleprocessing environments including TSO, IMS and CICS. Data may be integrated into an ADS application from DB2, DL/1, VSAM and SQL/DS. The modular architecture of ADS allows integration with other programs; knowledge bases can be embedded in existing programs and external programs can be called from the knowledge base. Cobol, PL/1, C and Fortran programs can be called to access databases such as Oracle, Adabas and IDMS indirectly. Spreadsheets, such as Lotus–123, can also be accessed.

NAME OF PRODUCT   *PC Beagle*

OTHER NAMES (previous names etc)   *None*

NAME OF VENDOR   *Warm Boot Ltd*

CONTACT PERSON   *Richard Forsyth*

ADDRESS OF VENDOR   *8 Grosvenor Avenue, Nottingham, NG3 5DX*

Telephone Nº.   *0602 - 621676*

Names of other vendors/supporters/collaborators

Telephone Nº. of other vendors

ENVIRONMENT FOR RUNNING PRODUCT

Machine   *IBM PC or compatible*

Operating System   *PCDOS or MSDOS v2.1 or later*

Other required software   *NIL*

PRICE *£125*   MAINTENANCE CHARGE   *NIL*

CURRENT RELEASE: *2.4*

COMMENTS
Inductive rule derivation system which extracts rules from examples using a Genetic Algorithm and generates program sourcecode in C, Basic, Pascal or Fortran. Consists of six modules, SEED, ROOT, HERB, STEM, LEAF and PLUM. Can be used for diagnosis, prediction etc. A version (BEAGLE/PLUS) is available for Data General minicomputers and DEC VAX.

NAME OF PRODUCT   *BIM Prolog*

OTHER NAMES (previous names etc)   *None*

NAME OF VENDOR   *BIM*

CONTACT PERSON   *Dani De Ridder*

ADDRESS OF VENDOR   *Kwikstraat 4, Everberg B-3078, Belgium*

Telephone №.   *(2) 759 5925*

Names of ~~other vendors/supporters~~/collaborators   *Catholic University Leuven (Dept of Computer Science), Celestijnenlaan 200A, B - 3030 Heverlee, Belgium*

Names of other vendors/~~supporters~~/collaborators *The Shure Group (US); ISL (UK); BIM SYSTEMES (F); NEXUS(D); ISS(SP); S&M(I)*

ENVIRONMENT FOR RUNNING PRODUCT

Machine   *Sun 3 and 4 workstation; VAX, MicroVAX*

Operating System   *Sun UNIX, Ultrix, VMS*

Other required software   *Optional DBMS (Ingres, Unify, Sybase, Oracle)*

PRICE *From £860 to £4300*   MAINTENANCE CHARGE   *£43p.m.*

CURRENT RELEASE: *2.4   (2.5 Jan 90)*

COMMENTS

Expert system language written in predicate calculus clauses, extended to include database accesses. Backward chaining. Can access Ingres, Unify , Oracle and Sybase databases. A general interface is provided to facilitate integration with other databases. Interfaces to/from C; interfaces to Fortran , Assembler and Pascal. Windowing & graphics. Algorithmic debugger with post-mortem analysis.

NAME OF PRODUCT   *CA–DB:Expert*

OTHER NAMES (previous names etc) *Application Expert; Enterprise Expert*

NAME OF VENDOR   *Computer Associates Ltd*

CONTACT PERSON *Simon Stevens*

ADDRESS OF VENDOR   *Computer Associates House, 183/187 Bath Road, Slough, Berks, SL1 4AA*

Telephone Nº.   *0753 — 77733*

Names of other vendors/supporters/collaborators
                                    NONE
Telephone Nº. of other vendors

ENVIRONMENT FOR RUNNING PRODUCT

Machine   *IBM mainframe; DEC VAX; MicroVAX*

Operating System   *VM, DOS, MVS; VMS*

Other required software   *Optional DBMS & Universal Communications Facility for CMS, TSO etc*

PRICE   *See below*   MAINTENANCE CHARGE   *15% approx*

CURRENT RELEASE: *1.1 (October 1988)*

COMMENTS
Expert system shell with capability to access IDMS/SQL (now called CA-DB/VAX), IDMS/R (now called CA-IDMS/DB), DB2, Oracle and other commercial DBMS on IBM or VAX hardware.
£2350-£7950 (MicroVAX)   £13 350 - £55 450 (VAX)   £30 650-£55 700 (IBM mainframe)

NAME OF PRODUCT   *Crystal*

OTHER NAMES (previous names etc)   *None*

NAME OF VENDOR   *Intelligent Environments Ltd*

CONTACT PERSON   *Nicki Katsikas*

ADDRESS OF VENDOR *Northumberland House, 15-19 Petersham Road, Richmond, Surrey TW10 6TP*

Telephone Nº.   *01 - 940 - 6333*

Names of other vendors/supporters/collaborators

NONE

Telephone Nº. of other vendors

ENVIRONMENT FOR RUNNING PRODUCT

Machine   *IBM PC/XT/AT/PS2 or 100% compatible, 350K RAM*

Operating System   *PCDOS v2.0 or later, OS/2*

Other required software   *Optional as required for interfaces*

PRICE   *£995*   MAINTENANCE CHARGE

CURRENT RELEASE:

COMMENTS

Menu-driven expert system shell. Supports data-driven and goal-driven applications. Interfaces to Lotus/Symphony spreadsheets, dBASE databases, ASCII files, Lattice, and Microsoft C. Can execute DOS commands. Inductive system. Applications are written in English-like language.

NAME OF PRODUCT   *DB–Edge*

OTHER NAMES (previous names etc)   *None*

NAME OF VENDOR   *Grafton Software Ltd (Northern Europe sole distributors)*

CONTACT PERSON   *Bill McDougall*

ADDRESS OF VENDOR   *Canbury Business Park, Elm Crescent, Kingston-upon-Thames, Surrey KT2 6HJ*

Telephone N⁰. *01 --541 5555*

Names of other vendors/supporters/collaborators   *TECSIEL, 00197 Rome, Via B. Oriania, 32 (manufacturers)*

Telephone N⁰. of other vendors   *+ 39 6 8870341*

ENVIRONMENT FOR RUNNING PRODUCT

Machine   *IBM PC or PS2/ IBM mainframe.*

Operating System

Other required software

PRICE | MAINTENANCE CHARGE

CURRENT RELEASE:

COMMENTS

Db–edge is intended for end-users; it applies knowledge–based technologies and solves problems of data navigation in relational database and presentation of extracted data. It is a pc front end for IBM's DB2 database.

NAME OF PRODUCT   *Expert–Ease*

OTHER NAMES (previous names etc)   *XpertRule/SuperExpert*

NAME OF VENDOR   *Knowledgelink (formerly Intelligent Terminals Ltd)*

CONTACT PERSON

ADDRESS OF VENDOR   *Douglas House, 116-118 Waterloo Street, Glasgow, G2 7DN*

Telephone Nº.   *041 221 9010*

Names of other vendors/supporters/collaborators
                                                      NONE
Telephone Nº. of other vendors

ENVIRONMENT FOR RUNNING PRODUCT

Machine   *IBM PC/XT and compatibles; DEC Rainbow; Sirius; Apricot*

Operating System   *PCDOS; MSDOS*

Other required software   *None*

PRICE *£495* | MAINTENANCE CHARGE

CURRENT RELEASE:

COMMENTS
Expert system heuristic tool; assimilates examples and derives rules. The rules can be refined in the light of further contradictory examples. The resulting system is usable at any stage of its development.

NAME OF PRODUCT   *Expert System Environment   (ESE)*

OTHER NAMES (previous names etc)   *None*

NAME OF VENDOR   *IBM United Kingdom Ltd*

CONTACT PERSON   *Chris Pollock, KBS Market Development*

ADDRESS OF VENDOR   *PO Box 118, Normandy House, Alencon Link, Basingstoke, Hampshire, RG21 1EJ*

Telephone Nº.   *0256 56144*

Names of other vendors/supporters/collaborators

NONE

Telephone Nº. of other vendors

ENVIRONMENT FOR RUNNING PRODUCT

Machine   *IBM System /370 processor or equivalent for development; IBM PC or equivalent can be used for consultation*

Operating System   *VM, MVS, IBM PC DOS*

Other required software   *Pascal run-time library (on S/370)*

PRICE   *POA only*   MAINTENANCE CHARGE   *None*

CURRENT RELEASE: *Version 1 Release 2.0*

COMMENTS

Expert system shell with forward and backward chaining, interfaces to SQL and DB2 databases. Can communicate with Cobol, PL1, Fortran, Assembler, REXX or Pascal programs. Demons and uncertainty are supported. Applications can be integrated with CICS or IMS/DC transactions.

NAME OF PRODUCT *ExTran*

OTHER NAMES (previous names etc) *None*

NAME OF VENDOR *Knowledgelink (formerly Intelligent Terminals Ltd)*

CONTACT PERSON

ADDRESS OF VENDOR *Douglas House, 116-118 Waterloo Street, Glasgow, G2 7DN*

Telephone N$^{\circ}$. *041 221 9010*

Names of other vendors/supporters/collaborators
                                    NONE
Telephone N$^{\circ}$. of other vendors

ENVIRONMENT FOR RUNNING PRODUCT

Machine *IBM mainframe; DEC VAX; CCC Supermini; Apollo workstation; IBM PC*

Operating System *MVS, TSO; VMS, UNIX; OS32; UNIX; PCDOS*

Other required software *Fortran-77 compiler*

PRICE *£2000(PC) - £18 000 (VAX)* | MAINTENANCE CHARGE

CURRENT RELEASE: *7.2*

COMMENTS
Induction system which has a spreadsheet type interface. Coded in Fortran and rules generated in Fortran.

NAME OF PRODUCT   *G-Base*

OTHER NAMES (previous names etc)   *None*

NAME OF VENDOR   *Scientific Computers Ltd   (British distributor)*

CONTACT PERSON   *Alan Gillmore*

ADDRESS OF VENDOR   *Scientific Computers Ltd, Victoria Road, Burgess Hill, West Sussex, RH15 9LW*

Telephone Nº.   *04446 5101*

Names of other vendors/supporters/collaborators   *University of Technology in Compeigne and Graphael*

Telephone Nº. of other vendors

ENVIRONMENT FOR RUNNING PRODUCT

Machine   *TI Explorer, Symbolics, Sun, Apollo*

Operating System

Other required software

PRICE   MAINTENANCE CHARGE

CURRENT RELEASE:

COMMENTS

Object oriented database management system, integrated with (and written in) common Lisp.
Can store many types of data including graphic, video-imaged and audio. Lisp methods and functions
are linked with the data to store information about how to manage facts, check them, display them, etc.
Interactive and menu driven query language. The data model and structure can be modified dynamically.
Control functions maintain data integrity and there are built in functions to maintain data consistency.

NAME OF PRODUCT   *Generis*

OTHER NAMES (previous names etc) *The Fact system*

NAME OF VENDOR   *Deductive Systems Ltd*

CONTACT PERSON   *Moya McNicholas (Uxbridge) Jim Williamson (Glasgow)*

ADDRESS OF VENDOR *3.06 Kelvin Campus, Glasgow G20 0SP;*
Brunel Science Park, Kingston Lane, Uxbridge, UB8 3PQ

Telephone Nº. *041 -946 0365 (Glasgow); 0895 73505 (Uxbridge)*

Names of other vendors/supporters/collaborators
NONE

Telephone Nº. of other vendors

ENVIRONMENT FOR RUNNING PRODUCT

Machine   *Sun 3 & 4; Apollo; HP9000; IBM 6150; DEC VAX   and MicroVAX*

Operating System   *UNIX (all but VAX); VMS (VAX, including MicroVAX)*

Other required software   *None*

PRICE *£4000 - £120 000*   MAINTENANCE CHARGE   *15% p.a.*

CURRENT RELEASE: *v 2.1 (Summer 1988)*

COMMENTS

Intelligent Knowledgebase Management System (IKBMS) combining features of relational database and expert system with AI representation in a single software environment. Claimed to eliminate ES/DBMS integration problems and support creation, maintenance and operation of knowledge-based systems in near-natural language.

NAME OF PRODUCT   *GoldWorks*

OTHER NAMES (previous names etc)   *None*

NAME OF VENDOR   *Artificial Intelligence Limited*

CONTACT PERSON   *Andy Smith and Alexis Figeac*

ADDRESS OF VENDOR   *Greycaine Road, Watford, Herts WD2 4JP*

Telephone N°.   *0923 - 247707*

Names of other vendors/supporters/collaborators
                                    NONE

Telephone N°. of other vendors

ENVIRONMENT FOR RUNNING PRODUCT

Machine   *IBM PC XT/AT; Compaq Deskpro 386. 512K RAM*

Operating System   *PCDOS or MSDOS*

Other required software   *Optional as required for links*

PRICE *£5500*   MAINTENANCE CHARGE   *£825*

CURRENT RELEASE: *1.1*

COMMENTS
   Expert system building tool. Forward, backward and goal-directed chaining; links to Lotus –123, dBASE III. Planned links to mainframe databases. Can call C and Assembler programs.

NAME OF PRODUCT   *Guru*

OTHER NAMES (previous names etc)   *None*

NAME OF VENDOR   *SystemStar Ltd*

CONTACT PERSON   *David Turley*

ADDRESS OF VENDOR   *1-3 Parliament Square, Hertford, SG14 1EX*

Telephone Nº.   *0992 500919*

Names of other vendors/supporters/collaborators

Telephone Nº. of other vendors

ENVIRONMENT FOR RUNNING PRODUCT

Machine   *IBM PC XT/AT/RT; PS/2; LAN; microVAX -> VAX 8800*

Operating System   *MS/PCDOS; OS/2; Novell; 3COM+; AIX; VMS*

Other required software   *Optional extended network DBMS interface - MDBS III*

PRICE   *£5850* | MAINTENANCE CHARGE   *15% after first year*

CURRENT RELEASE: *GURU version 1.1*

COMMENTS

Expert system environment offering natural language, menus, command language and customised interface. Integrates expert systems technology with built-in development tools such as spreadsheet, relational database, communications etc & can also access dBASE II/III files, the MDBS III database & Lotus–123 worksheets. Will chain forwards, backwards or in combination. Rule-firing may be controlled according to various criteria (eg, pursue least-cost solutions first) and 16 different mathematical models for uncertainty are supported. Many advanced development facilities.

NAME OF PRODUCT	IBM Prolog for 370
OTHER NAMES (previous names etc)	None

NAME OF VENDOR	IBM United Kingdom Ltd

CONTACT PERSON   Chris Pollock, KBS Market Development

ADDRESS OF VENDOR   PO Box 118, Normandy House, Alencon Link, Basingstoke, Hampshire RG21 1EJ

Telephone Nº. 0256 56144

Names of other vendors/supporters/collaborators

NONE

Telephone Nº. of other vendors

ENVIRONMENT FOR RUNNING PRODUCT

Machine   IBM System/370 processor or equivalent

Operating System   VM/SP Release 5 or later; VM/SP HPO Release 5 or later; VM/XA SP Release 2 or later

Other required software

PRICE POA	MAINTENANCE CHARGE None

CURRENT RELEASE: Version 1 Release 1 (available from January 1990)

COMMENTS

Implementation of Prolog for VM/CMS with language extensions; interfaces for DBMS, operating system, applications in other languages, screen handler; fast interpreter plus incremental and full compilation; interpreted and compiled code can co-exist; Edinburgh or IBM 'mixed' syntax; Prolog extended to include: arrays, attribute-value lists, character strings, large rational numbers, user-defined types, delayed evaluation and global terms.

NAME OF PRODUCT   *ICL–Adviser*

OTHER NAMES (previous names etc)   *See also SD–Adviser*

NAME OF VENDOR   *ICL*

CONTACT PERSON   *Peter Blacoe, David Young*

ADDRESS OF VENDOR   *Future Systems, ICL, Cardinal House, 18-20 St Marys Parsonage,*
Manchester, M3 2NL

Telephone Nº.   *061-833 9111*

Names of other vendors/supporters/collaborators   *NONE*

Telephone Nº. of other vendors

ENVIRONMENT FOR RUNNING PRODUCT

Machine   *ICL 2900 series and S39; DRS300; DRS PWS*

Operating System   *VME; CDOS v5.1 or later; MSDOS*

Other required software   *None for VME; an editor is needed for DRS300 and PWS*

PRICE   *£16 500   (£1500 for DRS)* | MAINTENANCE CHARGE   *10% p.a. (minimum £100)*

CURRENT RELEASE: *VME v 30.00; DRS 300 1.00; DRS PWS 1.00*

COMMENTS
Menu-driven expert system shell consisting of the Builder, the Interpreter, the Editor and the Manager.
The Interpreter runs the application, the Builder compiles it, the Manager front-ends the result.
Normally backward-chaining, but forward-chaining can be forced. Circular reasoning is trapped.
Demons - "whenever" conditions - are supported. May interface to Cobol, Fortran, Pascal,
SCL or any other language supported by VME.
DRS notes: No editor, WordStar recommended. Interfaces to Microsoft C, Pascal, Fortran, by which
any database access is made.

NAME OF PRODUCT	*Inference ART*
OTHER NAMES (previous names etc)	*NONE*

NAME OF VENDOR *Syseca Temps Reel (Third party vendors)*

CONTACT PERSON *Cyprienne Lancrey-Javal*

ADDRESS OF VENDOR *Syseca Temps Reel, 315 Bureaux de la Colline, 92213 Saint Cloud, CEDEX,*
Paris, France

Telephone Nº.   *(010 33) 1 4911 7151*

Names of other vendors/supporters/collaborators   *Inference Corp, Los Angeles*

Telephone Nº. of other vendors   *(USA)*

ENVIRONMENT FOR RUNNING PRODUCT

Machine   *Sun workstation; VAX mainframes, workstation II, GPX, T.I. Explorer,*
Apollo Domain 4000, Hewlett-Packard 9000, Symbolics 36XX, IBM PC

Operating System   *As per host machines*

Other required software   *Lisp*

PRICE *from US $30 000*	MAINTENANCE CHARGE *US $7500*

CURRENT RELEASE: *3.X*

COMMENTS
Expert system building tool offering Lisp-like language supporting forward and backward chaining,
hypothetical reasoning and object-oriented programming. Has a sophisticated debugging environment,
high-quality bit-mapped graphics, Wimp interface. Requires extensive training.

NAME OF PRODUCT *Intellect*

OTHER NAMES (previous names etc) *None*

NAME OF VENDOR *AICorp*

CONTACT PERSON *Geoff Smith*

ADDRESS OF VENDOR
                    Station House, 1 Harrow Road, Wembley HA9 6DE

Telephone N°. *01 900 2466*

Names of other vendors/supporters/collaborators
                                    NONE

Telephone N°. of other vendors

ENVIRONMENT FOR RUNNING PRODUCT

Machine   *IBM mainframe;*

Operating System   *VM, MVS; MVS/XA TP; TSO, CICS, IMS/DC, CMS*

Other required software *DBMS as required for linkage*

PRICE *£50 000-100 000*   MAINTENANCE CHARGE *15% pa*

CURRENT RELEASE: *403*

COMMENTS
        Natural language front-end to database; links to Focus, SQL/DS, Adabas, DFAM, DB2, IMS,
        CA-IDMS/DB, DBC/1012, sequential files.

NAME OF PRODUCT   *KBMS*

OTHER NAMES (previous names etc)   *None*

NAME OF VENDOR   *Al Corp*

CONTACT PERSON   *Geoff Smith*

ADDRESS OF VENDOR
Station House, 1 Harrow Road, Wembley HA9 6DE

Telephone N°.   *01 900 2466*

Names of other vendors/supporters/collaborators
NONE

Telephone N°. of other vendors

ENVIRONMENT FOR RUNNING PRODUCT

Machine   *IBM mainframe; IBM PC (OS/2 and MS-DOS)*

Operating System   *VM, MVS, MVS/XA; TP; TSO, CICS,IMS/DC, CMS, IDMS DC*

Other required software   *Intellect; DBMS for use with Intellect.*

PRICE   *£65 000- £160 000*   MAINTENANCE CHARGE   *15% p.a.*

CURRENT RELEASE: *403*

COMMENTS
*Knowledge-based application development system. Rule-based and object-oriented programming.
The higher price figure includes payment for Intellect by means of which it can access DB2,
SQL/DS, VSAM , CA-IDMS/DB, IMS-DB and Adabas. Forward and backward chaining,
hypothetical reasoning. Any IBM independent or DB machine eg Teradata has direct connections
with KBMS via the user defined object (UDO).*

NAME OF PRODUCT   *KEE*

OTHER NAMES (previous names etc)   *None*

NAME OF VENDOR   *Intellicorp Ltd*

CONTACT PERSON   *Russell Prince-Wright*

ADDRESS OF VENDOR   *Intellicorp Ltd UK Office, 10 Jewry Street, Winchester, Hampshire, SO23 8RZ*

Telephone Nº.   *0962 735348 or 61518*

Names of other vendors/supporters/collaborators   *Unisys; IBM*

Telephone Nº. of other vendors   *07072 69911; 01 995 1441*

ENVIRONMENT FOR RUNNING PRODUCT

Machine   *IBM mainframe, IBM pc and compatible, Sun, Symbolics, Explorer, Xerox, HP, Apollo, Dec Vax, etc*

Operating System   *Various*

Other required software

PRICE *POA*   MAINTENANCE CHARGE

CURRENT RELEASE: *3.1*

COMMENTS

Lisp-based expert system shell. Wimp interface, graphics, object-oriented programming, production rules, forward and backward chaining. Interfaces to Mapper databases and to IMS, DB2, VSAM, IDMS, Adabas, Total and System 2000 databases. KEE connection provides an interface to numerous databases including Ingres, Oracle and DB2. KEE–C integration package provides a bi-directional link (C-> KEE -> C). Intelliscope can be used in conjunction with KEE and databases.

NAME OF PRODUCT   KES

OTHER NAMES (previous names etc)   KES II (Unisys)

NAME OF VENDOR   Software Architecture and Engineering

CONTACT PERSON   Seamus Ross

ADDRESS OF VENDOR   Sussex Suite, City Gates, 2-4 Southgate, Chichester, PO19 2DJ

Telephone N°.   0243 789310

Names of developers   Software Architecture and Engineering, USA

Telephone N°. of other vendors   Some hardware vendors - contact Software A&E

ENVIRONMENT FOR RUNNING PRODUCT

Machine   IBM PC, AT, PS2, UNIX workstations, minis and mainframes

Operating System   DOS, OS2, Xenix, Unix, VMS, VM/CMS, MVS/TSO and others

Other required software   None

PRICE   £2500 to 40 000   MAINTENANCE CHARGE   Incl. 1st year; 15% thereafter

CURRENT RELEASE: KES 2.5 / 2.6

COMMENTS

KES is an object oriented expert system development toolkit which supports three inference engines, forward and backward chaining, classes and inheritance, and integral procedural language. Written in C, it has an Application Programmers Interface and is source code compatible across 70 platforms with graphical interface under X-windows. Several levels of interfacing to databases.

NAME OF PRODUCT   *Knowledgecraft*

OTHER NAMES (previous names etc)

NAME OF VENDOR   *Carnegie (UK) Ltd*

CONTACT PERSON

ADDRESS OF VENDOR

Telephone Nº.

Names of other vendors/supporters/collaborators   *Kingham Business Systems, Kingham House, East End, Newbury, Berks*

Telephone Nº. of other vendors   *0635 254710*

ENVIRONMENT FOR RUNNING PRODUCT

Machine   *VAX, Sun, 386*

Operating System   *Various*

Other required software

PRICE	MAINTENANCE CHARGE

CURRENT RELEASE: *3.2*

COMMENTS

Integrated set of tools with a flexible architecture, various knowledge representations and multiple inferencing strategies. KC/SQL provides connectivity to SQL databases including Oracle, DB2 and DEC Rdb.

NAME OF PRODUCT   *KnowledgePro*

OTHER NAMES (previous names etc)   *None*

NAME OF VENDOR   *Intellisoft (UK) Ltd*

CONTACT PERSON

ADDRESS OF VENDOR   *Intellisoft (UK) Ltd, 77A Packhorse Road, Gerrards Cross, Bucks, SL9 8PQ*

Telephone Nº.   *0753 889972*

Names of other vendors/supporters/collaborators   *None*

Telephone Nº. of other vendors

ENVIRONMENT FOR RUNNING PRODUCT

Machine   *286 and 386 clones*

Operating System

Other required software

PRICE   *£329 (£25 for demo)*   MAINTENANCE CHARGE

CURRENT RELEASE:

COMMENTS

KnowledgePro combines Hypertext and expert system technologies in a high level language. The symbolic language allows 'chunks of knowledge' containing rules, calculations, commands, text and graphics to be created. External files can be read and external programs called. Add-on extras include a Database Toolkit to allow reading of dBASE III and Lotus–123 files; Graphics Toolkit for hypergraphics; Video Toolkit to control a laser video disk player; KnowledgeMaker for rule induction.

NAME OF PRODUCT   *IBM KnowledgeTool*

OTHER NAMES (previous names etc)   *None*

NAME OF VENDOR   *IBM United Kingdom Ltd*

CONTACT PERSON   *Chris Pollock, KBS Market Development*

ADDRESS OF VENDOR   *PO Box 118, Normandy House, Alencon Link, Basingstoke, Hampshire, RG21 1EJ*

Telephone Nº.   *0256 56144*

Names of other vendors/supporters/collaborators
NONE
Telephone Nº. of other vendors

ENVIRONMENT FOR RUNNING PRODUCT

Machine   *IBM 1370 processor or equivalent; IBM AS/400*

Operating System   *MVS ,VM or OS/400*

Other required software   *IBM PL/1 optimising compiler and library*

PRICE *POA*   MAINTENANCE CHARGE *None*

CURRENT RELEASE: *version 2 release 1*

COMMENTS
KBS development tool providing rule-based language, high performance inference engine, application debugging environment. Can access IBM supported databases. Forward chaining, pattern matching, conflict resolution; can call and be called by Cobol, PL/1, Assembler, Fortran and Pascal. DBMS and program linkage in general is as for PL/1.

NAME OF PRODUCT *Leonardo*

OTHER NAMES (previous names etc) *None*

NAME OF VENDOR *Creative Logic Ltd*

CONTACT PERSON *R G Hunte*

ADDRESS OF VENDOR *Brunel Science Park, Kingston Lane, Uxbridge, Middlesex, UB8 3PQ*

Telephone N⁰. *0895 74468/9; 0895 70091* *Fax: 0895 - 70244*

Names of other vendors/supporters/collaborators

NONE

Telephone N⁰. of other vendors

ENVIRONMENT FOR RUNNING PRODUCT

Machine *IBM PC/compatible; DEC VAX (microVAX, 73x, 75x, 78x, 85xx - 89xx); Sun, Apollo*

Operating System *PCDOS/MSDOS; VMS; Sunos; Aegis*

Other required software *Optionally dBASE II/III, Lotus–123, Btrieve.*

PRICE *See below* | MAINTENANCE CHARGE *£150 - £300 pa (!st year free)*

CURRENT RELEASE: —

COMMENTS

Expert system development tool. Rule-based expert system shell, forward and backward chaining (for debugging, one at a time can be enforced) and procedural language. Links to dBASE, Lotus–123 and Btrieve. Leonardo 2 allows unlimited-size rulebases, frames & inheritance; Leonardo 3 also allows several forms of uncertainty, dynamic creation of instance objects & memberslots at runtime.
PC prices: Leonardo 1 - £149 Leonardo 2 - £695 Leonardo 3 - £1995. Upgradeable, trade-in available VAX prices: £4000 (microVAX, 73x - 75x) £8000 (85xx, 86xx) £12 000 (87xx - 89xx).

NAME OF PRODUCT   *Level5 Object*

OTHER NAMES (previous names etc)   *Insight, Insight 2, Insight 2+, Level5*

NAME OF VENDOR   *Information Builders (UK) Ltd*

CONTACT PERSON   *Peter Smith*

ADDRESS OF VENDOR   *Station House, Harrow Road, Wembley, Middlesex, HA9 6DE*

Telephone Nº.   *01 - 903 - 6111*

Names of other vendors/supporters/collaborators

NONE

Telephone Nº. of other vendors

ENVIRONMENT FOR RUNNING PRODUCT

Machine   *IBM PC/XT/AT or PS/2; IBM compatible; Macintosh Plus, SE or II; DEC VAX; IBM mainframe*

Operating System   *MS/DOS or PCDOS v 2.0 or later ; Macintosh system rel 4.2 or later; VMS v4.4 or later: CMS*

Other required software   *NONE*

PRICE *£950 (PC, Apple)* | MAINTENANCE CHARGE

CURRENT RELEASE: *Release 2.0*

COMMENTS

Integrated expert system shell: inference engine, editor, compiler, database access modules. English-like syntax. Backward chaining with goal outlines, knowledge-base chaining and shared facts. Full portability across hardware platforms. Production and Run-Only systems for all applications for a one-time cost of £4000. Educational discount available. Release 2.0 includes frames, forward chaining, mixed inference modes,Wimp interface and Ruletalk, an integrated window-based development environment.
Prices for VAX and IBM CMS are available on req uest.

NAME OF PRODUCT *LPA Prolog / flex*

OTHER NAMES (previous names etc)

NAME OF VENDOR *Logic Programming Associates Ltd*

CONTACT PERSON

ADDRESS OF VENDOR *Studio 4, The Royal Victoria Patriotic Building, Trinity Road, London, SW18 3SX*

Telephone Nº. *01 871 2016*

Names of other vendors/supporters/collaborators

Telephone Nº. of other vendors

ENVIRONMENT FOR RUNNING PRODUCT

Machine *IBM pcs and compatibles*

Operating System *MS-DOS*

Other required software

PRICE   **MAINTENANCE CHARGE**

CURRENT RELEASE:

COMMENTS
Edinburgh syntax system with a complete set of standard predicates. Software package comprises an incremental compiler, optimising compiler, GSX graphics interface and C/Assembler interfaces. Able to exit to DOS and direct running of .EXE files. Two toolkits are available to assist in building applications: the HCI toolkit can be used for constructing user interfaces; and flex can be used to build systems.
Flex combines frames, objects and rules, using KSL (Knowledge Specification Language). Flex has been incorporated into a number of other KBS tools, including Top-One.

NAME OF PRODUCT   *MacProlog*

OTHER NAMES (previous names etc)

NAME OF VENDOR   *Logic Programming Associates Ltd*

CONTACT PERSON

ADDRESS OF VENDOR   *Studio 4, The Royal Victoria Patriotic Building, Trinity Road, London, SW18 3SX*

Telephone Nº.   *01 871 2016*

Names of other vendors/supporters/collaborators

Telephone Nº. of other vendors

ENVIRONMENT FOR RUNNING PRODUCT

Machine   *Apple Macintosh MacII, SE, Plus*

Operating System

Other required software

PRICE   *£495 (£595 for colour)* | MAINTENANCE CHARGE

CURRENT RELEASE: *2.0*

COMMENTS

Combines artificial intelligence with the user friendly interface and enhanced graphics of the Apple Macintosh. Uses an extension of Edinburgh Prolog syntax, compatible with Quintus Prolog. Has a comprehensive set of primitives designed to exploit the Macintosh interface, for example to generate dialogues, install user defined menus, track the mouse, or draw and manipulate complex graphical objects.

NAME OF PRODUCT	*MVS/Prolog*
OTHER NAMES (previous names etc)	

NAME OF VENDOR	*IBM United Kingdom Ltd*
CONTACT PERSON	*Chris Pollock KBS Market Development*

ADDRESS OF VENDOR *PO Box 118, Normandy House, Alencon Link, Basingstoke, Hampshire, RG21 1EJ*

Telephone №. *0256 56144*

Names of other vendors/supporters/collaborators

NONE

Telephone №. of other vendors

ENVIRONMENT FOR RUNNING PRODUCT

Machine *IBM System/370 processor or equivalent*

Operating System *MVS*

Other required software *Optional DB2*

PRICE *P O A*	MAINTENANCE CHARGE *None*

CURRENT RELEASE:

COMMENTS

Implementation of Prolog to run under MVS supporting computable expressions, interfaces to TSO/E and ISPF, accessing DB2 databases and links to IBM Assembler programs.

NAME OF PRODUCT   *Natural Expert*

OTHER NAMES (previous names etc)   *None*

NAME OF VENDOR   *Software Ag*

CONTACT PERSON   *N Casson or A Yuill*

ADDRESS OF VENDOR   *Laurie House, 22 Colyear Street, Derby DE1 1LA*

Telephone Nº.   *0332 372535*

Names of other vendors/supporters/collaborators

NONE

Telephone Nº. of other vendors

ENVIRONMENT FOR RUNNING PRODUCT

Machine   *IBM 370, 3080, 3090, 4300, 9370; SIEMENS mainframes*

Operating System   *MVS, MVS/XA, BS2000, DOS*

Other required software   *Adabas version 4 or 5: Natural version 2*

PRICE   *Available on request* | MAINTENANCE CHARGE

CURRENT RELEASE: *Released 13.2.90 v1.1*

COMMENTS

Integrated with Natural, accessing and updating the Adabas knowledge database, including hypertext information. Forward and backward chaining. Integrated with Natural applications.
Can access DB2, DL/1 and VSAM files as well as Adabas production databases. Programming languages with standard IBM linkage conventions may be called from Natural, such as C, Cobol, PL/1, Fortran.

NAME OF PRODUCT   *Nexpert Object*

OTHER NAMES (previous names etc)   *None*

NAME OF VENDOR   *Neuron Data*

CONTACT PERSON

ADDRESS OF VENDOR   *34 South Moulton Street, London, W1Y 2BP*

Telephone N°.   *01 408 2333*

Names of other vendors/supporters/collaborators   *Software Sciences Ltd 0252 513739*
Megatron Computer Systems Ltd 0923 22 5278
Telephone N°. of other vendors   *Bechtel Ltd 01 846 6940*

ENVIRONMENT FOR RUNNING PRODUCT

Machine   *IBM PC AT/ PS2; Macintosh; DEC VAX; DEC station; VAX station;*
Sun, Apollo, HP workstations.

Operating System   *PCDOS/OS2; MAC OS; VMS/UIS and DEC windows; UNIX*

Other required software   *X-Windows (Sun, VAX); Microsoft Windows (PC)*

PRICE   *£7500 (£4500 on PC/MAC)*   MAINTENANCE CHARGE   *Price on application*

CURRENT RELEASE:

COMMENTS

Hybrid expert system building tool incorporating object and rule representation, pattern-matching, integrated forward and backward chaining, automatic goal generation, non-monotonic reasoning. Uses a windowing development environment. Incremental compiler. Can access DBIII, SQL or Rdb databases according to environment as well as Lotus 1-2-3 worksheets. Wimp interface can be built-in to the system, which may be integrated with application written in C, Fortran, Ada, Cobol, Pascal and others. System written in C, applications portable across supported hardware.

NAME OF PRODUCT *Parys*

OTHER NAMES (previous names etc) *None*

NAME OF VENDOR *Unibit*

CONTACT PERSON *S R Barr*

ADDRESS OF VENDOR *Unibit Holdings plc, Bradford University Science Park, 20-26 Campus Road, Bradford, West Yorkshire, BD7 1HR*

Telephone N⁰. *0274 736766*

Names of other vendors/supporters/collaborators *None*

Telephone N⁰. of other vendors

ENVIRONMENT FOR RUNNING PRODUCT

Machine *IBM pc or compatible*

Operating System

Other required software

PRICE | MAINTENANCE CHARGE

CURRENT RELEASE:

COMMENTS

Parys is an application environment designed for human resource managers as a set of software tools for customising applications (such as job design and vacancy management) to organisational needs. It can be integrated with word processing systems, spreadsheets and personnel record systems. Incorporated in Parys is an expert system application and a database

NAME OF PRODUCT   *Personal Consultant Series*

OTHER NAMES (previous names etc)   *None*

NAME OF VENDOR   *Texas Instruments Ltd*

CONTACT PERSON   *Martin Black*

ADDRESS OF VENDOR   *Manton Lane, Bedford MK41 7PA*

Telephone Nº.   *0234 - 270111*

Names of other vendors/supporters/collaborators

NONE

Telephone Nº. of other vendors

ENVIRONMENT FOR RUNNING PRODUCT

Machine   *IBM PC; IBM PS2; IBM compatible; TI Explorer*

Operating System   *PCDOS; OS2; MSDOS; MSDOS*

Other required software   *None*

PRICE   *See below*   MAINTENANCE CHARGE   ——————

CURRENT RELEASE: *3.02*

COMMENTS
*Two compatible expert system shells, PC Easy and PC Plus, and two add-on packages for the
latter, PC Images and PC Online. Either shell can access dBASE databases, Lotus–123 worksheets
or DOS text files. PC Plus can also use C and TurboPascal routines. Lisp is also accessible.
PC Easy applications can be moved to PC Plus with no modification. The same run-time system is
used for both.
Prices: PC Easy: £495   PC Plus: £1995   PC Images: £295   PC Online: £595*

NAME OF PRODUCT   *Prospect*

OTHER NAMES (previous names etc)

NAME OF VENDOR   *Lateral Systems Ltd*

CONTACT PERSON   *C J Cowland*

ADDRESS OF VENDOR   *Lateral Systems Ltd, 15 Barrons Row, Harpenden, Herts., AL5 1DS*

Telephone Nº.   *05827 3950*

Names of other vendors/supporters/collaborators   *Logic Programming Associates produce Flex;*
Information Management System produce ASPECT

Telephone Nº. of other vendors   *01 871 2016 (LPA)   01 948 8255*

ENVIRONMENT FOR RUNNING PRODUCT

Machine   *IBM pc or compatible*

Operating System

Other required software

PRICE | MAINTENANCE CHARGE

CURRENT RELEASE:

COMMENTS

Prospect is made up of Flex, a toolkit which provides a set of extensions to Prolog and Object
Orientation, and Aspect which is a database management system and application generator. New
facilities have been added, primarily rule induction, hypertext facilities and CASE tools.

NAME OF PRODUCT   *Quintec Prolog / flex*

OTHER NAMES (previous names etc)

NAME OF VENDOR   *Quintec Systems Ltd*

CONTACT PERSON   *Georges Saab*

ADDRESS OF VENDOR   *Quintec Systems Ltd, Wadham Court, Edgeway Road, Marston, Oxford,*
OX3 0HD

Telephone Nº.   *0865 791565*

Names of other vendors/supporters/collaborators

Telephone Nº. of other vendors

ENVIRONMENT FOR RUNNING PRODUCT

Machine   *32 bit workstations such as Sun and VAX station, VAX, PS/2*

Operating System   *UNIX, OS/2*

Other required software

PRICE   MAINTENANCE CHARGE

CURRENT RELEASE:

COMMENTS

Full implementation of Prolog with extended features. Incremental compiler which delivers compact
code. An interactive Environment Shell supports the compiler with menus, windows, dialogue boxes,
etc. Support for modularisation. Interfaces to C, Fortran and Pascal. Interfaces to Ingres and Oracle are
provided. Quintec flex is the same as LPA flex.

NAME OF PRODUCT   *Quintus Prolog*

OTHER NAMES (previous names etc)   *None*

NAME OF VENDOR   *Artificial Intelligence Limited*

CONTACT PERSON

ADDRESS OF VENDOR   *Greycaine Road, Watford, Herts WD2 4JP*

Telephone Nº.   *0923 - 247707*

Names of other ~~vendors/supporters/~~collaborators   *Prodata (Quintus / Oracle interface) marketed by*
Keylink Computers Ltd, 35 Pioneer Villas, Ogden,
Telephone Nº. of other vendors   *Newhey, Lancs, OL16 3TE*

ENVIRONMENT FOR RUNNING PRODUCT

Machine   *Sun ws; DEC VAX; Apollo Domain; Xerox 1100; IBM RT PC; NCR Tower; IBM mainframe*

Operating System   *UNIX; Ultrix, VMS; UNIX; MVS (IBM mainframe)*

Other required software

PRICE *£3250 to £9150*   MAINTENANCE CHARGE

CURRENT RELEASE:

COMMENTS
Prolog-based software development system with links to many languages,Unify & Oracle databases.
Stream-based I/O including random file access; floating-point arithmetic supported. Incremental
compiler, windowing screen editor, debugger, style checker.

NAME OF PRODUCT   *Reveal*

OTHER NAMES (previous names etc)   *None*

NAME OF VENDOR   *ICL*

CONTACT PERSON   *Peter Blacoe, David Young*

ADDRESS OF VENDOR   *Future Systems, ICL, Cardinal House, 18-20 St Marys Parsonage, Manchester, M3 2NL*

Telephone №.   *061 833 9111*

Names of other vendors/supporters/collaborators
                                    NONE

Telephone №. of other vendors

ENVIRONMENT FOR RUNNING PRODUCT

Machine   *ICL 2900 or S39 mainframe*

Operating System   *VME*

Other required software   *Cobol, Fortran optional*

PRICE   *See below*   MAINTENANCE CHARGE

CURRENT RELEASE:

COMMENTS
Business modelling tool allowing fuzzy-logic queries to a relational database. Links to Cobol and Fortran ,access to VME files, graphics and statistics functions. English-like command language.
Per quarter £435 (small 2900) to £762 (large S39)

NAME OF PRODUCT *Rulemaster*

OTHER NAMES (previous names etc)   *Rulemaker*

NAME OF VENDOR   *Radian Corporation*

CONTACT PERSON

ADDRESS OF VENDOR   *Texas, USA*

Telephone Nº.   *512 454 4797*

Names of other vendors/supporters/collaborators

Telephone Nº. of other vendors

ENVIRONMENT FOR RUNNING PRODUCT

Machine   *IBM pc and compatibles; Sun, Apollo, HP9000; DEC VAX*

Operating System   *DOS; UNIX; Ultrix*

Other required software

PRICE   MAINTENANCE CHARGE

CURRENT RELEASE:

COMMENTS
   Rulemaker is the rule generating part of Rulemaster. A C source code generator is available.
   Rulemaster is a rule based shell.

NAME OF PRODUCT *Savoir*

OTHER NAMES (previous names etc)

NAME OF VENDOR *Expertech (after a takeover of Intelligent Systems International Ltd)*

CONTACT PERSON

ADDRESS OF VENDOR *Expertech House, 163 Bestobell Road, Slough, Berkshire, SL1 4TY*

Telephone Nº. *0753 696321*

Names of other vendors/supporters/collaborators
                                    NONE
Telephone Nº. of other vendors

ENVIRONMENT FOR RUNNING PRODUCT

Machine *IBM PC and compatibles; VAX*

Operating System *MSDOS; VMS*

Other required software *Optional DBMS*

PRICE *See below*   MAINTENANCE CHARGE *10% per annum*

CURRENT RELEASE: *1.5*

COMMENTS
Expert system language and associated tools supporting forward and backward chaining, un-certainty handling, colour windowing displays, calls to external programs, dBASE III interface, demons, English-like language. Up to 2250 rules can be handled on a PC or similar, up to 20,000 on a mainframe. Source-compatible across supported hardware. Prices:
PC or similar - £1000   *Runtime systems: £50*
MicroVAX - £2000   *Low cost evaluation version: £200*
VAX   - £3000 or £4000

NAME OF PRODUCT   *SD–Adviser*

OTHER NAMES (previous names etc)   *Sage, Envisage*

NAME OF VENDOR   *SD–Scicon*

CONTACT PERSON

ADDRESS OF VENDOR   *Software Technology Centre, Pembroke House, Pembroke Broadway, Camberley, Surrey GU15 3XD*

Telephone Nº.   *0276 - 686200*

Names of other vendors/supporters/collaborators
                                        NONE

Telephone Nº. of other vendors

ENVIRONMENT FOR RUNNING PRODUCT

Machine   *IBM PC and compatibles; PDP-11; DEC VAX*

Operating System   *PCDOS, MSDOS; RSX11-M; VMS*

Other required software *None*

PRICE *£2.5K (PC) - £10K (VAX)*   MAINTENANCE CHARGE

CURRENT RELEASE:

COMMENTS
   Expert system shell. English-like knowledge representation language, database interface, fuzzy logic, Bayesian inferencing, links to Pascal and Fortran. Functionality is consistent with ICL–Adviser.

NAME OF PRODUCT   *Spices*

OTHER NAMES (previous names etc)   *None*

NAME OF VENDOR   *AEA Technology*

CONTACT PERSON

ADDRESS OF VENDOR   *Knowledge Engineering Services Centre, Harwell Laboratory, AEA Technology, Oxfordshire OX11 0RA*

Telephone Nº. *0235 24141 x 3434*

Names of other vendors/supporters/collaborators *Valerie Calderbank*
CASS, Culham Laboratory, AEA Technology Culham Abingdon, Oxfordshire OX14 3DB

Telephone Nº. of other vendors *0235 463356*

ENVIRONMENT FOR RUNNING PRODUCT

Machine   *IBM PC; DEC VAX; PRIME*

Operating System   *PCDOS; VMS; PRIMOS*

Other required software

PRICE   *£1500 (PC)*   MAINTENANCE CHARGE   *£300 pa (PC)*

CURRENT RELEASE: *3.0*

COMMENTS

Rule-based expert system tool supporting forward and backward chaining. It is written in Prolog, and statements in Prolog can be included in a Spices rule. Extensive knowledge base segmentation facilities are provided. Spices commands may be amended or added by the builder. Sophisticated off-line knowledge base analysis tools called Spick and Span are also available.
Prices for VAX and Prime are available on request.

NAME OF PRODUCT   *Today*

OTHER NAMES (previous names etc)   *None*

NAME OF VENDOR   *Computer Power Europe Ltd*

CONTACT PERSON   *Ed Barker*

ADDRESS OF VENDOR   *Berkeley House, 51-53 High St., Redhill, Surrey RH1 1RX*

Telephone Nº.   *0737 764500*

Names of other vendors/supporters/collaborators
                                    NONE
Telephone Nº. of other vendors

ENVIRONMENT FOR RUNNING PRODUCT

Machine   *IBM, HP, Sun, NCR, Pyramid, Prime, Unisys, etc*

Operating System   *MS-DOS, VAX/VMS, HP MPE, PRIMOS, UNIX, etc*

Other required software

PRICE *According to hardware*   MAINTENANCE CHARGE

CURRENT RELEASE: *Version 3*

COMMENTS
Inductive learning expert system environment designed to derive decision trees from supplied examples of expertise. Rules can be added explicitly. Occasional inaccurate examples can be "gracefully" handled. "Don't know" and "don't care" values are supported. Integration with Today 4GL allows report-writing, database access etc.

NAME OF PRODUCT   *Top–One*

OTHER NAMES (previous names etc)

NAME OF VENDOR   *Telecomputing plc*

CONTACT PERSON

ADDRESS OF VENDOR   *244 Barn's Road, Oxford OX4 3RW*

Telephone Nº.   *0865 - 777755*

Names of other vendors/supporters/collaborators

NONE

Telephone Nº. of other vendors

ENVIRONMENT FOR RUNNING PRODUCT

Machine   *IBM PC; IBM and ICL mainframes*

Operating System   *PCDOS; MVS(XA), VM,VSE; VME*

Other required software   *Optional CICS, IMS/DC, TSO, TPMS, QB*

PRICE   *£1 000 to £88 000* | MAINTENANCE CHARGE

CURRENT RELEASE:

COMMENTS

Top–One consists of Top–One /Flex and Top–One/Prolog. The former provides an English-like syntax for specifying rules, frames, etc. Top–One/Prolog has added facilities for integration with other applications. On-line and batch access to conventional files and databases is provided. The system can be integrated with TP systems.

NAME OF PRODUCT   *VM/Prolog*

OTHER NAMES (previous names etc)

NAME OF VENDOR   *IBM United Kingdom Ltd*

CONTACT PERSON   *Chris Pollock, KBS Market Development*

ADDRESS OF VENDOR *PO Box 118, Normandy House, Alencon Link, Basingstoke, Hampshire,*
                                                                           RG21 1EJ

Telephone Nº. *0256 56144*

Names of other vendors/supporters/collaborators
                                        None

Telephone Nº. of other vendors

ENVIRONMENT FOR RUNNING PRODUCT

Machine   *IBM System/370 processor or equivalent*

Operating System   *VM /SP release 3*

Other required software *Optional SQL/DS*

PRICE   *P O A*   MAINTENANCE CHARGE   *None*

CURRENT RELEASE:

COMMENTS
   Implementation of Prolog to run under VM/SP supporting computable expressions, interfaces to
   VM/SP and Lisp/VM, accessing SQL/DS databases . Optimised tail recursion, ability to define
   non-updatable rules as static for increased interpretation speed. Handles 32-bit integers, floating-
   point and character strings. Extra predicates can be written in Assembler language and loaded as
   needed.

NAME OF PRODUCT *XiPlus*

OTHER NAMES (previous names etc) *None*

NAME OF VENDOR *Expertech*

CONTACT PERSON

ADDRESS OF VENDOR *Expertech House, 163 Bestobell Road, Slough, Berkshire SL1 4TY*

Telephone Nº. *0753 696321*

Names of other vendors/supporters/collaborators

NONE

Telephone Nº. of other vendors

ENVIRONMENT FOR RUNNING PRODUCT

Machine *IBM PC and compatibles; VAX*

Operating System *PCDOS/MSDOS v2.0 and later; VMS*

Other required software *None*

PRICE *£1995* | MAINTENANCE CHARGE *£275 pa*

CURRENT RELEASE: *Release 3*

COMMENTS

Expert system shell with interface to Assembler , Basic and C, able to read ASCII text files, DIF files, Multiplan symbolic link files and Lotus–123 worksheets. Graphic displays can be produced. dBASE III databases can be accessed. Executable files can be invoked such as dBASE III, Lotus–123 etc. XiRule Plus provides rule induction facilities. Can call DOS directly from knowledge base.

NAME OF PRODUCT   *XpertRule*

OTHER NAMES (previous names etc)

NAME OF VENDOR   *Attar Software Ltd*

CONTACT PERSON   *David Isherwood*

ADDRESS OF VENDOR   *Attar Software Ltd, Newlands Road, Leigh, Lancashire, WN7 4HN*

Telephone Nº. *0942 608844*

Names of other vendors/supporters/collaborators *Dataflex (Information Management) Services Ltd*

Telephone Nº. of other vendors   *01 729 4460*

ENVIRONMENT FOR RUNNING PRODUCT

Machine   *IBM pc or compatible*

Operating System   *MS–DOS*

Other required software

PRICE   MAINTENANCE CHARGE

CURRENT RELEASE:

COMMENTS

Rule induction system, written in Turbo Pascal, which can use examples input by the user or examples extracted from data files. Rules can be exported as Pascal, Cobol, Basic, C, Fortran, dBASE III commands, SQL or production rules.
The Dataflex version is a customised version of Xpertrule which just exports Dataflex and C.

Annex C

Matrix of KBS versus DBMS, Spreadsheet, Languages and Environments

Many knowledge-based system (KBS) tools are used throughout the book as examples. The matrices on the following pages indicate some of the combinations of KBS tools and database management systems, spreadsheets, languages, operating system and transaction processing environments which are available. All combinations are not necessarily available on all possible hardware platforms; readers should confirm availability with the appropriate software vendors. The tables are not complete: the range of KBS tools on the vertical axis could be extended, and since tool vendors are continually enhancing their products to integrate with other software, the entries for each tool may be incomplete. The tables should be seen as illustrative and neither representative nor comprehensive.

Key

D	direct access to DBMS from KBS tool
I	indirect access to DBMS via other software
?	access to DBMS is likely, but uncertain
X	access to spreadsheet, language, operating system or TP environment

KBS Tool \ DBMS	Adabas	Aspect	DB2	dBASE III	DL/1 (IMS/DB)	Focus	IDMS (VME)	CA-IDMS/DB	CA-DB/VAX	Informix
Advisor-2				D						
ADS	I		D	I	D			I	I	
Beagle				I						
BIM Prolog										
CA-DB:Expert	I		D		I	I		D	D	
Crystal				D						
Db-Edge			D							
ESE	I		D	I	I					
Extran										
Goldworks				D						
Guru				D						
ICL-Adviser							I			
Inference ART					I					
Intellect	D		D			D		D		
KBMS	D		D		D			D		
KEE	I		I/D		I			I		
KES	I		I	I	I	I		I	I	I
Knowledgecraft			I							
KnowledgePro				D						
Knowledgetool	?		D		D			D		
Leonardo				I						
Level5 Object			D	D		D			D	
MVS/Prolog			D							
Natural Expert	D		D		D			D	D	D
Nexpert Object			D MVS only	I						I
Parys										
Personal Consultant				D						
Prospect		D								
Quintus Prolog			I							
Reveal							I			
Rulemaster										
Savoir				D/I						
SD-Adviser										
Spices				I						
Today			D							D
Top-One	I		I	D	I		D			
VM/Prolog										
Xiplus				I						
XpertRule				I						

KBS Tool \ DBMS	Ingres	Mapper	Oracle	Rdb	SQL/DS	Status	Sybase	Total	Unify	Lotus-123
Advisor-2										X
ADS	I		I		D					X
Beagle										X
BIM Prolog	D		D				D		D	
CA-DB:Expert	I		D	I	I		I			
Crystal										X
Db-Edge										
ESE	?		?		D					
Extran										
Goldworks										X
Guru										X
ICL-Adviser	I		I			I				
Inference ART	I									
Intellect				D	D					
KBMS			I		D			I		
KEE	D/I	I	D					I		
KES	I	I	D	I	I		I		I	X
Knowledgecraft			I	I						
KnowledgePro										X
Knowledgetool	?		?		D			?		
Leonardo										X
Level5 Object			D	D	D					
MVS/Prolog										
Natural Expert	D		D	D			D	I	D	X
Nexpert Object	I		I	D	I		I			X
Parys										X
Personal Consultant										X
Prospect										X
Quintus Prolog			D						D	
Reveal	I					I				
Rulemaster										
Savoir										
SD-Adviser										
Spices						D				X
Today			D	D						
Top-One	I		I		I			I		X
VM/Prolog					D					
Xiplus										X
XpertRule										

KBS Tool \ Language or Env.	Ada	Algol	Assembler	Basic	C	Cobol	Fortran	Pascal	PL/1	Op system	TPMS (VME)	CICS	TSO	IMS
Advisor-2					X		X	X		X				
ADS			X		X	X	X	X	X	X		X	X	X
Beagle				X	X		X	X						
BIM Prolog			X		X		X	X						
CA-DB:Expert			X			X						X	X	
Crystal					X					X				
Db-Edge														
ESE			X			X	X	X	X			X		X
Extran							X							
Goldworks			X		X									
Guru														
ICL-Adviser					X	X	X	X		X				
Inference ART					X		X							
Intellect												X	X	X
KBMS			X			X			X	X		X	X	X
KEE					X	X	X	X					X	
KES					X	X				X		X	X	X
Knowledgecraft														
KnowledgePro														
Knowledgetool			X		X	X	X	X	X			X		X
Leonardo					X	X	X	X						
Level5 Object													X	
MVS/Prolog			X							X			X	
Natural Expert		X	X	X	X	X	X	X	X			X	X	X
Nexpert Object	X				X	X	X	X				X	X	X
Parys														
Personal Consultant					X			X						
Prospect														
Quintus Prolog					X		X	X						
Reveal		X				X	X			X				
Rulemaster					X									
Savoir					X		X	X						
SD-Adviser							X	X						
Spices					X		X	X		X				
Today			X		X	X	X	X		X				
Top-One			X	X	X	X	X	X	X	X	X	X	X	X
VM/Prolog			X							X				
Xiplus			X	X	X	X VAX/X VAX	X VAX	X						
XpertRule				X	X	X	X	X						

Annex D

Examples of database and spreadsheet access

The mechanisms employed by a number of tools for specifying an interface to a database or a spreadsheet in a KBS application are described here. The following tools are included in alphabetical order:

1.   Aion Development System (ADS)

2.   BIM Prolog

3.   CA–DB:Expert

4.   Crystal

5.   Expert Systems Environment

6.   GURU

7.   ICL–Adviser

8.   Inference ART

9.   KBMS

10.   KEEconnection

11.   KEE (Unisys)

12.   KES

13.   Knowledgecraft

14.   Knowledgetool

15.   Leonardo

16.   Level5 Object

17.   MVS/Prolog and VM/Prolog

18.   Natural Expert

19.   Nexpert Object

20.   Prospect / flex

21.   Quintec Prolog

22.   Quintus Prolog

23.   Reveal

24.   Savoir

25.   Spices

26.   Today

27.   Top–One

28.   XiPlus

D1   AION DEVELOPMENT SYSTEM

D1.1   Overview of mechanism

Aion Development System (ADS) can access directly DB2, DL/1, VSAM, QSAM and SQL/DS databases and files. Any database which can be accessed by an external program (written in a conventional language) can be accessed by ADS, including Oracle, Ingres, Adabas and IDMS. ADS applications which access data can be delivered to run in a number of teleprocessing environments.

D1.2   Data types

No information given.

D1.3   Data access

Mainframe

Figure D1.1 illustrates the architecture of the CICS Option for ADS/MVS within the CICS environment and shows how databases and files can be accessed. An ADS/CICS transaction uses standard CICS services for terminal interaction and database communication.

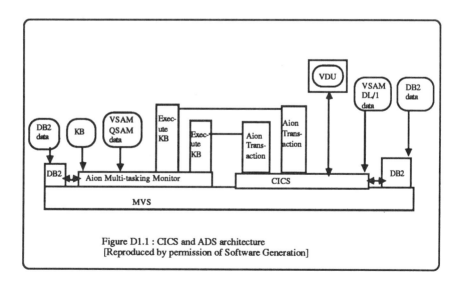

Figure D1.1 : CICS and ADS architecture
[Reproduced by permission of Software Generation]

The Aion region contains the multi–tasking monitor, which controls multiple concurrent sessions of knowledge–base execution. When the Aion transaction is invoked, it allocates a VTAM session and exchanges information with the Aion multi–tasking monitor. All screen interaction is handled by CICS through the requests generated by the Aion transaction.

DB2, VSAM and DL/1 data that exists under the control of CICS are accessed through requests generated by the Aion transaction, so data integrity remains under the control of CICS. Data that exists outside of CICS can be accessed directly from the Aion address space. In both cases, the data request is generated automatically by ADS based on statements within the knowledge–base.

This well integrated architecture illustrates a number of useful features:

- ADS applications can be moved between CICS/VS and IMS/VS without redesign or translation;

- this architecture is compatible with existing security packages;

- multiple Aion address spaces can be used and multiple CICS regions can be supported with a single Aion address space.

The above architecture shows how data can be accessed directly by an ADS application. Indirect access to data can be achieved by calling external programs; all languages which follow standard S/370 linkage conventions on IBM mainframes are supported, which includes Cobol, C, PL/1 and Assembler. A 'call' is made through an ADS Process object and the Aion Data Transfer Interface. The developer specifies the program he wishes to call, data to be passed out and data to be received.

The modular architecture of ADS allows full integration with other systems. For example:

- ADS applications can be called from conventional applications;

- the user interface, report generation, graphics and data access can be embedded in conventional applications or the ADS application;

- data transfer between the ADS application and calling or called programs is performed in memory;

- ADS 'code' is fully re–entrant, allowing for multi–tasking support.

Personal computers

The Aion Cooperative Processing Option (CPO) provides access from Aion applications running on micros to data residing on mainframes. The databases remain secure since CPO uses CICS and security interfaces. VSAM, DB2 and DL/1 databases under CICS control can be accessed. Remote knowledge–bases (on the mainframe) can also be called, which in turn may access data files as given above.

Pre–supplied routines are provided to Lotus–123 spreadsheets, dBASE III and R:base files, so that ADS applications can read and update these files.

External program calls can be made to any languages supporting Microsoft Pascal or C calling conventions, which includes Microsoft C, Microsoft Pascal, Microsoft Fortran, Micro Focus and Cobol/2.

D2   BIM PROLOG

D2.1   Overview of mechanism

Different levels of access to database systems (Unify, Ingres, Oracle and Sybase) are possible from BIM Prolog. Transparent access to relational databases may be given; or the Prolog programmer may use procedural language interfaces; or SQL may be embedded in Prolog.

The transparent access mode only uses one database specific command to open a database. From then on, all the tables in the relational database are known to the BIM Prolog system, and access and manipulation is exactly as if they were in-core predicates of BIM Prolog.

When embedded SQL is used for database access the SQL strings are forwarded to the database for processing. The results can be printed, displayed on the screen or returned to BIM Prolog variables.

D2.2   Interface to Ingres

Data types

Ingres	BIM Prolog
i1, i2, i4 (1, 2 or 4 byte integers)	integer

note: passing integers to Ingres which are out of range (such as passing 300 to an i2 declared integer) places unpredictable values in the database.

f4 or f8 (4 or 8 byte floating point number)	real
c	character string
text	character string
date	
money (8 byte floating point number)	real

Data access

Data can be read using the predicates *retrieve, join* or *printr*. The predicate backtracks so that all tuples (not just the first) which satisfy the condition(s) are retrieved from the database.

```
retrieve ( person( _code, _name, _town),
[ _code > 2, _code < 5] ), ......
```

The above statement will return the code, name and town of all tuples from the person table where the code is greater than two and less than five.

> *join([person(_code, _name, _town),*
> *town(_codetown, _town)],*
> *[_code > 1, _codetown <> 1000]), ...*

The above statement joins the two tables person and town on the common field town, and selects tuples which satisfy the given criteria. The processing of the query does not necessarily occur in that order.

The database can be updated using the predicates, *insert, delete, deleteall, create, destroy,* and *modify.*

> *insert(person(3, Alice, Brussels)).*

>> will insert a single tuple in the person table.

> *deleteall(person(_x, _y, Brussels)), ...*

>> will delete all person records where town = Brussels,

> *create(age, 'name = c20, years = 12').*

>> will create a new table called age, with two columns or attributes,

> *modify(age/2, 'hash unique', [name]).*

>> will change the storage structure of the table age so that it is hashed on the unique key of name.

Other facilities are provided such as counting of records, summation of a column, maximum and minimum values and averages.

D2.3   Interface to Unify

Data types

Unify	BIM Prolog
numeric short integer (1–4)	integer
numeric long integer (5–9)	integer
floating point number	real
string	string

Unify	BIM Prolog
date (month/day/year)	AND–list of (day, month, year)
combination fields	list of sub–fields

Data access

Data can be returned to Prolog using *retrieve* and *printr*, and the database changed using *insert* and *delete,* as for Ingres. Attributes on all records within a table which satisfy a given condition can be changed as follows:

> retrieve(person(_code, _name, Brussels)),
> replace(person(_code, _name, Bruxelles)).

The above statement will cause the spelling of Brussels to be changed on all records in the person table.

SQL commands which conform to SunUnify standards can be passed to the DBMS by specifying *sql(...).* The SQL statement can be an update, insert or delete command.

D2.4   Interface to Sybase

BIM Prolog provides two levels of interface to the relational database Sybase: a high level interface for the casual user, and a low level interface allowing the direct exploitation of the advanced features of Sybase by the BIM Prolog user.

The high level is a user friendly interface which provides about 20 predicates to access the Sybase database.

The low level interface is the implementation in BIM Prolog of most of the Sybase DBLIBRARY routines, plus some extra predicates added for convenience.

Data types

Sybase	BIM Prolog
int	integer
smallint	integer
tinyint	integer
float	real
char	atom
varchar	atom
binary	atom

	Sybase	**BIM Prolog**
	varbinary	atom
	bit	atom
	money	atom
	datetime	atom

Data access

The example below illustrates the functionality of the interface. Note that any standard SQL call can be sent by using the sql/1, sqlcmd/1, sqlexec/0 predicates; thus tables can be created, modified and deleted.

> *?–openSYBASEdb.*
> *?–schema.*

person/3
town/2

> *?–schema(person).*

person/3 (U)
        code   int   4
        name   char   32
        town   char   32

> *?–printr(person).*

person(0003, Alice, Brussels)
person(1234, Jim, London)

> *?– person(_code,_name,_town),*
    write(_name),nl,fail.

Alice
Jim

> *?–sqlcmd('select * from person'),*
    sqlexec([_code,_name,_town]),
    write(_code,_name,_town), nl, fail.

        0003   Alice   Brussels
        1234   Jim   London

> *?– closeSYBASEdb.*

D3   CA–DB:EXPERT

D3.1   Overview of mechanism

CA–DB:Expert can access all databases which run on IBM or VAX hardware using two mechanisms. SQL statements can be embedded in the knowledge–base to access any DBMS which supports standard SQL, such as CA–DB/VAX (which used to be called IDMS/SQL), CA–IDMS/DB (which used to be called IDMS/R), DB2 and Oracle. SQL can also be used to access VSAM or RMS files. A data dictionary associated with CA–DB:Expert issues SQL commands and maps the database items on to knowledge–base facts and temporary work fields in cache (an area of memory used to pass parameters across communicating programs).

Alternatively, a Cobol (or any other language which links to Cobol) sub–routine can be called, which then accesses the database in the usual way.

D3.2   Data types

CA–DB:Expert is written in a mixture of Cobol and Assembler, therefore data items from a database map easily on to knowledge–base facts (or variables). The corresponding columns and variables must be of the same data type, that is, numeric to numeric and alphanumeric to alphanumeric, and be of the same length.

D3.3   Data access

SQL statements are included in the knowledge–base associated with goals. Data can be read with up to five concurrent queries; a maximum of five cursors are used to perform the I/O operations. The database can also be updated and the coder can control when the update takes effect by using a 'commit' statement. Alternatively, the database update can be abandoned using 'rollback'.

When a query of any type is processed a value is assigned to a variable to indicate whether or not the query was successful; a value of zero indicates success and one represents a failure.

SQL_SELECT selects data from columns in a DBMS table as follows:

> *QUERY SELECT[1] QTYPE SQL_SELECT*

> *SELECT CODE, NAME, TOWN*
> *FROM PERSON*
> *WHERE NAME = @NOM*

> *FETCH_ID SQL_F_SWITCH[1]*

> *FETCH CODE, NAME, TOWN*

The above query selects data from the person table where name has the same value as that currently assigned to NOM in cache. 'AND END_SQL_QUERY (query name)' can be specified at the end of the query to free the cursor for future I/O operations.

QUERY SQL_STAT[1] QTYPE SQL_UPDATE

UPDATE PERSON
SET CODE = @CODE,
     NAME = @NAME,
     TOWN = @TOWN
WHERE CODE = @CODE

The above query specifies the columns (code, name and town) in the table (person) to be updated, the values they are to be updated with (@CODE, @NAME and @TOWN) and the condition which limits the rows which are to be updated (those where CODE equals the value in @CODE). Multiple conditions can be specified in the where clause to cause update of many rows. An SQL_SELECT query can be included in the where clause to specify which rows of a table should be updated.

QUERY SQL_STAT[1] QTYPE SQL_INSERT

INSERT INTO PERSON
VALUES @CODE, @NAME, @TOWN

The above command will insert one new row into the person table. There must be a one to one correspondence between the values listed and the columns in the table.

QUERY SQL_DELETE[1] QTYPE SQL_DELETE

DELETE FROM PERSON
WHERE NAME = 'BLOGGS'

One or more rows may be deleted by a single query depending upon the condition specified in the where clause.

QUERY COMMIT_ALL_SQL_QUERIES[1] QTYPE
SQL_COMMIT

Autocommit can be switched off so that all updates, deletes and inserts can be committed at the same time by specifying SQL_COMMIT as above. SQL_ROLLBACK will undo all updates since the previous commit or rollback and has a similar format to commit.

D4   CRYSTAL

D4.1   Overview of mechanism

The Crystal dBASE III interface allows multiple database files to be accessed in read and write mode. Interfaces to ASCII data files, the DOS operating system and Lotus are also available.

D4.2   Data types

Crystal allows arrays of up to 3 dimensions and 8192 elements to be specified, but only one dimensional arrays can be used to accept data directly from the dBASE III interface. In version 2, only a single field could be passed via the interface on any one call. Version 3 allows multiple fields from a single record to be read and written.

Crystal	dBASE III
floating variables, up to 15 significant digits	integer, real, logical or date
text variables up to 50 characters	character

An array in Crystal is either of text or numeric type. If a record has mixed character and numeric fields then two arrays, which must be as large as the total number of fields on the record, are needed for reading and writing. If the array is of text type, all the character fields will be read into or written from it. If the array is of numeric type, then numeric and date fields will be read into or written from it. Therefore, two read or write statements are needed to retrieve or update records of mixed types.

D4.3   dBASE III access

Calls to the dBASE III interface are included in a Crystal knowledge–base associated with rules. The interface commands are entered in 'edit text' boxes (windows provided by the editor for Crystal) in the same way that other Crystal operations are specified.

There are facilities for creating, opening and closing both databases and indexes. Searches for data can be specified as:

- go to a particular record;

- go to the first, last, next or previous record;

- search for a matching field;

- find a record using an index;

- read a record.

Version 3 of Crystal includes facilities for changing a database as follows:

- writing a new record;

- updating an existing record;

- marking a record for deletion;

- preventing deletion of a marked record (which provides a limited 'rollback' facility);

- removing deleted records (which is a limited 'commit' facility).

A window on the screen is used to input database functions as follows:

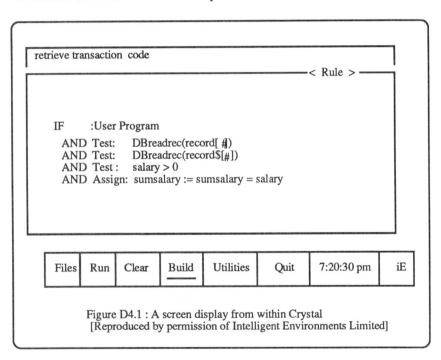

retrieve transaction code

———< Rule >———

```
IF      :User Program
  AND Test:   DBreadrec(record[ #])
  AND Test:   DBreadrec(record$[#])
  AND Test :  salary > 0
  AND Assign: sumsalary := sumsalary = salary
```

| Files | Run | Clear | Build | Utilities | Quit | 7:20:30 pm | iE |

Figure D4.1 : A screen display from within Crystal
[Reproduced by permission of Intelligent Environments Limited]

The above code causes data to be read from a dBASE III file into the arrays record (numeric fields only) and record$ (character fields only). Validation can be associated with variables in Crystal, such as range checking (see the test included in the above code).

The rule content (the instructions enclosed in the rule box) specifies data access. This could include code to open a file:

Assign: personf := DBopen('person.dbf)

or to write a record:

Test: DBwriterec(record[#])

Test: DBwriterec(record$[#])

or to create a new database file:

Assign:
personf := DBcreate('person' , 5, nm$[#], tp$[#], ln[#], dps[#]).

The parameters in the above file creation code are the file name, the number of fields and arrays containing the record descriptions. The array nm$ must contain the names of the fields, tp$ contains the field types, ln contains the lengths of the fields and dps contains the number of decimal places required for numeric fields.

D4.4   Lotus–123   access

The Lotus interface enables Crystal applications to contain function calls which will read, write, create and update Lotus–123 and Symphony spreadsheet files. The interface software can buffer parts of spreadsheet files for direct access and thereby improve performance. Cells are held in the interface buffer, with their current display format and current values, as follows:

numbers	integers or double precision form
text	up to 50 characters
blanks	held as blanks
formulae	are NOT stored, only the associated number is stored.

Cells in the buffered range can be read and changed individually using the read and write functions. The whole range can be read using direct Crystal array functions.

The interface functions fall into a number of logical groupings:

- creating, opening and closing files;

- defining, loading and saving ranges in the interface;

- reading the range into an array and writing an array into the range;

- reading cells from the range as dates, numerics or text;

- writing cells to the range in the interface;

- loading cells directly from a spreadsheet file;

- creating a column heading in a spreadsheet.

Array handling

A two dimensional, numeric Crystal array can be populated using the command LTarrread(numbers[#,#]) to read cells from the range in the interface. The first dimension of the array corresponds to the columns of the range in the interface, the second corresponds to the rows. An error will be displayed if the array is not large enough to hold the range. A similar function LTarrwrite(names$[#,#]) writes cells from a Crystal array into a range in the interface.

D4.5 ASCII file interface

ASCII files can be used to pass data between systems. Crystal can read from and write to ASCII files, but only one file can be open at any one time. A pre–defined record or field structure is not assumed, therefore a wide range of data structures can be used. However, guidelines are given within the Crystal documentation, suggesting that records should have a fixed number of fields, commas should separate fields, text should be delimited by quotes, and a new record should be denoted by a new line.

There are three read functions: one for reading data in the format of text, regardless of whether the data is text or numeric to give a Crystal string; a second for reading a number; and a third to read a date returning a Crystal internal date number. The 'errok' function can be used to test whether or not the read was successful.

Data written to a file is always sent to the end of a file. Two functions, AScomma and ASnewline, must be used to format written data, the former to delimit fields, the latter to separate records. Text, numbers and dates can be written to a file. The number function must be called with the number to be written, the field width to be used and the number of decimal places. The number will be output right justified with leading spaces. Dates will be output in the format YYYYMMDD.

D5   EXPERT SYSTEMS ENVIRONMENT

D5.1   Overview of mechanism

Expert Systems Environment (ESE) runs on IBM mainframes under both MVS and VM operating systems, and can be used to access SQL/DS and DB2 databases using SQL queries. SQL commands can be embedded explicitly in ESE code, or they may be generated by the system from a database access specification or they may be implicitly generated by ESE as a result of a value being required for a parameter (fact). ESE controls the passing of SQL commands to the DBMS and the return of data.

Other databases and files can be accessed using external routines written in languages such as Cobol. DL/1 databases can be accessed under CICS or IMS. When embedded in CICS or IMS transactions, it is recommended that all database activity is controlled by the TP system, for integrity and back–up.

IBM Expert System Consultation Environment/PC (ESCE/PC) enables knowledge–based systems created by ESE under MVS or VM to be deployed under DOS on IBM Personal Computers. Databases or files residing on the micro are accessed by external routines written in Pascal, C or Assembler.

D5.2   Data types

ESE uses Pascal data types, which are numeric (integer, decimal and real numbers) and strings. Dates in DB2 translate into strings. DB2 numbers can also be transferred into an ESE string. NULL values are transferred as a single BLANK value with a certainty of 0 (in the range –1 to +1); this is not the same as UNKNOWN. Boolean parameters can take the values true and false.

D5.3   Data access

There are two methods of specifying access to data: there is an 'ACCESS' control verb within ESE which explicitly causes the database to be accessed; or the external sourcing sequence interface used in the backward chaining process can be used to implicitly obtain data. A windowed interface is provided to allow easy input of ESE details.

Implicit data access

Parameters, which are equivalent to facts or program variables, are defined along with various attributes to the system through a window as shown in figure D5.1 on the next page.

If the 'sourcing seq' attribute is set equal to 'external procedure' then the top window (Edit : Procedure name) is displayed. If 'SQL' is entered the bottom window is displayed so that the coder can specify which data item (column of a table in the database) this parameter maps on to, and under what conditions. The system will then generate SQL (which is not visible to the developer or the end user) to obtain this parameter from the database, when required, using the given details. For example,

$$SELECT \quad name \quad FROM \quad person \quad WHERE \quad code \ = \ :VL \ *code$$

would be generated from information given on the screen below. :VL *code indicates that a value in that variable should be used. Therefore, an explicit 'read database' statement is not required and need not be coded; when a parameter becomes a goal at run time (as part of the backward chaining process) ESE will automatically access the database to obtain a value.

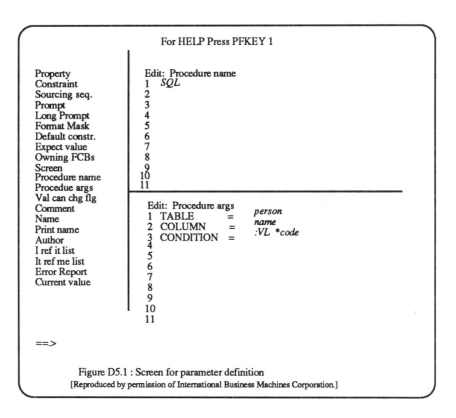

Figure D5.1 : Screen for parameter definition
[Reproduced by permission of International Business Machines Corporation.]

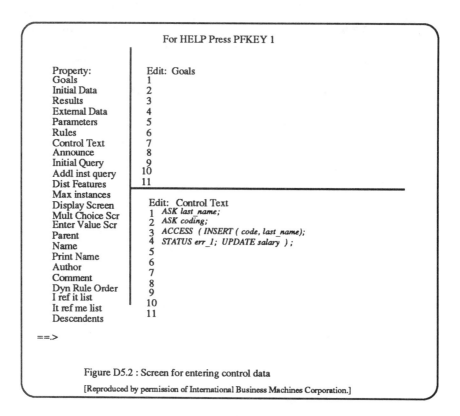

Figure D5.2 : Screen for entering control data

[Reproduced by permission of International Business Machines Corporation.]

Explicit data access

ESE is a goal driven (backward chaining) system. Goals are associated with Focus Control Blocks (FCBs, which are broadly equivalent to modules) which will evaluate those goals. FCBs are structured hierarchically, since one FCB will generate subgoals, to be evaluated by other FCBs and so on. It is not always desirable that all actions should be executed in the default, goal driven order and the developer may choose to over–ride this. The user may, for example, specify when the database should be accessed either to read data or update the database. Some control text can be associated with each FCB which allows the coder to impose some order (forward chaining) on actions. 'Access' is a control verb which can be included to cause database access – either reading to evaluate goals or to update the database. Figure D5.2 shows the window through which control text is entered.

Data can be read by specifying:

ACCESS (SELECT (code, name, town))

The system will generate one or more SQL queries from the Procedure arguments specified with each of the parameters code, name and town. More than one database table can be accessed by a single SQL statement (that is joins can be generated), providing that the columns on which to join have been specified in the conditions associated with parameters.

A new row or record can be inserted in a table as follows:

ACCESS (INSERT (code, name, town))

or one or more rows can be deleted from a table:

ACCESS (DELETE (person))

or columns in a table can be modified:

ACCESS (UPDATE (name))

In all of the above examples, the SQL command is generated from the Procedure arguments associated with the given parameters. Note that in the second example it has been assumed that person has been defined as a group parameter of code, name and town. Group parameters can be used in all types of database access.

Generalised access to a DB2 or SQL/DS database is allowed, in that any SQL command can be specified, not just those supported by ESE through use of the predicate REQUEST. For example a new table can be created as follows:

ACCESS (REQUEST 'create table finance
(code integer, salary integer, bankmanager varchar(30) ')

Some control information can also be obtained concerning the success or otherwise of SQL queries. Status, code and warning values can be retrieved and cause following database access statements to be ignored. For example, if a database update fails, then further updates can be abandoned. In the example in figure D5.2, salary will not be updated if a person record fails to be inserted.

D6   GURU

D6.1   Overview of mechanism

Guru can access dBASE III, MDBS III databases and Lotus–123 spreadsheets. dBASE III files are accessed as though they are GURU tables. SQL is used to access MDBS files. Cells within spreadsheets can be accessed and updated directly.

D6.2   Data types

No information given.

D6.3   Data access

SQL like commands are used to access MDBS databases. For example:

> *SELECT town, name FROM person–table*
> *FOR age > 25*
>
> *PLUCK index–name FROM person–table USING index–on–name*
>
> *OBTAIN NEXT RECORD FROM person–table.*

Up to 45 tables can be used simultaneously.

Spreadsheet processing is an integral part of Guru and the inference engine has immediate access to the value of any cell of a currently loaded spreadsheet. The spreadsheet need not be displayed on the screen before access.

There are two ways to refer to a spreadsheet cell.

> *VARIABLE: SALARY*
> *FIND: PERSONCOL = LOOKUP (PER, #Y2, #Y13, #Z2)*
> *SALARY = LOOKUP (SAL, #A18, #A31, #(18, PERSONCOL))*

One possibility is to use a hash in front of the cell column and row (eg #Y2). Alternatively, row and column numbers can be specified, as in the example #(2,25). In the above example person data given in column Z2 is found between person 2 and person 13; then the salary between A18 and A31 is found.

Large spreadsheets can be manipulated: maxima of 65,535 cells and 255 windows are allowed.

D7   ICL–ADVISER

D7.1   Overview of mechanism

ICL–Adviser runs on ICL mainframes and DRS.300 terminals and can access any database within the environment through a sub–routine written in Pascal, Cobol, Fortran, any other language supported by VME or SCL (System Control Language or operating system commands). Databases such as IDMS can be read or updated but the database access is totally under the control of the sub–routine.

D7.2   Data types

ICL–ADVISER	Cobol
integer	numeric
object	numeric
assertion (probability, cert. or odds held as a real number)	numeric
string	alphanumeric
array (group of items of same type)	map each individual item as above
record (group of items of different types)	map each individual item as above

D7.3   Data access

Data is retrieved from, or written to, a database in the normal way for the sub–routine language. For example, the appropriate DML (data manipulation language) statements must be encoded in a Cobol or Fortran program to access an IDMS database. Data can be passed between the sub–routine and an ICL–Adviser application using a number of supplied procedures. There are different procedures for passing each of the fact types (integer, real and string) in each direction. Calls to these procedures are coded in the ICL–Adviser expert system application as procedures and functions, according to whether they are passing or receiving data. Only a single fact or data item is passed on any one call to a procedure;   the ICL–Adviser code does not reflect this, but multiple calls are coded in the Cobol program with which it communicates. Facts which are members of arrays or records must be passed individually on repeated calls. For example, FUNCTION 3001 below appears to retrieve a record consisting of three data items in one call. However, there are six calls to ICL procedures in the corresponding Cobol sub–routine, two for each data item.

Assuming that an IDMS database holds a record type PERSON, with data items CODE, NAME and TOWN, reading a record for someone with the name 'Smith' would require the following code:

```
PROCEDURE  3000 :  'passes the name'
  stringpass( STRING  s1)

FUNCTION 3001  : ' returns a person record'
  recordreturn ( )  : RECORD  personmode

MODE personmode : 'describes person record'
  INTEGER  code :  'first data item'
  STRING  name :  'second data item'
  STRING  town  :  'third data item'

RECORD  personmode recordreturned : 'record of the above
                                           layout'

ACTION actionl :  'send parameter'
  CALL stringpass (Smith)

ACTION action2 : 'receive record'
  CONSIDER  code, name, town

RULE getrecord:  'rule to get the record'
  recordreturned IS  recordreturn ( )
```

The associated Cobol sub–routine would include a call to a procedure in order to accept the string s1(CALL 'ICL9QSGGETSTR' with parameters). The IDMS database would be accessed by the Cobol program to retrieve a single record and the data items would be returned in the record personmode using CALL ICL9QSGSETFIELD and ICL9QSGSETSTR for each of the strings town and name, and ICL9QSGSETFIELD and ICL9QSGSETINT for the numeric field code.

The procedure and function could be combined as:

```
FUNCTION 3001  : ' returns a person record'
  recordreturn ( STRING s1)  : RECORD  personmode
```

However, the same Cobol calls to procedures would be required. If a number of records were to be returned, an array of the record could be used; there would only be one rule and function in the ICL–Adviser code associated with the call to get data, but there would be repeated calls within the Cobol program to return the data items of all records individually.

Since IDMS accesses are under the control of the Cobol or Fortran sub–routine, the latter must monitor IDMS–STATUS parameters (error codes with respect to failed database access) and return appropriate error details to the ICL–Adviser application.

External procedures and functions are accessed through a 'firewall', with the effect that failures in user supplied code do not cause ICL–Adviser to crash – the UNKNOWN value is returned instead.

D8 Inference ART

D8.1 Overview of mechanism

Inference ART runs on Sun workstations, Symbolics, TI Explorer, micro Explorer and VAX machines. There is no direct access function which allows access to databases, but an indirect route via an external call facility to programs can be used. Links to C and Fortran are provided in the current release on the Sun workstation; a future release is expected to allow interfaces to any foreign language. Inference ART running on a VAX can trigger access to databases using operating system commands and the results are placed in a log file, which can then be interrogated. In theory, any DBMS running within the same environment as Inference ART can be accessed.

A large application has been developed by Ferranti using ART running on a Symbolics workstation and accessing a database on an IBM mainframe.

D8.2 Data types

Integer, real, string, literal and sequence.

D8.3 Data access

On SUN or VAX machines the external calls can be made by linking a list symbol (in ART) to the foreign function label and then loading the foreign object file into the ART/Lisp system. This is achieved using two function calls from within ART, namely:

> *(define_C_function...)*

and

> *(load_foreign_files...)*.

A C program can then be called in the same way that Lisp programs can be invoked. The ART process can continue inferencing while there is a pending request for data from a database.

An alternative method is available on VAX machines; database commands are constructed by a network of Inference ART *methods* as a text file under the operating system. This text file is executed as a database command file (that is the database queries encoded in the file are executed) by a call to the VMS system from ART. The results of the query are written to a log file which can be interrogated from ART. See figure D8.1 for a representation of this access method.

The ART program uses a set of forward chaining rules which operates on an object oriented data structure. There are two classes of objects, 'commands' and 'databases'. 'Commands' contains a family of generic database commands. 'Databases' contains a hierarchy of database packages, possibly containing a number of versions. A 'method' is attached to a 'vector' of each database package and each primitive task.

There are two rule sets corresponding to two program phases: in the first phase, primitive command instances are created and related; in the second phase, a single rule steps through the command network sending a message to a vector of each command and the database package version. Each method returns an appropriate code fragment which is written to the command file. The command file is then executed by calling *lib$spawn* (operating system).

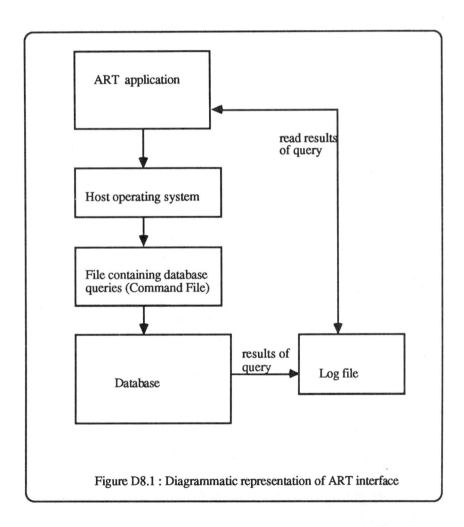

Figure D8.1 : Diagrammatic representation of ART interface

D9   KBMS

D9.1   Overview of mechanism

KBMS provides an interface to IBM mainframe database management systems, such as DB2 and SQL/DS and VSAM files. SQL commands are automatically generated to read the database; update SQL commands can be embedded in the application. A generalised interface called the User Defined Object (UDO) provides access to all other IBM databases such as DL1 and IMS, and those of independent vendors such as IDMS, Adabas, Datacom and Oracle.

KBMS may call, or be called from, traditional programming languages, such as PL/1 and Cobol, via the KBMS high level interface, AISQL. Using standard IBM linkage conventions, it may call or be called from newer programming languages such as Natural, ADs, Telon, etc.

KBMS operates under CICS, TSO, CMS and IMS/DC TP monitors. It has a central server, allowing multiple users from different TP monitors or batch programs to access a single copy of KBMS.

D9.2   Data types

Database tables are automatically mapped on to objects and all DB2, SQL/DS and other DBMS data types are available within KBMS.

D9.3   Data access

KBMS applications are built using an intelligent editor, therefore underlying code (as might be provided in a listing) is not visible. When the developer defines an object which is to be populated from a DB2 table, for example, KBMS accesses the DB2 catalogue and retrieves a description (list of column names, etc) of that table. All the columns are made available but the developer can blank out those not required. An object is multi–valued, in that all tuples in the corresponding table map on to the object. LINK definitions enable automatic joins on tables.

When an object is to be evaluated, that is the object is a goal in the application which is running, KBMS uses automatically generated SQL to retrieve the data. If the table description in the DB2 catalogue has changed since the KBS application was written, the KBMS version will automatically be amended. If columns have been deleted from the table, then KBMS will mark them as unavailable.

Database update is achieved through SQL commands associated with rules.

Multiple databases can be accessed simultaneously. For example, a single rule can request information from a DB2 database to be joined with information from a VSAM file.

Data storage for micro implementations of KBMS use AICorp's internal data storage facility, KDB, or external sequential files. Rule syntax is independent of where the data is stored.

D10   KEEconnection

D10.1 Overview of mechanism

KEEconnection is marketed by Intellicorp to build bridges between KEE applications and SQL relational databases. A graphics interface using multiple windows, allows mappings between database relations and attributes and knowledge–base objects to be specified. KEEconnection then creates a bridge between them by generating SQL commands. Data can be accessed in multiple databases, possibly on different machines. KEEconnection facilitates access to Oracle and Ingres on VAX machines and Britton Lee database machines; DB2 databases on IBM mainframes can also be accessed.

D10.2 Data mappings

KEE is object oriented, therefore tables and attributes must be mapped on to objects. A number of transformations are provided by KEEconnection:

- mapping multiple tables to a single class;

- mapping one table to multiple classes;

- mapping multiple columns of a table or tables to the values of a single slot;

- mapping one column of a table to values of multiple slots;

- transformation of column values into knowledge–base units such as numbers and strings;

- computation of new values by the database or by the knowledge–base (reasoning).

Table to class mappings

'Membership conditions' within KEE can be used to restrict the download of data from the database. This would be the equivalent of specifying a condition on a 'SELECT' statement. Membership conditions can also be used for sorting rows of data from a single table into members of different sub–classes. For example, a table containing data of PERSONs might contain a 'COUNTY' attribute; sub–classes could be defined for PERSONs living in each of Norfolk, Suffolk, Essex, etc using membership conditions. KEEconnection would classify rows of data on retrieval and place them in appropriate KEE units for each of these categories.

Alternatively, tables may be split, such that different columns are attributed to different classes, but both classes holding the key field so that they could be 'rejoined'. For example, it might be desirable to split PERSON details into PERSON–ADDRESS (for labels for printing) and PERSON–OTHER.

The converse of the above can be carried out, such that two tables retrieved from a database can be joined on a common attribute and stored as one sub–class within a KEE application.

Column to slot mappings

KEE slots can accommodate multiple values and it is possible to map multiple columns from one or more tables or multiple rows into a single slot. For example, an address is commonly held as five columns, which could all be mapped on to one KEE slot.

Transformation of database values can be achieved by specifying a 'one of' translation table. For example, POSTCODEs could perhaps be decoded into postal areas. An expression can also be associated with a slot so that a slot value can be computed from one or more column values.

D10.3 Data access

When the mappings of data to slots and classes has been specified, data retrieval is mostly handled by KEEconnection, through generation of SQL. This can be over–ridden by developers writing their own SQL if required. Down loading of the data is under the control of the developer; the data can be transferred as a single data set or incrementally.

KEEconnection utilities allow update of tables; rows can be created and deleted and column values can be changed. There are instructions for 'uploading' data and to 'commit' the changes to the database. Database access permissions are controlled by the DBMS.

The KEEconnection data communications module performs all network processing required to enable access to remote databases. In a typical operation, KEEconnection sends an SQL request through the network; the communications software on the remote machine receives the request and passes it to the DBMS. The reply takes the reverse path. The communications module detects crashes and unavailability of the DBMS and reports them to the user. Faulty connections will be reopened automatically.

D10.4 KEElink

KEElink makes data from non–relational databases and configurations, not supported by KEEconnection, accessible to KEE applications. KEElink translates queries from its TellAndAsk language (similar to predicate calculus) into database queries. The query statement returns results which are then mapped into KEE structures for knowledge processing. Processing is specific to each database, so multiple databases can be accessed simultaneously.

D10.5   KEE–C Integration Toolkit

The KEE–C Integration Toolkit[†] provides the following:

- calling C functions from Lisp/KEE as methods or functions;

- calling Lisp/KEE functions from C;

- reference to Lisp/KEE objects in C functions;

- parameter passing and conversion between Lisp/KEE and C.

The toolkit can be used in a number of ways, such as building a real–time data acquisition system and creation of a knowledge server.

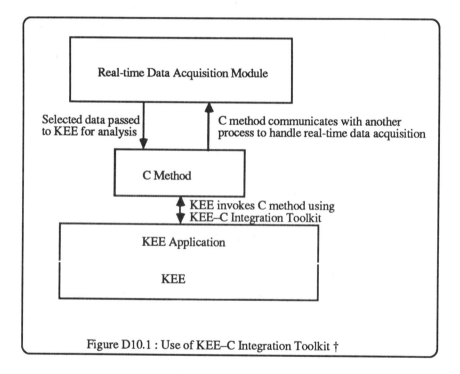

Figure D10.1 : Use of KEE–C Integration Toolkit †

D10.6   Use of languages

Languages such as C, Fortran and Pascal can be used with KEE on a UNIX workstation if the Lisp on that platform provides the appropriate interfaces. For example, Sun Microsystems Lisp provides three types of interface: foreign function calls from Lisp, C callable Lisp functions and interprocess communication.

[†] KEE–C Integration Toolkit is a trademark of Intellicorp, Intellicorp is a registered trademark of Intellicorp Inc (copyright by Intellicorp Inc).

Foreign function calls

C or Fortran subroutines may be called from KEE (or Lisp) as if they were Lisp functions; the parameters and the type of value the sub–routine returns must be known to Lisp. The C and Fortran sub–routines can in turn call other sub–routines, possibly written in other languages, providing indirect access mechanisms between KEE and, for example, Pascal.

Interprocess communications

Using a 'stream' mechanism, KEE can communicate with other UNIX programs via the standard input and output mechanisms provided by UNIX. In simple terms, the communication consists of strings sent between two communicating programs. More sophisticated data structures may require the development of a custom protocol. This mechanism provides a gateway to any UNIX functionality.

D11   KEE (UNISYS)

D11.1 Overview of mechanism

Unisys markets KEE software on Explorer workstations (Lisp machines) and has
released Explorer software (KS/A) for linking KEE to IBM mainframe databases,
such as IMS, DB2, VSAM, IDMS, Adabas, Total and System 2000. The
databases can only be read, not updated. Additionally, Unisys have developed a
technique for interfacing KEE on the Explorer to Unisys 1100 series Mapper
databases by defining an interface to a mainframe resident transaction program.
A Mapper database can be read and updated.

D11.2 Data types

No information given.

D11.3 Data access

KS/A link

The KS/A software operates on a standard Explorer system with the SNA
software and a protocol converter. It can access any IBM mainframe system with
Answer/DB software. The IBM operating system can be MVS or DOS/VSE,
and both IMS/DC and CICS environments are accessible. The KS/A commands
can be used in any KEE or common Lisp application running on an Explorer.

Answer/DB provides a consistent interface to a variety of IBM host databases.
Requests for data from the same database can be combined and extracted in a
single pass of the database. Answer/DB holds the extracted data until it is
requested to be sent to the Explorer system. Queries can also be stored allowing
previously defined queries to be executed. The Answer/DB software on the IBM
mainframe handles security, database access and scheduling.

A number of Lisp 'forms' comprise the KS/A system. Firstly, an instance of
the KS/A structure and a logon procedure to the converter, mainframe and
Answer/DB must be created. The glossary (database definition) may be
explicitly down–loaded if desired, but this will automatically occur on the first
query to a database. The link can then be used.

A query is built and submitted through the following Lisp form, for example:

```
(KSA: BUILD–AND–SUBMIT K : query–name 'start1'
                         : database 'personnel'
                         : fields 'code name  town'
                         : conditions 'dept = "21" '
                         : sort 'code' )
```

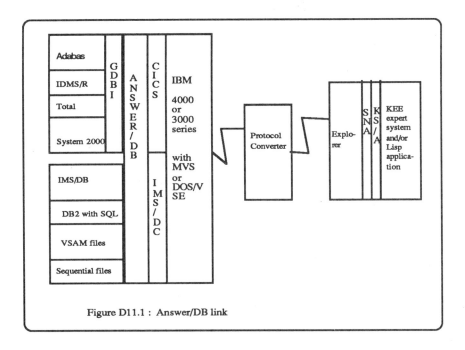

Figure D11.1 : Answer/DB link

The status of the query (while running) can be checked. A single record may be returned as a Lisp list using the deliver–extract record form. The record (list) can be entered into a KEE frame structure using a 'put.value' function. This form must be evaluated a number of times to receive all the data sequentially. Alternatively, a number of records can be returned in one call, using the following form for example:

(KSA: DELIVER–EXTRACTED–DATA k : QUERY–NAME 'start2'
: DATA–PATHNAME 'person–file'
: MAX–RECORDS–DELIVER 30
: SCHEMA–PATHNAME nil
: EXPOSE–BEFORE t
: DEEXPOSE_AFTER t)

Normally, functions will be defined within KEE which will submit more than one query and return data in KEE frames. A facility to list databases which can be accessed using this connection is available.

Explorer–Mapper link

The method is based on an implementation of Mapper Level 33 on the host machine, which provides Mapper Transaction Queuing (MTQ). This enables Unisys 1100 transaction programs to initiate Mapper runs and receive the results. The transaction programs can be invoked by a TTY–compatible terminal. The Explorer system includes an RS232 interface which can send and receive TTY protocol and so can connect via an asynchronous communications line to the Unisys1100 host, appearing in the host communications configuration as a standard TTY device. (The TTY protocol used between Explorer and the Unisys 1100 host does not have message integrity or recovery capability.)

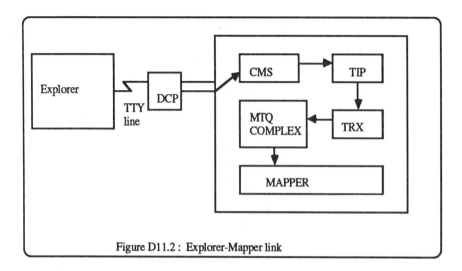

Figure D11.2 : Explorer-Mapper link

In the Explorer system there are some Lisp functions to send and receive messages via the Explorer RS232 interface. A typical message to the host would include the name of the transaction program, name of a user–defined Mapper Run and Mapper variable names.

The transaction program on the Unisys 1100 host, written in Cobol, reads the Explorer message and issues sub–routine calls to the MTQ, to execute the named Mapper run. Any results are returned to the Explorer system.

D12   KES

D12.1 Overview of mechanism

KES runs on, and is source compatible across, over 70 platforms including micros, UNIX workstations, minis and mainframes. A database gateway (The Link) allows direct access to SQL databases. There are two techniques for interfacing KES and other applications, including databases. Most simply, an external application can be defined within the knowledge–base to be called and run as an operating system executable. For more flexibility, KES can be embedded in C, which provides the ability to embed both the database and KES in an overall C control program using the KES Application Programmers interface.

On IBM mainframes, KES runs under VM/CMS, MVS/TSO, IMS and CICS with a Cobol interface, in addition to the other KES interfacing mechanisms.

D12.2 Data types

Real, integer, string, single and multiple valued symbolic variables (like enumerated types, unordered), reference variables (holding a reference to a class member or object instance) and user defined objects (classes). A near future release will support lists.

D12.3 Data access

Two techniques exist. The simpler technique is called the EXTERNAL mechanism. The more general technique is referred to as EMBEDDING.

In the EXTERNAL mechanism, KES permits an external program to be defined as the source of an attribute value. When the attribute value is required during inferencing, KES will call the external program and receive control to continue inferencing when the external program terminates. The external program can be any program that can be run from the operating system command line. KES invokes a program and passes optional command line parameters as defined in the knowledge–base. Any optionally defined inputs to the external program are passed via a text file, and any optionally defined return arguments are passed back via a text file.

A more elegant and efficient way of integrating KES with other software is by EMBEDDING it with other software. The Application Programmers Interface allows programmers to manipulate a knowledge–base and control the inference engine. In particular, the values of KES variables and classes can be read and assigned, and KES inference goals can be set.

Providing that a DBMS has a programmer interface, then both KES and a database can be manipulated together. For example, the members of a KES class can be instantiated from database data. KES informs the C program that it requires the class members, the C program reads the database (optionally using an SQL statement declared in the KES knowledge–base) and uses the data to instantiate and assign values to KES class members. The KES knowledge–base can then be manipulated, adding or deleting class instances and values, and the results be written back to the database if required.

Software Architecture and Engineering provide a bolt–on product called The Link which provides these gateway functions to SQL databases. Oracle was the first database to be supported, but gateways to other databases will be added.

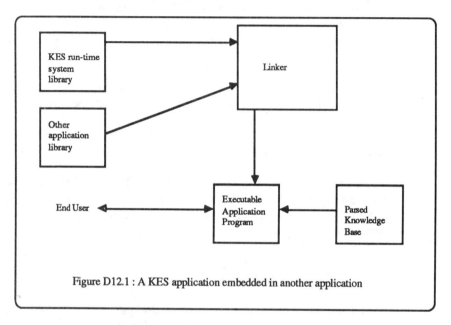

Figure D12.1 : A KES application embedded in another application

D13 KNOWLEDGECRAFT

D13.1 Overview of mechanism

Carnegie Group Inc provide SQL Database Connection Package for interfacing Knowledgecraft applications with Oracle databases. Tables and views cannot be created but most other SQL operations are available to read and update databases. Table locking (not record locking), record rollbacks and record auto commits are available.

D13.2 Data types

One table–template schema is created for each database table that is to be accessed. This schema contains the conversion information that allows Knowledgecraft to transfer data from a database table. For each table–template instance that is created, a prototype schema is also created. For each column in a database table there is a corresponding slot in the prototype schema. By default, each record retrieved from a table is represented as an instance of this schema.

D13.3 Data access

Multiple databases and multiple tables within databases may be accessed via dynamic clauses. Selected records are automatically stored as application schemata. The SQL functionality which is supported includes:

- opening and closing network connections;

- opening and closing databases;

- locking and unlocking tables;

- retrieving records;

- inserting, updating and deleting records.

The SQL Database Connection Package (SQL/DCP) is made up of three parts:

- a Lisp–based functional user connection, which is part of the standard Lisp/KC image. The connection is responsible for parsing user requests and returning database records in the form of schemata;

- a C program responsible for database communication;

- network routines for passing data between the connection and C program. The connection and C program do not have to reside on the same machine since the network is used for communication.

The following is a system level view of using the SQL/DCP. The user sends a sql–connect message to the oracle–db–manager causing a VMS command file to be executed. The VMS file starts a C language process and opens a network connection between Lisp and the C process. The sql–connect message returns a schema that contains information about the network connection. The connection has a unique identity since it is possible to have simultaneous connections to different databases.

The user sends a sql–open message to the schema, including a password. The Lisp interface sends a command to the C program which opens the database. A response (success or error) is returned to the Lisp program. Providing that the database has been opened successfully, the user then sends a sql–create–template specifying the name of a database table, causing information to be retrieved from the data dictionary about that table (column names, field types, etc). This information is stored in a table–template schema in the Lisp program.

Sql–query messages, updates, deletions and insertions are passed in a similar manner. A sql–close message closes the database, and sql–disconnect deletes the C process and closes the network connection.

D14   KNOWLEDGETOOL

D14.1 Overview of mechanism

IBM KnowledgeTool can access any database within the environment in which it runs. For example, data held in DB2, SQL/DS and DL/I databases can be directly accessed by KnowledgeTool applications. The translator associated with the expert system converts KnowledgeTool source into PL/I source code, hence database accesses are coded as PL/I statements.

KnowledgeTool applications can call and be called by programs coded in Cobol, PL/1, Assembler, C, Fortran and Pascal, therefore allowing the application to be linked with existing systems which may already access a database.

D14.2 Data types

Since KnowledgeTool source is converted to PL/1 there is no difficulty in mapping database data items into facts. All PL/1 data types are available, with some minor restrictions.

D14.3 Data access

KnowledgeTool source can be a mixture of rule constructs and PL/1 source, therefore SQL calls conform to PL/1 standards. Data can be read into an application as follows:

```
EXEC SQL BEGIN DECLARE SECTION;
  DCL CODE FIXED BIN(15);
   DCL NAME CHAR(30) VARYING;
   DCL TOWN CHAR(£)) VARYING;
EXEC SQL END DECLARE SECTION;

EXEC SQL DECLARE C1 CURSOR FOR
  SELECT * FROM PERSON;

EXEC SQL OPEN C1;
EXEC SQL FETCH C1 INTO :CODE, :NAME, :TOWN;
DO WHILE (SQLCODE = 0 )
 ALLOCATE item SET(t);
 t => code1 = CODE;
 t => name1  = NAME;
 t => town1  = TOWN;
 EXEC SQL FETCH C1 INTO :CODE, :NAME, :TOWN;
 END;
 EXEC SQL CLOSE C1;
```

The variables into which data will be placed are first declared, followed by a cursor for reading the person table in the database. The first record or row is returned by a fetch statement; all subsequent records are retrieved using the do loop. A database can also be updated; for example, records can be inserted as follows:

```
EXEC SQL DECLARE C2 CURSOR FOR
    INSERT INTO PERSON
    VALUES (:CODE, :NAME, :TOWN);

EXEC SQL OPEN C2;
EXEC SQL PUT C2;
EXEC SQL CLOSE C2;
```

A record will be written containing the values in the specified variables.

D15   LEONARDO

D15.1 Overview of mechanism

A full input–output interface is available from within the procedural language to allow direct access to formatted and unformatted files. Some libraries, provided as an optional extra, support reading of Lotus–123 spreadsheets and dBASE III files; access to Oracle is planned.

Leonardo can execute external procedures written in any language. Parameters can be passed to and from the interface, so that data can be retrieved and stored by the external procedures.

D15.2 Data types

No information given.

D15.3 Data access

The dBASE III interface package allows the developer to invoke access to dBASE files from within the procedural language component of Leonardo. A number of operations are supported including opening and closing files; reading the first, next, last and previous record; appending a record; replacing the current record; marking the current record as deleted; and getting the nth record. Functions within the procedural language can be used to manipulate the buffer string which is returned after reading a file.

The interface to Lotus–123 spreadsheets is also a callable function from the procedural language. Two functions enable the developer to read a range of cells from a spreadsheet (GETLOTUS) and write a range of cells to a spreadsheet (PUTLOTUS). Three parameters must be given on each call: the name of the file, the range of cells to be read and the location for storing the cell values. These arguments may be literal constants or any text type object. Cells which are referenced may be real, text or formulae; in the latter case, values derived from the formulae will be returned.

D16   LEVEL5 OBJECT

D16.1 Overview of mechanism

Level5 Object provides direct access to data stored in external files. Interfaces to the following are available: Focus, dBASEII, III, III+, RS/1, CDD, TDF and ASCII files.

Level5 Object will be available under TSO with versions for OS/2, UNIX and Wang VS to follow. Focus Read/Write interfaces will be made available for OS/2, TSO, UNIX and Wang VS. The existing database interfaces will be extended to include most major proprietary database products. Interfaces to DB2, SQL/DS, VSAM, Oracle, Rdb, IMS and IDMS will be added. There are also plans to closely integrate Level5 Object and Focus by allowing Level5 Object knowledge–bases to be embedded within Focus applications.

D16.2 Data types

Simple fact (boolean)
String
Numeric
Attribute–value (single and multi–valued).

D16.3 Data access

The database interface is provided as part of the rule grammar, not indirectly via subroutine calls or external programs. Records can be read, updated and deleted from within a KBS application. The following example code would reference a dBASE III database.

A database of 'person' records is opened as follows:

> *OPEN person.dbf AS DB3 FOR WRITE CALLED person*

A record can be read as follows:

> *RULE to select a record based on person id*
> *ASK person id number*
> *IF   LOCATE person id number = person.id IN person*
> *THEN selected person record*

Once the record has been located by the above command, it can be updated as follows:

> *RULE to update salary and grade*
> *IF selected person record*
> *AND ASK person.salary*
> *AND ASK person.grade*
> *THEN updated person record*

A record can be deleted as follows:

> *RULE to remove a person from the database*
> *ASK person id number*
> *IF LOCATE person id number = person.id IN person*
> *AND NOT EOF person*
> *AND DELETE FROM person*
> *THEN deleted person record*
> *ELSE DISPLAY person record not found*

D16.4   Release 2.0

The architecture of release 2.0 has been designed to isolate major areas of functionality into libraries of modules. Database Interface modules will contain the read/write access capabilities for all the supported database management systems for the current platform. The library is used by the inference engine, RuleTalk (editor) and the PRL compiler. Level5 Object will have a consistent internal representation of an ideal database into which all 'real world' databases will be mapped.

D17   MVS/PROLOG and VM/PROLOG

D17.1 Overview of mechanism

MVS/Prolog can directly access DB2 databases using embedded SQL queries. The DB2 interface must be purchased to use these facilities. The Call Attach Facility (CAF) communicates with DB2. VM/Prolog works in a very similar way to MVS/Prolog in order to access SQL/DS databases, rather than DB2.

D17.2 Data types

MVS/Prolog	DB2
integer	short integer
	long integer
floating point number	floating point number
floating point number	decimal number
character string	char
character string	varchar

Data typing between MVS/Prolog and DB2 is controlled automatically with the above conversions taking place when data is transferred. The same matches exist for VM/Prolog and SQL/DS.

D17.3 Data access

Associated with the SQL predicate are a number of types of call. The SELECT statement reads records from a table. A single row is placed in a Prolog list, where the elements of the list must be in the same order as the column names in the select statement.

SQL ('select code, name, town from person where town = "Norwich" ',
code1.name1.town1.nil).

The above statement will return the first tuple which has town equal to 'Norwich' into the fields in the list given (code1, name1 and town1). Backtracking in Prolog will cause the second and further tuples to be returned to the same items in the list.

Database updates are achieved using standard SQL commands such as:

> *SQL ('delete from person where town = "Norwich" ')*

or,

> *SQL ('update person set code = code2,*
> *name = name2,*
> *town = town2*
> *where code = 123456 ')*

All such SQL statements are passed without alteration to DB2 or SQL/DS. Commit and rollback statements are available to allow updates to be grouped into transactions. All open cursors are automatically closed by such statements; up to ten cursors may be open at any one time.

Information about the success or otherwise of SQL commands can be obtained by including a return code with each SQL command as a third parameter. SQL messages which provide information about failed SQL statements are displayed at the terminal.

D18   NATURAL EXPERT

D18.1 Overview of mechanism

Natural Expert is part of Software AG's Fourth Generation Open Integrated Software Architecture, which enables data to be accessed from Adabas, DB2 and VSAM files. It is integrated with other Software AG products, such as Predict, a data dictionary and Natural, which is a fourth generation language. It is available on IBM and Siemens mainframes and can run under some operating systems including TSO and CICS.

Natural Expert can be triggered in stand alone mode or from within a Natural application. Natural Expert applications can also call Natural programs.

D18.2 Data types

A wide variety of data types are supported by Natural Expert, including basic types (range, integer and text), structured types (such as conditional, having values of true or false), constructed types (such as lists), tuple types (like records in a database), free types (functions which can apply to any data type) and higher–order types (which cause transformation or type mapping).

Natural Expert	Natural data
Text	A253
Integer	I4
Range	F4/1:2 I these are one dimensional arrays
Probability	F4/1:2 I with 2 single precision, floating I point elements to represent the I lower and upper limits.
Conditional	L

D18.3 Data access

Natural Expert is a functional programming language, where a function is an operation which transforms one set of objects to another set of objects using a pre–defined formula. Gateway functions enable execution of Natural sub–programs directly from a Natural Expert model at run–time. This direct access to the Natural environment enables the import and export of data objects. These data objects may be derived from a number of proprietary databases, not just Adabas.

A framework for a Natural subprogram is generated by the knowledge processing environment from the declaration of a gateway function. The data definition corresponding to that declared within the knowledge–base is created. This can be modified, for example the length of fields might be changed, and processing commands included.

D19   NEXPERT OBJECT

D19.1 Overview of mechanism

Nexpert Object runs on IBM mainframes, DEC VAX machines, Sun workstations, Macintosh II and IBM AT, PS/2 and 386 machines. Applications can access several DBMS including Oracle, Ingres, Rdb and dBASEIII. Dynamic links between objects and database records are established so that data can be read and updated. Links to any custom, proprietary database can be developed by the user of the tool. Bridges to Oracle and HyperCard are provided as peripheral, add–on products.

D19.2 Data types

Nexpert Object is object oriented and uses classes, properties and meta–slots, and has multiple and user–defined inheritance. There is a one–to–one mapping between tables, records and fields in databases, and classes, objects and properties in knowledge–bases respectively.

D19.3 Data access

Links to a database are effected either through rules within the knowledge–base or through an external call to the system via a callable interface. Two types of database 'read' functions are available. One or more values of existing properties in Nexpert Object can be read. That is, a declared property for an object can be instantiated. Alternatively, new objects can be created on reading from a database.

Nexpert Object can be integrated with other systems in a number of ways, depending upon the hardware on which it is mounted. On VAX machines, for example, knowledge–bases can be integrated with external programs and make standard VMS calls. Nexpert is also delivered as a shareable image so that many users can develop and execute knowledge–bases using the same copy of the software. On Sun workstations standard UNIX calls can be made and multi–tasking is allowed.

On IBM mainframes, systems will be available to run under both VM and MVS. The Nexpert mainframe products have been registered in IBM's SAA catalogue of approved products. The SAA features include integration with SAA compliant languages such as Cobol, C and PL/1, integration with databases such as SQL/DS and DB2, and common user access across operating systems and windowing environments.

D20 PROSPECT /FLEX

D20.1 Overview of mechanism

Flex is a hybrid expert system development toolkit (developed by LPA) for building knowledge–based systems; it has been incorporated into a number of tools including Top–One, Quintec Prolog and Prospect. Lateral Systems Ltd has built a product called Prospect, which includes flex and Aspect (a DBMS and application generator). Aspect can also read and write ASCII and Lotus–123 files.

D20.2 Data types

Flex uses objects and frames to store data and facts.

D20.3 Data access

Flex includes some 'sentences' which allow database access; for instance, 'access' open a database file, 'for' specifies database usage and 'switch' gives control to the database. The application generator part of Aspect includes the database access commands.

D21 QUINTEC PROLOG AND FLEX

D21.1 Overview of mechanism

Quintec Prolog and Flex are available on 32–bit workstations such as Sun and VAX workstations, VAX machines and personal computers such as IBM PS/2. Direct interfaces to relational databases such as Ingres and Oracle are provided for Quintec Prolog. Indirect access to data can be made through language interfaces to C, Fortran and Pascal.

D21.2 Data types

Quintec Prolog uses atoms (which can hold up to 255 characters), strings of up to 65 535 characters, 24–bit signed integers, double precision floating point numbers, lists and tuples.

Quintec flex uses hierarchies and networks of frames and instances. Each frame has a set of defined slots, which may hold one or more values; these values may be explicitly stored, inherited or calculated by slot specific formulae. Pieces of flex or Prolog code (attached procedures) can be associated with frames or slots, which are triggered when the data to which they belong are created, accessed or updated.

D21.3 Data access

Interfaces to relational databases such as Ingres and Oracle are provided with the software. These interfaces allow external databases to be used as part of Prolog with external relations accessed as Prolog clauses. The normal Prolog mechanisms of pattern matching and backtracking may be used transparently with external data tables. Prolog expressions of constraints may be passed to the interface to increase the efficiency of queries; in particular, the database interfaces optimise joins on tables using the host SQL support system.

Indirect data access can be made using external language interfaces to C, Fortran and Pascal. An external function, sub–routine or procedure can be called directly as a predicate from Prolog and may access Prolog objects which are passed as arguments, create new Prolog data structures and instantiate Prolog variables. Library functions are provided to perform most data access functions and to allow access to the Prolog unification and backtracking mechanisms.

File streams (conventional files) may be opened for read, read–write or append access by Quintec Prolog. Random access file handling is also supported.

A general interface to the host operating system (UNIX, VMS, ULTRIX or OS/2) is provided, whereby a command string may be issued to the operating system from within a Prolog program for immediate execution. Operating system facilities, such as deleting or renaming files, listing directories, invoking sub–processes, etc are thereby made available.

D22   QUINTUS PROLOG

D22.1 Overview of mechanism

Quintus Prolog runs on a number of machines including Sun workstations and
DEC VAX machines. Interfaces to the DBMS Unify and Oracle are provided by
Artificial Intelligence Ltd. There are interfaces to languages such as C, Fortran
and Pascal which could be used to access any database within the environment.
A cross–compiler allows applications to be delivered to the IBM System/370
environment in which DB2 databases can be accessed.

Databases are accessed using database predicates, which are similar to constructs
in a query language. Data can be read implicitly and updated explicitly. For
practical purposes, the external database can be considered to be completely
integrated with Quintus Prolog and the programmer does not need to know about
the underlying query language of the database system. The user of a Quintus
Prolog application can simultaneously access multiple external Unify databases.

D22.2 Data types for SunUnify

Quintus Prolog	Unify
integer	long or short numeric

Note that Prolog uses 29 bits for an integer, Unify uses up to 32, therefore there
may be a loss of precision (the three most significant bits may be lost).

integer	date
integer	time
integer or float	amount
float	float

Note that Prolog uses a 20 bit mantissa but Unify uses 24 bits, therefore
precision may be lost.

string	string, text and combined*

*subfields of combined fields are converted to strings, separated by a vertical bar.

All Prolog data types can be stored in a Unify database. The above conversions
take place when data is retrieved from Unify databases. There is no support for
retrieving BINARY data items from a Unify database in Quintus Prolog.

D22.3 Access mechanism for SunUnify

There are two levels to the interface: the relational level, at which single facts
are implicitly retrieved from the database and the view level, at which a Prolog
clause is translated into a single query clause for the underlying database.

Database predicates are used to access a database and they can be used anywhere that a Prolog predicate can be used. A single record is retrieved on each database access via the interface; when control within Prolog backtracks into the predicate the next record is retrieved, and so on. The order of retrieval is determined by the underlying database.

The table layouts must be defined in the Prolog program to provide the mappings on to Prolog facts. The view level interface allows the programmer to define derived relations in the database. Aggregations such as average, sum, count, maximum and minimum, may be included in these views.

The following code declares a personnel database with one table for person details, to be used in the application.

```
db_name ( personnel, unify,  'personnel.db' )

db (person, personnel,
        person ( 'code'  :  integer,
                 'name'  :  string,
                 'town'  :  string  )).
```

Use of a database is initiated through the predicate dbconnect and more than one can be in use concurrently. A database can be disenabled using the dbdisconnect predicate. After a dbconnect call, all predicates declared as database predicates (data) can be used just like any other Prolog predicate. That is, there is no specific predicate for reading the database. The above predicates or facts (code, name, town) can be used in Prolog predicates and values will automatically be attributed to the facts through a transparent interface to the Unify database. Backtracking to the same predicate would cause the next value to be read, and so on.

A Unify database can be updated explicitly, using the predicates dbassert and dbretract to insert and delete single tuples respectively. Another predicate, dbretractall, will delete all tuples in a relation which match the condition. The following code:

```
db_assert (personnel:person( '123456', 'Brown', 'Norwich' )
```

would insert a record into the person table with the given data values. The changes to the database are immediate as there is no concept of transactions and committing data to the database. Consistency constraints are maintained through the interface; for example, key values must be specified and a field that references another relation must have a value which is already stored in the referenced relation.

A trace facility is provided to determine how the database is accessed and all calls to the database cause a trace message to be printed. For a view level query the trace message will give the SQL query that is sent to the database system (which may include joins).

D22.4 Data types for Oracle

Quintus Prolog	Oracle
integer or float	number(Precision, Scale)
integer	date
string	char(len)

D22.5 Data access in Oracle

The Oracle interface is very similar to the Unify interface with a few minor differences as follows:

- Oracle views are available to the Prolog programmer and are used in the same way as relations or tables;

- Oracle supports a simple transaction concept which is accessible to the Prolog database interface. Db_commit causes all updates to the database to be made permanent; dbroll_back_work causes all updates which have not been committed to be discarded;

- only one Oracle database can be connected to a program at any one time;

- indexes can be created on a table;

- tables can be created (db_create_table) and removed (db_drop_table) from the database.

D22.6 PRODATA

The Prodata Quintus/Oracle interface has been produced by Keylink Computers Ltd. The interface allows Oracle tables to be accessed from Prolog as though they existed within the Prolog environment as facts. All database accesses are dynamic. The interface allows: concurrent access and update; automatic use of indexes; execution of any database function which can be achieved using SQL; programmer configured error messages; automatic data conversions; and full access to the data dictionary.

The interface data types which cannot be handled are well documented. For example, the Oracle data types LONG and LONG RAW are not supported. Also, when updating Oracle tables, any fields which cannot be converted to the Oracle defined types in the data dictionary will cause an error to be issued.

D23   REVEAL

D23.1 Overview of mechanism

REVEAL has its own 'relational' database management capability. Facilities are provided for grouping datasets (two dimensional tables) into three dimensional tables or hierarchies, and selecting data. This facility is not described below, since this book is concerned with accessing external databases.

There are in–built functions in Reveal which allow applications to read from and write to host system files. Records can be assembled and disassembled so that individual data items can be used. There is also an interface to call user supplied procedures written in other languages, such as Cobol, Fortran and Algol. As a result, host files and any databases (such as IDMS) within the host environment can be manipulated by these procedures, and data be passed to and from associated Reveal applications.

D23.2 Data types

Reveal	External files
F, floating decimal (width and decimal places specified)	real number
B, floating binary (4 bytes)	binary
I, binary integer	binary
string (width specified)	character string

D23.3 Data access

Data can be read from and written to VME files using the external file functions, READ and WRITE. Up to 40 serial external files may be accessed simultaneously and each must be assigned a unique identifier as follows:

ASSIGN (20, 'PERSONDATA')

A single record is read by calling:

READ (20, PERSON)

where 'person' has been declared as a string variable within Reveal. Repeated calls will retrieve further records from the assigned file. The data items within the record can be 'unpacked' using string operators (if the files are in free format having variable length fields) or using the function RLAYOUT (for which a record layout must have been specified). A record layout is specified in an interactive session with the editor as follows:

```
MODE  >EDIT LAYOUT PERSONLAYOUT
.....CREATING A NEW LAYOUT?> Y

...FIELD NAME > CODE
...FIELD TYPE > B
...FIRST TERM > 6
...    REPEATS > 1

...FIELD NAME > NAME
...FIELD TYPE  > S
...    WIDTH   > 30

...FIELD NAME > TOWN
...FIELD TYPE  > S
...    WIDTH    > 30
```

The record retrieved in the string person can be converted to the above layout using:

> *RLAYOUT (PERSONLAYOUT, PERSON)*

Data may be written to a file as follows:

> *WRITE (20, PERSON)*

where PERSON is a string containing the record contents to be sent to the file. The record contents may be assembled using the WLAYOUT function (the reverse of RLAYOUT).

When all accesses to a file are complete, the file can be closed using:

> *RELEASE (20).*

Reveal is a procedural language and data access is specified in a similar way to that in a Cobol program.

D24   SAVOIR

D24.1 Overview of mechanism

Savoir is provided with an interface to dBASE III, but functions can be written to link Savoir with any database within the environment (which may be on an IBM micro, a VAX machines and others). Savoir is written in Pascal and the linking functions can be written in Pascal, Fortran, C and some other languages. The functions provided for the dBASE III interface are written in C.

The Traphandler (a routing procedure written in Pascal which invokes functions when a call is made from Savoir) passes parameters between Savoir and external C functions. A skeleton traphandler is provided with the Savoir software. The C functions access dBASE lattice routines; they are efficient, in that the database need not be repeatedly accessed in response to calls if parameters to be returned are all contained on the last record accessed.

External routines can be used to access other databases, but the traphandler must be modified to include calls to these routines and to ensure that parameters passed from and to Savoir are 'popped' off and 'pushed' on to the stack respectively.

D24.2 Data types

Savoir can only handle single facts, having no concept of records or arrays, and only one fact can be used to send data to or accept data from a database on any single call to an external function. The mappings of data are as follows:

Savoir	dBASE III
number (a pair of numbers representing the range)	integer or real
probability (range pair)	real
condition (true, false or unknown)	logical
string	character, integer, date, logical

D24.3 Data access

Calls to external routines can be included in Savoir code in three ways. They can be part of questions, so that instead of the user being prompted for input, a database value can be retrieved. They can also be attached to MADE variables (which have their values set or reset by demons), or attached to demons themselves when no data is being passed. The following examples illustrate these various methods of including calls in Savoir code.

When a call to a dBASE III external function is executed a reply status is returned to a variable DBstatus. This is set to zero to indicate success and other values represent various error codes.

Database files must be opened and closed. The maximum number of files which can be open is limited by the operating system; dBASE III allows a maximum of ten files for each of the database, index and memo files (a total of 30). Since data is not returned when opening and closing files, the call is associated with a demon as follows:

> *DO opendBASE ('PARTS.DBF')*
> *ASSOONAS AT_START*
>
> *DO DBend*
> *ASSOONAS AT_QUIT OR AT_END*

Functions are provided to open and close index and memo files. DBdump dumps all open files before closing them and DBrestore closes all files which are open, restores a dumped file and opens any files that were dumped, thus providing a rollback facility.

Data can be read from dBASE III files as follows:

> *QUESTION town ' Where does this person live?'*
> *ReadDBstring ('PERSON.DBF', code, 'TOWN',)*

or,

> *STRING town 'where person lives'*
> *CALL ReadDBstring ('PERSON.DBF', mycode, 'TOWN',)*

or,

> *STRING town MADE*
> *NUMBER status MADE*
> *MAKE town ReadDBstring ('PERSON.DBF', mycode,*
> *   'TOWN',)*
> *MAKE STATUS DBstatus*
> *ASSOONAS KNOWN mycode*

The external function readDBstring will read a record from the person.dbf file, where the code is equal to the value in the Savoir variable 'mycode' and return the value in the item town on that record. There are other functions such as readDBnum and readDBcond, to return different types of data.

Single values can also be written to dBASE III files as follows:

> *DO writeDBstring ('PERSON.DBF', mycode, 'TOWN',*
> *'Norwich')*
> *ASSOONAS KNOWN town*

The town item on a single record where code equals the value in 'mycode' will
be changed to 'Norwich'. Again, there are functions to write numerics and
conditions. Related index files are updated when new numbers and strings are
written to data items on dBASE III files. In addition, a new empty record can be
appended at the end of an existing file using DBnewrec and a new database file
can be created using the createDB function.

A number of functions are provided to manipulate indexes, such as getting the
record number of the first, last, previous and next entry on the file, creating an
index file and updating the index file. Some housekeeping functions are
available which cause the return of a status code, display the dBASE III file
structure and list files which are open, among others.

It is possible to use a scratchpad which can contain up to 1000 data items and
can be read from or written to by Savoir programs and functions. It is therefore
possible to write a database read function which reads a whole record and writes
it on to the scratchpad for use by the Savoir program. Users would, however,
need to write these functions themselves as they are not provided with the
Savoir software.

D25   SPICES

D25.1 Overview of mechanism

Spices may be used to build KBS applications in a stand alone mode but it also allows users to access Status (a free–text information retrieval system developed by AEA Technology) databases. There are two methods of using Status. Either, the Spices session can be suspended and a Status session invoked, or Status can be invoked by a macro in order to read text into Spices. Ongoing work is attempting to generalise this interface so that SQL commands can be called to access other databases, such as Oracle.

Spices is implemented in Prolog and access is allowed to this lower level. External software, such as Lotus–123 or C programs can be invoked from Prolog and hence this provides a general mechanism for accessing other databases.

D25.2 Data types

A Status database is composed of articles within chapters, and each article may be split into several named sections. The article can be further sub–divided into paragraphs. Each word in every article may be indexed, and hence used as a criterion to retrieve the article. Key fields may be numeric, date or string types.

D25.3 Data access

A number of User Commands are provided for the end user of Spices applications, including one to suspend Spices and invoke a Status session (STATUS). This enables the user to browse through articles in the Status database. When the Status session is ENDed control is automatically passed back to the Spices application and processing is resumed.

Alternatively, a Spices command can be implemented to invoke Status and execute a Status macro. This macro could carry out a display function or retrieve information from the database to be returned to Spices. This method has been implemented in the user command 'source'. The Status database can have a chapter devoted to articles from which rules can be derived. Each article has a named section indicating which rules were derived from it. If, during a consultation the Spices user asks for the source of a particular rule by using this command, Status is invoked and a search is made for any articles which contain the rule identification in the appropriate named section. The text of these articles is automatically displayed at the terminal.

D26   TODAY

D26.1 Overview of mechanism

Today is a fourth generation language and knowledge–based system combined, and databases can be accessed using the 4GL Today commands. Today can access many proprietary file systems and DBMS including Oracle, Informix, Prime Midas and Rdb. Applications can be run across a variety of hardware platforms, including a number of UNIX machines.

D26.2 Data types

The knowledge–base and the fourth generation language use the same data types.

D26.3 Data access

The knowledge–based system part of Today is integrated with the dictionary and data structures of the fourth generation language part of Today, therefore it can use logic blocks, screens and external programs. An evaluation method is associated with each attribute in the knowledge–base, which can be any one of the following actions:

- a function, to use an algorithm to determine a value;

- a screen, to invite the user to input a value;

- a decision tree or rule set, if inferencing is needed to determine a value;

- a database access.

Today can update and retrieve databases directly.

A number of third generation languages can be called from Today including Assembler, Pascal, Fortran, Cobol and C. Subroutines written in these languages can be used to access databases.

D27   TOP–ONE

D27.1 Overview of mechanism

Top–One runs on ICL mainframes under VME, IBM mainframes under VM, VSE or MVS(XA) and micro–computers under MS–DOS. DEC VAX and UNIX versions are under development and are expected to become available in 1990. At present, direct access to database is available for IDMS (VME) and dBASE III. Other databases can be accessed via a general interface to other languages. This general interface, using built–in functions, allows applications to directly access conventional file structures or call modules written in languages such as second generation Assembler, third generation Cobol and fourth generation MANTIS. This will allow access to any database within the environment.

D27.2 Data types

Top–One can handle all Cobol data definitions, therefore all database types which map on to Cobol can be accessed. For example, zero suppression, signs and implied decimal points can be handled. Top–One can manipulate integers, decimal, packed decimal, floating point numbers and strings.

D27.3 Data access

Telecomputing envisage that a Top–One application will most likely be integrated with existing systems and a likely scenario is depicted below.

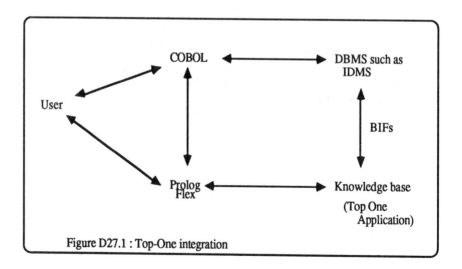

Figure D27.1 : Top-One integration

A conventional application will already be in service; this will access any data needed by the KBS application, then call the KBS application, passing the necessary data. When the knowledge–based system finishes, data will be passed back to the calling program and the latter will update the database as necessary. This type of knowledge–based system and database integration is generally called loose coupling (see chapter 6).

In addition, it is possible to extract data from a database while the knowledge–based system is running. The above mechanism can be used, in that the system can return control to Cobol to access data, and then the Cobol program invokes a continuation of the knowledge–based system consultation. A buffer area is declared for passing data.

A second method for accessing a database from Top–One code is through Built–In Functions (BIFs). The code can invoke a procedural module written in Assembler, PL/1, C, Cobol, Fortran or Pascal by invoking a BIF of the format:

cobol(module–name, functor),

where functor specifies a data structure to be passed to and from the Cobol module. Data can be both read and updated. Error codes are returned to the KBS application so that recovery procedures can be invoked if necessary.

A third method of data access is via a 4GL, Compass. Within Compass a logical user view (LUV) can be defined, made up of up to twelve record layouts. The latter may relate to conventional files or records within an IDMS database schema. Data can be both read and updated via a Compass mapping.

Future releases of Top–One will allow direct database access through some new BIFs. Telecomputing also state that direct access from Top–One production rule and object oriented environments will also be supported. They are standardising on embedded SQL for data manipulation, which will give access to SQL standard DBMS such as DB2, Oracle and Ingres.

D28   XiPlus

D28.1 Overview of mechanism

XiPlus can interface to dBASE III through a general interface which can be used to access any database within the environment in which XiPlus is running. A command file (using dBASE and XiPlus commands) or a C program needs to be written to provide the direct link between an XiPlus knowledge–base and a dBASE III database. The amount of memory required by the called program can be specified in the XiPlus knowledge–base, so that data can be rolled out of memory to disk.

Data can be read from and written to a database indirectly through another data file. A predefined interface for accessing data on external files in ASCII and DIF (data interchange format) format is provided.

Culham Laboratory, AEA Technology have successfully front–ended Oracle with XiPlus via a C interface (using Microsoft C). [See SPICES contacts in annex B if more details are required].

D28.2 Data types

Variables in XiPlus can be simple variables, multiple variables, floating variables and complex variables. Data can be read into any of these types. It is the coders responsibility to ensure that numeric items map on to numerics, character on to character, and so on. Any number of records can be retrieved in one call and the results are placed in a file. If the number of records is known, it is possible to return values directly to knowledge–base variables.

D28.3 Data access

Calls to the interface are associated with rules in the XiPlus knowledge–base. Data can be retrieved as follows:

> *Rule 1*
>> *if database access is needed*
>> *then command reset file read.prg*
>> *and report to file read.prg from file read.rpt*
>> *and do dbase access using ('c:\fix \read', 224)*
>> *and database has been read*
>
> *Rule 2*
>> *if database has been read*
>> *then do read database results using ('c:\fix\flt.txt' , next cells)*
>> *giving (code , name , town)*

An external program interface form for 'dBASE access' is set up in XiPlus using a 'program' window; that is, the coder can define the program specification using a template as follows:

> *Procedure name: dbase access*
> *User program:*
> > *program function name: dbase*
> > *file path: \dbase3   file name: dbase.exe*
> > *program to stay resident during execution: n (y/n)*
> *Language interface program:*
> > *file path: \xip   file name: rollprog.exe*[†]

'do dbase access' on line 4 of rule 1 links with the above program specification and causes dBASE III to be accessed. The file read.rpt (third line of rule 1) needs to contain the database query, which could take the following format:

> *erase c:\fix\flt.txt*
> *use c:\fix\known*
> *copy to c:\fix\flt   FOR ;*
> *(town = 'Norwich');*
> *delimited*
> *quit*

This query requests all records where town is equal to Norwich to be returned to the file c:\fix\flt. Rule 2 causes data to be read from this external ASCII file and placed in XiPlus variables: code, name and town.

Writing data to a dBASE III database uses a similar mechanism to a read, but the process is reversed. Rules contain the same function calls (do dBASE access) but use different parameters referring to different template files, containing append, replace or delete commands to dBASE III. Consider the following code:

> *rule 10*
> > *if current action is to append new details*
> > *then report to file new1.prg append blank*
> > *and report to file new1.prg replace name with 'CCTA'*
> > *and report to file new1.prg quit*
> > *and dbase commands are prepared*
>
> *rule 11*
> > *if dbase commands are prepared*
> > *then do dbase access using ('c:\fix\new1', 224)*
> > *and appending record is complete.*

[†] Reproduced by permission of Expertech.

D28.4 VAX XiPlus

A VAX implementation based on XiPlus release 3 has been produced. Program interfaces to multiple languages, including C, Cobol, Fortran and Pascal, have been added. Some new facilities are also provided, including: the ability to start asynchronous external programs and receive interrupts; and file locking to maintain application integrity in a multi–user environment.

References

AHME89 : Ahmedzai, S, Mallett, K, Teather, D, Wroe, B, (1989). The Leicester Palliation Support System: A computer–based approach to learning palliative medicine and nursing.

AION89 : Aion Corporation, (1989). Aion Development System Object Processing: Concepts and Facilities (ADS documentation).

ALZO87 : Al–Zobaidie, A, Grimson, J B, (1987). 'Expert systems and database systems: how can they serve each other?'. Expert Systems 1987, Vol 4.

BECK88 : Beckman, J, (1988). Discussion paper 'Some factors to consider when integrating KBS with information processing and database systems in a mainframe environment', Swedish Agency for Administrative Development (SAFAD), 1988.

BEEC88 : Beech, D, (1988). 'A foundation for evolution from relational to object databases', Hewlett–Packard Laboratories, Palo Alto, 1988.

BEYN88(1) : Beynon–Davies, P, (1988). 'Frames and relations'. Computing Techniques 1988.

BEYN88(2) : Beynon–Davies, P, (1988). 'Using knowledge based systems for relational database query optimisation', Computing, November 1988.

BIC86 : Bic, L, Gilbert, J P, (1986). 'Learning from AI: New Trends in Database Technology'. IEEE Computer.

BUTL83 : Butler Cox Foundation (1983). Report Series Number 37, Expert Systems, September 1983.

BUTL87 : Butler Cox Foundation (1987). Research report 60, Expert Systems in Business, October 1987.

CCTA86 : CCTA, ISE Division, Norwich, (1986). Appraisal of RTI's INGRES, Report Number 6.

CCTA88(1) : CCTA, ISE Division, Norwich, (1988). Appraisal of ICL–ADVISER, Report Number 19.

CCTA88(2) : CCTA, ISE Division, Norwich (1988). Development study, Appraisal of Hypercard, Report Number 20.

CCTA88(3) : CCTA, ISE Division, Norwich, (1988). Data dictionary reporting, Report Number 22.

CCTA88(4) : CCTA, ISE Division, Norwich, (1988). Application Generators, Appraisal and Evaluation, Report Number 32.

CCTA88(5) : CCTA, ISE Division, Norwich, (1988). Database Management Systems, Appraisal and Evaluation, Report Number 33.

CCTA89 : CCTA, ISE Division, Norwich, (1989). Appraisal of Sybase, Report Number 37.

CCTA89(2) : CCTA, ISE Division, Norwich, (1989). SSADM, The Open Approach to Information Management.

CHU89 : Chu, C H, (1989). 'Design Issues for Intelligent Microcomputer–based Decision Support Systems', Journal of Information Systems Management, Spring 1989.

CONW88 : Conway, G (1988). 'CCTA Technology brief: an introduction to rule induction'.

DAGA87 : d'Agapeyeff, A, Hawkins, C J B, (1987). Report to the Alvey Directorate on the Second Short Survey of Expert Systems in UK Business. Pub. IEE for Alvey Directorate, August 1987.

DATE86 : Date, C J, (1986). Introduction to Database Systems, Volume I, 4th Edition, Pub. Addison–Wesley.

DEE88 : Dee, E G, (1988). Draft CCTA ISE paper on distributed database.

DEE87(1) : Dee, E G, Kerridge, J M, (1987). Design notes on Proposal for Triggers (un–published).

DEE87(2) : Dee, E G, Kerridge, J M, (1987). Examples of triggers (unpublished).

DOGA89 : Dogac, A, Yuruten, B, Spaccapietra, S, (1989). 'A generalised expert system for database design', IEEE Transactions on Software Engineering, Vol. 15, No. 4, April 1989.

DUFF87 : Duffin, P, (Ed), (1987). KBS in Government, Proceedings of Conference 87, Pub. Online.

DURH89 : Durham, T, (1989). 'Having the last word on information retrieval', Computing, 18 May 1989.

EUSI88 : EUSIDIC (1988). 'Artificial Intelligence: Potential for Application in the Information Industry', European Association of Information Services.

EVET87 : Evett, I W, Spiehler, E J, (1987). 'Rule induction in forensic science'. KBS in Government 1987.

FAVA87 : Favaro, J, (1987). 'Artificial intelligence in information technology State of the art', paper in Industrial Software Technology, pub. Peter Peregrinus Ltd on behalf of IEE, IEE Computing Series 10, Ed. R Mitchell, 1987.

FEIG88 : Feigenbaum, E, McCorduck, P, Penny Nii, H, (1988). The rise of the Expert Company, pub. Macmillan, ISBN 0–333–49659–0.

FOLL89 : Folland, D, (1989). Framework for open systems, internal CCTA paper.

GAUC89 : Gauch, S, Smith, J B, (1989). 'An expert system for searching in full–text', Information Processing and Management Vol. 25, No. 3, 1989.

GLOW89 : Glowinski, A, O'Neil, M, Fox, J, (1989). 'Knowledge–based decision support for general practitioners: designing very large and versatile systems', Proc 5th International Expert Systems Conference 1989.

GRAY89 : Gray, P M D, (1989). 'Interfacing a knowledge base to a large database', submitted to Knowledge Engineering Review January 1989.

GRAY88(1) : Gray, P M D, Lucas, R J, (1988). Prolog and Databases – implementations and new directions, pub. Ellis Horwood.

GRAY88(2) : Gray, P M D, Storrs, G E, du Boulay, J B H, (1988). 'Knowledge representations for database metadata'. Artificial Intelligence Review.

GRAY88(3) : Gray, P M D, (1988). 'Expert systems and object oriented databases: evolving a new software architecture', Research and Development in Expert Systems V, Proceedings of Expert Systems 88, Edited by B Kelly and A Rector, Pub. Cambridge Press for BCS.

GUES89 : Guest, D, (1989). 'Brains stop play', Datalink, May 8 1989.

HELD89 : Held, J P, Carlis, J V, (1989). Conceptual data modeling of expert systems, IEEE Expert, Spring 1989.

HEWE86 : Hewett, J, Timms, S, d'Aumale, G, (1986). Commercial Expert Systems in Europe, Pub. Ovum Ltd.

HOLS86 : Holsapple, C W, Whinston, A B, (1986). Manager's Guide to Expert Systems using GURU, pub. Dow Jones–Irwin, ISBN 0–87094–916–0.

HOWA87 : Howard, H C, Rehak, D R, (1987). 'KADBASE – A Prototype Expert System – Database Interface for Integrated CAE Environment'. Proceedings of AAAI 87.

HOWA89 : Howard, H C, Rehak, D R, (1989). 'KADBASE – Interfacing Expert Systems with Databases'. IEEE Expert Autumn 89.

HOWE88 : Howells, D I, Fiddian, N J, Gray, W A, (1988). 'A source–to–source meta–translation system for database query languages – implementation in Prolog', in Prolog and Databases GRAY88(1) reference.

IBM89 : IBM Corporation (1989). AD/Cycle Concepts, GC26–4531–0, September 1989.

ICL : ICL Quickbuild and TPMS Manuals.

INFO89 : Information Builders (1989). Level5 Release 2.0: A Technical Overview, Second Annual Users Conference Proceedings.

ISO88 : ISO–ANSI, (1988). Working draft database language SQL2 and SQL3 papers.

ISO89 : ISO (1989). Draft ISO–IEC/JTC1/SC21/WG3\N1007, Reference Model for Data Management, November 1989.

JANS89 : Jansen, B, Compton, P, (1989). 'Data dictionary approach to the maintenance of expert systems: The Knowledge Dictionary', Knowledge Based Systems, Vol. 2 No. 1, March 1989.

JARK84 : Jarke, M, Vassiliou, Y, (1984). 'Databases and Expert Systems: Opportunities and Archtectures for Integration'. New Applications of Databases.

JOHN88 : Johnson, T, Hewett, J, Guilfoyle, C, Jeffcoate, J, (1988). Expert Systems and Market Suppliers, Ovum Ltd, ISBN 0–903969–37–8.

JONE89 : Jones, K, (1989). 'Untouched by Human Hand', Computer Weekly, January 1989.

JONE89(2) : Jones, K, (1989). 'Hypercard deals an expert hand', Computer Weekly, August 1989.

JONE89(3) : Jones, R, (1989). 'Leave it in expert hands', Computing, 26 October 1989.

KELL86 : Kellogg, C, (1986). 'From Data Management to Knowledge Management'. IEEE Computer.

KERR88 : Kerry, R E, CCTA (1988). Integrating Expert Systems and Databases, CCTA ISE Report Number 29.

KERS87 : Kerschberg, L, (1987). 'Expert database systems', BCS Computer Bulletin June 1987.

KING86 : King, R, (1986). 'A database management system based on an object oriented model', Expert Database Systems, 1986.

KIWI88 : KIWI, The team (1988), contact Mecchia, A. 'A system for managing data and knowledge bases', Proceedings of an ESPRIT technical meeting held in Brussels, November 1988.

KOTZ88 : Kotz, A M, Dittrich, K R, Mulle, J A, (1988). Supporting semantic rules by a generalized event/trigger mechanism.

KULL89 : Kull, D, (1989). 'Cutting through DBMS complexity', Computer Decisions, April 1989.

LOU88 : Loucopoulos, P, (1988). 'Information systems: a knowledge–based perspective', Knowledge–Based Systems, Vol. 1 No. 4, September 1988.

LUCA88 : Lucas, R, (1988). Database applications using Prolog, pub. Ellis Horwood.

LUCA89 : Lucas, R, (1989). 'Systems integration', ICL Technical Journal, May 1989.

LUNN87 : Lunn, S, Nomura, T, (1987). Prolog, Transaction Processing and Databases, Knowledge Based Systems Vol. 1, No. 1, Dec 87.

MARA88 : Maraschini, F, (1988/89). Easyfind – methods and tools for intelligent database access, Unisys Italia report.

MCCA89 : McCandless, H, (1989). 'Smarter than the average program', article in Practical Computing September 1989.

MEWE89 : Mewes, A, (1989). Migration to open systems, internal CCTA report.

MORR89 : Morrison, A W, (1989). Hypertext and Expert Systems – Experiences and Prospects, Proc. 5th International Expert Systems Conference 1989.

MOTR84 : Motro, A, (1984). 'Query generalisation: A technique for handling query failure', Proc. of Workshop on Expert Database Systems, 1984.

NOMU87 : Nomura, T, Lunn, S, (1987). Integration of Knowledge Based Systems with Data Processing, Telecomputing plc, December 1987.

PARK86 : Parker, D S, Carey, M, Golshami, F, Jarke, M, Sciore, E, Walker, A, (1986). Logic Programming and Databases. Expert Database Systems.

PARS83 : Parsaye, K, (1983). 'Database Management, Knowledge Base Management and Expert System Development in PROLOG'. Proc. of the Logic Programming Workshop 83.

POPO88 : Popolizio, J J, (1988). 'Embedding Expert Systems: An Issue of Integration', Artificial Intelligence Research October 1988.

POPO89 : Popolizio, J J, Cappelli, W S, (1989). 'New shells for old iron', Datamation April 15, 1989.

PUNC88 : Puncello, P P, Torrigiani, P, Pietri, F, Burion, R, Cardile, B, Conti, M, (1988). 'ASPIS: A knowledge–based CASE environment', IEEE Software, March 1988.

RAUC86 : Rauch–Hindin, W, (1986). 'Software integrates AI, standard systems', article in Mini–Micro Systems October 1986.

REIN87 : Reinstein, H, Cohn, L, (1987). 'The database role in expert systems', InfoDB, Volume 2, Number 4, Winter 1987/88.

RICH86 : Rich, E, (1986). Artificial Intelligence, International Student Edition, McGraw–Hill.

RISC88 : Risch, T, Reboh, R, Hart, P, Duda, R, (1988). 'A functional approach to integrating database and expert systems', Communications of the ACM, Number 12, Volume 31, December 1988.

SALV87 : Salvini, S, (1987). 'An internal representation for expert system knowledge in a logic database', Computer Science Technical Report 87/13, Heriot–Watt University, Edinburgh.

SALV89 : Salvini, S, Williams, M H, (1989). 'Knowledge sharing for expert systems using a deductive database', Computer Science Technical Report 89/11, Heriot–Watt University, Edinburgh.

SALV89(2) : Salvini, S, (1989). 'Towards a knowledge–base management systems', Computer Science Technical Report 89/12, Heriot–Watt University, Edinburgh.

SHAN88 : Shan, M, (1988). 'Optimal plan search in a rule–based query optimiser', Hewlett–Packard Laboratories Research Report.

SIMO86 : Simons, G L, (1986). Expert Systems and Micros, NCC Publications.

SMIT86 : Smith, J M, (1986). 'Expert Database Systems: A Database Perspective'. Expert Database Systems 1986.

SOFT89 : Software AG, Germany (1989). Natural Expert Reference Manual, 1989.

SPIE89 : Spiers, J, (1989). 'Bringing Intelligence into the DBMS', presented at the 'Breaking Down Software Development Barriers' Conference, 1989.

STEW89 : Stewart, D, (1989). 'Integrated systems on PCs', article in Expert System User, March 1989.

STON86 : Stonebraker, M, Rowe, L A, (1986). The Design of Postgres.

SZUP89 : Szuprowicz, B, (1989). 'Planned promotion to strategic status', Systems International, July/August 1989.

TEXA89 : Texas Instruments, (1989). Intelligence – International Journal on Artificial Intelligence, Number 15, April, 1989.

THOM89 : Thomas, D, (1989). 'What's in an Object?', BYTE, March 1989.

TSUR88 : Tsur, S, (1988). 'LDL – A technology for the realisation of tightly coupled expert database systems', IEEE Expert, Autumn 1988.

WALK87 : Walker, A, McCord, M, Sowa, J F, Wilson, W G, (1987). Knowledge Systems and Prolog, A Logical Approach to Expert Systems and Natural Language Processing, Addison Wesley.

WAUG89 : Waugh, K G, (1989). Squirrel: an extended SQL for a deductive database system, Technical report number 89/1, Department of Computer Science, Heriot–Watt University, Edinburgh.

WHITE88 : White, C J, (1988). 'Expert DBMSs aren't hype', Computer Decisions, March 1988.

WILL88 : Williamson, M, (1988). 'KnowledgePro Disperses Complex Data Efficiently', PC Week Volume 5, No. 33, August 15, 1988.

WIND89 : Windebank, C, (1989). 'Open Systems Standards', internal CCTA paper.

WINS87 : Winstanley, G, (1987). Program Design for Knowledge Based Systems, Sigma Press (UK) and Halsted Press.

Index

access control, 36, 37, 40, 50, 78, 88, 98, 108, 115, 126, 229, 235, 238, 323
AG, *see application generator*
AI, *see artificial intelligence*
analysis and design, 42–43, 44, 46, 47, 99, 100, 103, 104, 124, 125, 126, 130,
    132, 133, 225, 233, 237, *see also SSADM*
analyst workbench, 42, 47, *see also CASE*
ANSI, 68, 107, 219, 220
ANSI–SPARC 3, 36
application generator, 20, 30, 42, 46, 101, 117, 120, 127, 135–137, 140, 170,
    181–186, 342, *see also 4GL*
        Application Master, 42, 101
        Focus, 137, 177, 183, 336
        Ingres, 136, 140 *see also DBMS Ingres*
        Oracle, 136, 209 *see also DBMS Oracle*
applications
        KBS, 13, 19, 20, 21, 22, 25, 26, 27, 28, 29, 30, 31, 32, 33, 38, 65,
            66, 76, 89–98, 100, 102, 108, 115, 122, 137–139, 142–143, 144,
            145, 150, 157, 159, 188, 211–212, 229, 230, 236, 238, 246
        other, 38, 40, 42–43, 51, 54, 58, 61, 68, 69, 71, 73, 75, 95, 104, 120,
            173–174, 199, 205, 275, 354
architecture, 12, 13, 16, 18, 19, 26, 29, 33, 34, 36, 38, Ch. 4, 59–118, 124,
    127–128, 129, 172, 174, 181–182, 183, 188, 214, 220–223, 227,
    228–232, 239, 245, 265, 298, 340, *see also client/server*
artificial intelligence, 10, 34, 63, 77, 89–90, 102, 124, 205, 255, 271
ASCII, 40, 150, 152, 193
        files, 249, 288, 306, 309, 336, 342, 356–357
ASG, *see automatic system generation*
ASPIS, 103
assertion, 68–69
audit trail, 51
automatic system generation, 46, 47, 99, 100, 101–102, 104, 124, 236–237

backtracking, 139, 300, 338, 343, 345
backward chaining, 29, 32, 64–66, 71–72, 74, 75, 77, 78, 185, 247, 249, 252,
    256, 257, 259, 260, 262, 263, 264, 268, 269, 273, 274, 282, 284, 311
BCS, 25
blackboard systems, 115, 213, 214, 215
boolean, 87, 94, 112–113, 161, 310
British Computer Society, *see BCS*
British Standards Institute (BSI), 43, 107, 219, 220